HINDU AND MUSLIM RELIGIOUS INSTITUTIONS

Andhra Desa, 1300-1600

HINDU AND MUSLIM RELIGIOUS INSTITUTIONS
Andhra Desa, 1300-1600

R. Soma Reddy

RESEARCH INDIA PRESS
New Delhi (INDIA)

Cataloging in Publication Data--DK

Courtesy: D. K. Agencies (P) Ltd. <docinfo@dkagencies.com>

Soma Reddy, R. (Ravula), 1943-

Hindu and Muslim religious institutions : Andhra Desa, 1300-1600 / R. Soma Reddy.

p. cm.

Includes bibliographical references (p.) and index.

ISBN : 9788189131340

1. Religious institutions--India--Andhra Pradesh--History. 2. Hindu temples--India--Andhra Pradesh--History. 3. Mosques--India--Andhra Pradesh--History. 4. Religion and state--India--Andhra Pradesh--History. I. Title

DDC 306.6095484 22

ISBN : 978-81-89131-340

Price : 750/-

First Edition: 2011

Typesetting by
G. R. Sharma
9968281826

Published by :
RESEARCH INDIA PRESS
E-6/34, Sangam Vihar
New Delhi-110062
Phone: 011-26047013, (M) 9818085794
E-mail: researchindiapress@yahoo.co.in

Contents

Foreword

The most satisfying experience for a University Teacher is when one's own student takes up a research problem suggested to him and works on it to fruition. I have now that experience when writing this foreword to Dr. R. Soma Reddy's *Hindu and Muslim Religious Institutions: Andhra Desa, 1300-1600*. I congratulate him for having been able to publish his Ph.D., thesis so soon after obtaining the Degree of Doctor of Philosophy, which does not happen often. My congratulations to Dr. S. Srinivasan, the cultured publishers, naturally follow.

At the present day, religion has become a subject of critical and scientific enquiry, quite logically. Whenever the ethical or moral value of activities or conditions in a given society are questioned, the value of religion is involved. Historian has a very responsible role to play in this meaningful enquiry. Micro-studies at the regional level are yet to be made ready in India, for a scholar to be able to generalize on theses matters for the whole of the country. It is from this context that Dr. Soma Reddy's work from the Osmania University acquires its special significance. Appropriately the venerable Dr. G. S. Dikshit remarked, "This thesis breaks new ground".

The period of study, A. D. 1300-1600, was one of continuous rule over the greater part of Andhra, successively, under the Tughlaqs, the Bahmanis and the Qutb-Shahis and there lies its distinctiveness and source of the problems of study. Further, there was so far no work which comprehensively dealt with the religious institutions of Medieval Andhra. This work fills the gap.

M. Radhakrishna Sarma

Professor of Ancient India History,
Culture and Archaelogy,
Osamania University, Hyderabad-500 007

Acknowledgements

I owe a debt of gratitude to several individuals and institutions. My foremost indebtedness belongs to Dr. M. Radhakrishna Sarma, Professor and Head (Retd.) Department of Ancient Indian History, Culture and Archaeology, Osmania University, under whose scholarly guidance I completed this study. I am also thankful to him for his learned foreward to this work.

I take this opportunity to express my debt to my teacher Prof. T. Surendar (Retd.) Department of Political Science, Osmania University, whose concern for my well-being has been a grate source of strength and inspiration in my career. My late wife Sumathi, daughter Vasudha and son Dheeraj made possible the effort that created this book, which I dedicate to the fond memory of my wife late Sumathi.

I express a deep sense of indebtedness to all the scholars whose published works and opinions in the field have benefited me. The first edition of this book was brought out in 1984 by New Era Publications, Madras.

Finally, it is with great pleasure that I acknowledge my obligation to Research India Press for bringing out the second edition of this book. I thank the staff of the Balussery Press Mr. N. Dharmarajan, Manager, Mrs. Aysha Begum Ahmad Basha and Mrs. Laxmi Prasanna, type setters: Mr. A Gurumurthy, Machine Operator and others for the excellent manner in which the printing of the book has been carried out. I also thank Mr. Suman Pathak of Research India Press, New Delhi for preparing the index.

Prof. R. Soma Reddy (Retd.)
Department of History, Osmania University
Hyderabad-500 007

Abbreviations

AR	*Annual Report on Indian Epigraphy and South Indian Epigraphy.*
Aravidu Dynasty	*Aravīdu Dynasty of Vijayanagara, Henry Heras.*
ASPP	*Āndhra Sāhitya Parishat Patrika.*
Bahmanis	*The Bahmanis of the Decan, H. K. Sherwani.*
Bhandarkar	*Vaishnavism, Saivism and Minor Religious Systems, R. G. Bhandarkar.*
Briggs	*History of the Rise of the Mahomedan Power in India, (Translation of Ferishta), John Briggs.*
Briggs (Anon.)	*The History of Mahomed Kolly Kootb Shah : Translation of Anonymous Historian, John Briggs.*
CP	*Copper Plates.*
Ct. Mm.	*Chatupadya Manimanjari, V. Prabhakara Sastri, (ed.)*
Cudd. Ins.	*Cuddapah Inscriptions, N. Venkataramanayya.*
EC	*Epigraphia Carnatica.*
ED	*History of India as told by its own historians, H. M. Elliot & John Dowson.*
EI	*Epigraphia Indica.*
EIM	*Epigraphia Indo-Moslemica.*
Elliot	*The History of India (as told by her own Historians) The Mohammadan period-Tarik-i-Ferozshah, Ziauddin Barni, M. Elliot (ed.)*
Foreign Notices	*Foreign Notices of South India, K. A. Nilakanta Sastri.*
Forgotton Chapter	*A Forgotten Chapter of Andhra History, M. Somasekhara Sarma.*
Forgotten Empire	*The Forgotten Empire, Robert Sewell.*
FS	*Futuhus-Salatin, Amir Khusru.*

Further Sources	*Further Sources of Vijayanagara History, comp. K. A. Nilakanta Sastri & N. Venkataramanayya.*
Glossary	*A Glossary of Judicial & Revenue Terms and c. of British India, H. H. Wilson*
Hr. Vm.	*Hari Vamsamu: Errapragada.*
IA	*Indian Antiquary.*
IAP. Cu.	*Inscriptions of Andhra Pradesh, Cuddapah District.*
IAP. Kn.	*Inscription of Andhra Pradesh, Karimnagar District.*
IAP. Ng.	*Inscription of Andhra Pradesh, Nalgonda District.*
IAP. Wg.	*Inscription of Andhra Pradesh, Warangal District.*
IC	*Islamic Culture, Hyderabad.*
Ins. Gloss.	*Inscriptional Glossary of Andhra Pradesh, K. Iswara Dutt.*
JAHRS	*Journal of Andhra Historical Research Society.*
JTA	*Journal of Telugu Academy.*
Kakatiyas	*The Kakatiyas of Warangal, P. V. Parabrahma Sastri.*
Karmarkar	*The Religions of India, A. P. Karmarkar.*
Kr. Rm.	*Kridabhiramam, Vallabhamatya.*
Landmarks	*Landmarks of the Deccan, A. A. Bilgrami.*
LR	*Local Records.*
Mac. Mss. (S.A.)	*Mackenzie Manuscripts (Andhra Pradesh Government State Archives copy).*
Malkapuri	*Mahbūbu-i-dhil-manam Tadhkira Āuliya-i-Dakhan, Abdul Jabbār Khān Malkāpuri.*
MAR	*Mysore Archaeological Report.*
Medieval Deccan	*History of Medieval Deccan, H. K. Sherwani & P. M. Joshi (eds.)*
MER	*Madras Epigraphical Report*
NI	*Nellore District Inscriptions, A. Butter-worth & Venugopal Chetty.*
Ob	*Obsequy.*
Qutbshah Dynasty	*History of the Qutbshah Dynasty, H. K. Sherwani.*
Reddi Kingdoms	*History of the Reddi Kingdom, M. Somasekhara Sarma.*
Relations	*Relations of Golkonda in the Early Seventeenth Century, W. H. Moreland.*
Religion in Andhra	*Religion in Andhra, B. S. L. Hanumanta Rao.*

Siddesvara Charitramu	*Siddesvara Charitramu (Kakatiya Rajula Charitra—Pratapa Charitra), Kase Sarvappa, (ed.) K. Laxmiranjanam.*
SII	*South Indian Inscriptions.*
Simhachalam Temple	*The Simhāchalam Temple, K. Sundaram.*
Sources	*Sources of Vijayanagara Ḥistory, S. K. Ayyangar.*
Studies in the Third Dynasty	*Studies in the History of the Third Dynasty of Vijayanagara, N. Venkataramanayya*
Suryavamsi Gajapatis	*The Suryavamsi Gajapatis of Orissa, R. Subrahmanyam.*
TDER	*Tirupati Devasthanam Epigraphical Report Sadhu Subrahmanya Sastri.*
TTDE	*Tirumala-Tirupati Devasthanam Epigraphical Series.*
Vij. Sex. Comm. Vol.	*Vijayanagàra Sexcentenary Commemoration Volume.*
VR	*Topographical List of Inscriptions from the Madras Presidency, V. Rangacharya.*
Vv. Vm.	*Velugōtivāri Vamśāvalli, N. Venkataramanayya (ed.).*

MAP

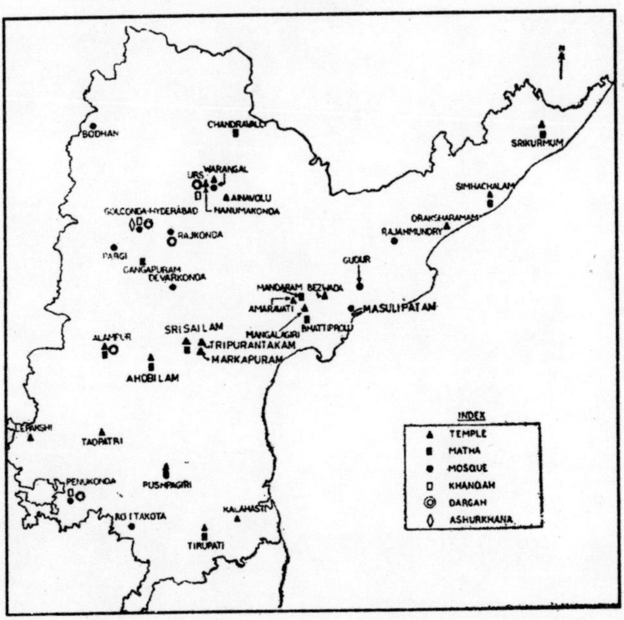

1

INTRODUCTION

I

Religion had been the most dominant of the factors that shaped the course of history of Ancient and Medieval Andhra Desa, as it had been the case with the whole of Indian history. Religious institutions acted as the most powerful agencies of the times and governed every aspect of life in the society.

Considerable work has been done on the various aspects of the history of the Hindu and Muslim religious institutions in Andhra Desa of the period under study. There are some independent works dealing exclusively with the general history of the individual temples. *The Simhachalam Temple* by K. Sundaram, *History of Tirupati* by S. K. Aiyangar, *History of Tirupati by* T.K.T. Veera Raghavacharya and *The Tirumala Temple* by N. Ramesan may be mentioned as examples for this type of work. There are a few scholarly articles which deal with the social, cultural and economic aspects of the history of the religious institutions of the period. "Mana Pracheena Vidya Samasthalu" (Telugu) by M. Soma Sekhara Sarma[1], "The Economic Function of a Medieval South Indian Temple" (Tirupati) by Burton Stein[2] "Hyderabad-Ke Muqadas Tabarrukat" (Urdu) by Rahat Azmi[3] and "Hyderabad-Ke-Qadim Ashurkhana" (Urdu) by Hadi Ali Baquri[4] are some of the articles belonging to this category. The general histories like *The Early History of Deccan* edited by G. Yazdani, *The History of Reddi Kingdoms* by M. Somasekhara Sarma, *The Studies in the History of Third Dynasty of Vijayanagara* by N. Venkataramanayya and *Life in Medieval Andhra* (Unpublished thesis) by R. Narasimha Rao contain a few pages giving a sketch of the religious institutions.

But, no comprehensive and systematic account of the religious institutions, both Hindu and Muslim, in Andhra Desa, tracing their interactions and vicissitudes during the three centuries from A.D. 1300 to 1600 is available. An attempt is made in this book to fill up this gap.

The period under study (A.D. 1300-1600) constitutes a distinctive epoch in the history of Andhra Desa. The beginning and closing years of this period are characterised by momentous political and cultural changes. The beginning of the 14th century A.D. where the present study, starts, is marked by the commencement of the decline of the Hindu political power and the advent of Muslim political force into Andhra Desa. The Kakatiya Kingdom of Warangal, which under its last ruler Prataparudra II (A.D. 1280-1323) held sway over practically the whole of Andhra, Desa attained the zenith of its political and cultural development by the end of the 13th century A.D. It was exposed in the first quarter of the 14th century A.D. to a number of Muslim invasions from A.D. 1303 onwards culminated in the annexation of this Kingdom to the Muslim empire of Delhi in the year A.D. 1323. Similarly, the Ganga Kingdom of Orissa which included the Northern Coastal Andhra comprising roughly the three modern districts of Srikakulam, Visakhapatnam and Vijayanagaram, was also very much weakened by the Tughluq invasion the Muslim invasions led not only to the advent of Muslim Political power but also to the emergence of Islam as a powerful element in the religious life of the area. The development of Islam as the state religion which naturally gave a great fillip to the growth and spread of its own institutions, adversely affected the fortunes of the Hindu religion and its institutions, which had hitherto been in a predominant position.

Similarly, the end of the 16th century A.D. where the study closes is also characterised by notable political and cultural changes. It marks the end of the Hindu predominance and the consolidation of the Muslim rule in Andhra Desa. The Vijayanagara Empire was the last Hindu political power to rule over the Telugu country. Its last important ruler Venka II (A.D. 1586-1614) had, at this juncture, only a semblance of this authority over the Telugu districts. On the other hand, the close of the 16th century A.D. marks the high watermark of the political power and the cultural development of the Qutbshahi Kingdom of Golkonda. By that time, almost the entire Telugu country came under the sway of Muhammad Quli Qutbshah (A.D. 1580-1612).

Two other events—the advent of the Mughal and the European influence on the area–also make the close of the 16th century quite important. After establishing its sway over Ahammadnagar Kingdom by the year 1600 A.D., the Mughal Empire of Delhi came into direct contact with the Qutbshahi Kingdom. Though the latter accepted the Mughal suzerainty in the year 1636 A.D. when its ruler Abdulla signed the *Inqiyad Nama,* and though it was annexed to the Mughal Empire only in the year 1687 A.D., the advent of Mughal influence was to have a demoralising effect on its political and religious system. Threatened with Mughal aggression, the Qutbshahi rulers began to feel insecure. They realised that sooner or later their Kingdom would also be swept away by the fast advancing Mughals. The advent of Mughal influence also signalled the ascendancy of Sunni sect to which the Mughals belonged, over the Shi'ism which was the Qutbshahi state religion. Similarly, by the year 1599 A.D. the Portuguese missionaries established their Churches at Chandragiri, the Vijayanagara capital. The Dutch established their factories at Masulipatnam by the year 1606 A.D. and the English also a established settlement at Masulipatnam by 1611 A.D. Though the advent of the Europeans was not to have any significant impact on the political life of the Telugu country in near future, it laid the seeds of Christianity, another major world religion, on the Telugu soil for the first time.

II

The period covered by the study witnessed notable political changes. The Muslim invasions which commenced at the beginning of the 14th century A.D. destroyed the political unity and stability which had characterised the Kakatiya rule in Andhra Desa. Under the Tughlqu rule which lasted for a brief period of a decade or so in the Telugu country, though it lost the political independence, continued to be under the rule of a single political power. After the liberation from the yoke of Delhi Sultan, it lost its political unity also. Now it came to be parceled out among a number of independent Kingdoms, both Hindu and Muslim. It witnessed during the remaining period, the rule of Musunuri, Bahmani, Vijayanagara, Reddi, Velama, Ganga, Gajapati, Qutbshahi and a host of other minor dynasties, some of them ruling over it simultaneously and some in succession. Some of them were minor Kingdoms and had a short life. Some of them were major ones and more enduring.

Similarly, on the religious side also the period was equally crucial. While Buddhism, Jainism and Christianity had practically no adherents, the major and active religions that claimed the allegiance of the people in the area during the period were– Hinduism and Islam. The two major religious systems and especially some of their principal sects, underwent many fluctuations in their fortunes during this period. These fluctuations depended to a great extent upon the political and dynastic changes of the corresponding period, their (religions) mutual competition and rivalry and finally their inherent strength and weakness.

Hinduism comprised mainly the following sects and subsects: the Vedic religion; Saivism and its sub-sects such as–Pasupatas, Kalamukhas, Kapalikas and Veera-Saivas (both Basava and Aradhya schools); Vaishnavism and its sub-sects, such as– Vaikhanasas, Srivaishnavas (both *Vadagalai* and *Tengalai* schools) Madhwas, Vallabhas, Chaitanyas and Vithalas; Sakti cult and the cult of Hero-worship.

Besides these, there existed a number of minor and primitive religious cults, such as the cult of Siddhas, the cult of minor deities of Hindu pantheon like Veerabhadra, Ganapati, Skanda (Kartikeya or Subrahmanya), Surya, Hanuman, Pandavas, Potaraju, and the cult of animal and plant-worship, which also played a significant role in the popular religious beliefs.[5]

Islam consisted of two major sects, viz., Sunnism and Shi`ism. Of the two religious systems i.e. Hinduism and Islam, the former, with its sects and sub-sects, was the most predominant religious system throughout the Telugu country at the beginning of the 14th century A.D. Among its sects again, it was Saivism with its sub-sects that was the most important one in the royal courts as well as among the common people throughout the Kakatiya dominions. Vaishnavism occupied the second place. It was the religion of the Eastern Ganga rules and therefore was influential in the North-Coastal Andhra. The next position among the Hindu sects, was occupied by the old Vedic religion: then came the cults of minor deities and popular beliefs. In the post-Kakatiya period, Saivism and Vaishnavism underwent major fluctuations in their fortunes. Saivism, though did not experience any significant doctrinal changes, maintained its influential edge over all the other sects of the Hindu religion till the middle of the 15th century A.D. Subsequently, it declined loosing its first place of importance. Vaishnavism, which occupied the second influential position at the beginning of the period, gradually gained influence and finally came to occupy the first place among the Hindu sects. The advent of a few new Vaishnavite sub-sects like Vallabhas, Chaitanyas, Vithalas etc. into the region and the further sub-division of some of its sub-sects like Srivaishnavism, on doctrinal matters, strengthened the position of Vaishnavism. The first part of the 16th century A.D. when the major part of Andhra Desa was under the Vijayanagara rule, can be regarded as the golden age of Vaishnavism in the Telugu country.

At the beginning of the 14th century A.D., Islam had only a limited following in the Telugu country. Its influence was confined to a few places. The Muslim invasions in the first quarter of the 14th century A.D. and the brief Tughluq rule over Andhra Desa gave a new impetus to Islam. The influx of new Muslims, local conversions, and the state patronage enabled it to take its roots firmly in the local soil. The emergence of Islam as the state-religion was naturally to have serious repercussions on the fortunes of the other religious systems of the area. The subsequent Bahmani and Qutbshahi rule over the Telugu country enabled Islam to strengthen its position still further. By the end of the 16th century A.D., it came to have a considerable following in this area. However, its followers were only a fraction of the total population and were concentrated mainly in the principal towns that were the bases of Muslim political power. Among the three regions of Andhra Desa, it was telangana which had the greater population of Muslims.

During the period of Tughluq and Bahmani rule, when the Sunni sect of Islam was the state religion, the followers of Islam in Andhra Desa belonged mainly to the Sunni sect. During the Qutbshahi period the Shia sect became the state religion and naturally came to have a good number of its followers in the area. Inspite of this, the Sunni sect continued to have greater number of adherents than that of the former.

The religious institutions whose fortunes in Andhra Desa, as elsewhere, were inextricably linked with the contemporary political and religious changes underwent correspondingly a number of fluctuations during this period.

At the beginning of the 14th century A.D., the Hindu religious institutions were at the height of their influence and prosperity. This corresponded to the political strength of the Kakatiya Kingdom and the influential position enjoyed by the Hindu religion in the area. Among them again, those of the Saiva sects were in a most predominant position at that juncture. Next in position were the religious institutions belonging to Vaishnavism, Sakti cult, Advaitism and other minor sects in that order. The religious institutions belonging to Islam were very few in number in Andhra Desa and their influence and activities were nominal.

The Hindu religious institutions in general received a great setback in their fortunes and activities during the period of Muslim invasions and the Tughluq rule. The Muslim religious institutions and especially those of Sunnis became strengthened and took firm roots in Andhra Desa during this period.

Consequent on the re-establishment of the Hindu political power in the Telugu country by the Musunuris, the Reddis, the Velamas and the Sangamas, there was a revival in the fortunes of the Hind religious institutions, though not to the same level of prosperity enjoyed under the Kakatiyas. During this period, the growth of Muslim religious institutions in Andhra Desa, except in the Western parts of Telangana region which was under Bahmany rule, was very slow.

The Hindu religious institutions, especially in the Telangana region received another great setback in their fortunes, with the fall of the Velama rule in the middle of the 15th century A.D. from then on under continuous Muslim rule, that of Bahmanis at the beginning and the Qutbshahis afterwards, their condition further declined. At this time, the Muslim religious institutions received a new boost and gradually spread to the entire region. Especially under the Qutbshahis, the Shia religious institutions became most predominant.

In the other two regions i.e., Rayalaseema and Coastal Andhra the Hindu religious institutions continued to be active and prospecrous even after the middle of the 15th century. But the Saiva religious institutions, began to decline after the fall of the Reddi Kingdoms and the Sangama dynasties Vijayanagara. The rule of Suryavamsi Gajapatis of Orissa and Saluvas and Tuluvas of Vijanagara was a period of the ascendancy of Vaishnava religious institutions.

The Hindu religious institutions received the final setback with the decline of Gajapatis after 1540 A.D. and of Vijayanagara after 1565 A.D. and with the gradual establishment of the Qutbshahi rule over the coastal Andhra and Rayalaseema region. Towards the end of the 16th century A.D., the Hindu religious institutions, in general, were in declining condition with no hope of revival in near future. The Muslim religious institutions and especially those of the Shia sect were at the height of their influence and prosperity in Andhra Desa.

The religious institutions which are covered in the present study are, the Temple, the *Maṭha,* the *Agrahāra*, the Mosque, the *Khānqah,* the *Dargah* and the *Āshūrkhāna*, the first three of Hinduism and the remaining four of Islam.

The Hindu Temple is basically a seat or an abode of God and a place of worship for Hindus. Some of the terms used in the epigraphs of Andhra Desa to designate the Temple are *Dēvalayamu*[6], *Dēgulamu*[7] *Surāgāramu*[8], *Tirumuṭṭamu*[9], *Prāsādamu*[10], *Rāgudi*[11], *Mēḍa*[12] *Dēvulamu*[13], *Dēvaḍumu*[14], *Dēvasthānamu*[15], *Alukamu*[16], *Sthānamu*[17], *Nagaru*[18], and *Kōyil*[19]. Most of these terms means, etymologically, the residence or the dwelling that enshrines the image of a deity or some symbol of worship.

The term *Maṭha*, in its etymological meaning, is a place of residence for an order of Hindu monks whose lives are devoted to the service of that particular religious order. The Hindu monk known as *Sanyasi* is one who has renounced the world and leads an ascetic life under the monastic vows such as poverty and chastity. The other terms, used to denote the Hindu monk, are *Yōgi*, *Muni*, *Paramahamsa, Parivrājaka, Avadhūta* etc.[20].

The Sanskrit term *Agrahāra* literally means "a village granted to Brahmans, in general, for sustance".[21] The are also referred to, in the local epigraphs, as *Chaturvēdimaṅgalam* or *maṅgalam*[22] and *Naḷḷillu.*[23] Besides being the centre of learning, the *Agrahāra* was an important centre of Hindu religious activity.[24]

The Mosque is a place of public worship and prayers for the Muslims. *Masjid,* the Arabic term denoting the Mosque, literally means "a place where one prostrates oneself (before God), or in other words, completely surrenders oneself to God."[25].

The Persian term *Khānqh* means etymologically "a house where mystics live and pray, according to the rules of their order."[26] It can be regarded almost as the counterpart of the Hindu *Matha.* Different terms such as, *Zāwiyah, Tekke, Rābita, Ribāt,* besides *Khānqh,* were used to denote the Muslim monastery.[27]

The term *Dargāh* is defined in the *Dictionary of Islam* as "a Muhammadan Shrine or tomb of some reputed holy person and which is the object of pilgrimage and adoration".

The term *Āshūrkhāna* has been defined as "the building which houses the *Ālams* or conventional copies of the standard carried by Imam Hussain".[28] It belonged excessively to the Shia sect of Islam.

Hindu as well as Muslim scriptures stress very much the religious merit accruing from building or establishing the religious institutions of their respective religious systems. The religious merit accruing from the building of temples to God was equated with that of performing sacrifices, the deeds of piety and charity. *Bṛhat Samhita* declares, "Let him, who wishes to enter the worlds that are reached by sacrificial offerings and the performance of religious obligations, (*Iṣtapūrta*), build a temple to the Gods, by doing which he attains both the results of sacrifice and the performance of religious obligations." [29] The scriptures ascribe equal merit to the rich as well as to the poor people who build temples according to their resources. *Agni Purana* says "A poor man building the smallest shrine reaps the same benefit which a rich man does by building the largest temple."30 The building of a temple and also the granting of an *Agrahāra* to the Brahmans are included among the *Sapta Santanāmulu* i.e. the seven acts productive of religious merit, to be pursued by people as laudable object.[31] Similarly, the building of a Mosque was also considered as an act of religious merit. A tradition, attributed tot he Prophet, says "...for him who builds a mosque, God will build a home in paradise...[39]

Hence the establishment of the Hindu and Muslim religious foundations became an essential feature of their respective religions in Andhra Desa during the medieval period. These institutions, being basically religious in character, acted as the nerve centres of their respective faiths and helped the latter's propagation and preservation. Patronised by the rulers and the ruled alike, they became very rich institutions possessing large number of landed estates, buildings and other sources of income. They evolved their own organizations to manage their affairs. The government of the day also took lot of care to see that they functioned on proper lines. Finally, besides being great religious and spiritual centres, they were the institutions of multifarious activities and exerted a profound influence on the political, social, economic and cultural life of the contemporary society.

Their various aspects—the general history, organizations and functionaries of each category of religious institutions, their relations with the state and finally their various activities and their impact on the contemporary society—are discussed in detail in the following chapters.

The geographical limits of Andhra Desa, the area covered by this study, correspond roughly to the present state boundaries of Andhra Pradesh. The term Telugu country is also used as synonym for Andhra Desa in the following pages. Similarly, the terms—the Telengana, Rayalaseema and Coastal Andhra, which are used at present to denote the principal regions of Andhra Pradesh, are used with the same connotation in the work.

III

SOURCES

The primary sources for this study are principally epigraphic and the literary. Of these, again, the epigraphic sources constitute the major protion. In the case of the Muslim religious institutions, due to paucity of information for reconstructing their history, sources falling slightly outside the period and the region of study also have been utilized, wherever needed and with caution.

Epigraphic Sources

The surviving and known lithic and copper-plate inscriptions of the period are abundant. But an analysis of them would show that they are not equal in number or even in information relating to each category of the religious institutions dealt in this work. The religion-wise distribution of these inscriptions is also unequal. For example, the bulk of the epigraphs of the period belong to the Hindu religious institutions. Among these again, the inscriptions belonging to the temples are more in number compared to those referring to the *Maṭhas* and the *Agrahāras*. The majority of the Temple epigraphs belong to the major shrines like those of Tirumalai-Tirupati, Srisailam, Simhachalam, and Ahobilam. A majority of the epigraphs belonging to the Hindu religious institutions, if they are considered region-wise are from the Rayalaseema and the Coastal Andhra region. Compared to them, those of the Telengana region are less in number. A majority, within the inscriptions of the Telenganga region, belonged to the Kakatiya period and a few of them to that of the remaining dynasties namely, the Velama, the Qutbshahi, the Bahmani, the Gajapati and the Vijayanagara. The non-availability of sufficient number of these epigraphs from Telengana region must be attributed to the political instability prevailing there during the post-Kakatiya period. But the case of the Coastal Andhra and the Rayalaseema districts is different in this regard. As these two regions were, more or less throughout this period, under the continuous Hindu rule, they provided large number of epigraphs. In the case of Rayalaseema, the availability of epigraphs is more or less continuous and enables us to give a chronological picture of the things. While a majority of the epigraphs from the Coastal Andhra belong, in order of importance, to the Reddi, the Kakatiya, the Vijayanagara, and the Gajapati dynasties, and in the Rayalaseema region, to mainly Vijayanagara and Kakatiya dynasties.

The epigraphs belonging to the Muslim religious institutions are very few and contain meagre information compared to those of the Hindu religious institutions. They belong mainly to the Bahmani and the Qutbshahi periods; and the majority of them came from the Telengana region. Even of the Muslim epigraphs, those of the Mosques are more in number, than those of the other Muslim religious institutions.

The inscriptions of the period are found in several languages-Sanskrit, Telugu, Tamil, Kannada, Persian and Arabic. Some of them are bi-lingual and most of them are in one language. Almost all of them are published either with English translations or summaries in the journals such as *South Indian Inscriptions, Epigraphia India, Epigraphia Indo-Moslemica, Epigraphia Carnatica, Andhra Pradesh Government Epigraphy Series,*

Tirumalai-Tirupati Devasthanam Epigraphical Series, Inscriptions of Nellore Districts, Telengana Sasanamulu., etc.

Most of the inscriptions are *Dāna-sāsanās* recording the establishment of the new religious institutions, additions made to the exiting institutions, grants of land and cash made to them and their functionaries by the rulers and private individuals. They contain innumerable details about the history of the religious institutions—their income and expenditure, organization, management, charities and other religious and social activities. Being contemporary documents, these epigraphs provide valuable first hand source material. By way of illustration, a few important epigraphs, especially belonging to the Hindu religious institutions can be cited.

The Vilasa c.p. grant of Musunuri Prolaya Nayaka[33] and the Anitalli c. p. grant of 1423 A.D.[34] are remarkable records having a lot of information for the history of religious institutions. They give a graphic account of the life in the Telugu country during the period of Tughluq rule. They describe the impact of Muslim rule on the fortunes of the Hindu religious institutions like the temples and *Agrahāras,* and the efforts of Musunuri Prolaya Nayaka and Prolaya Vema Reddi to revive them. As these c. p. grants, like many of their type, were issued mainly for recording the grant of *Agrahāra* villages to Brahmans engaged in scholarly and sacrificial activities they throw very useful light on the life of those villages.

The Malkapuram inscription of Kakatiya queen Rudramadevi, dated 1261 A.D.[35], though its date precedes the period under study by about four decades, furnishes may interesting details about the organisation, management, finances and activities of the Golaki *Maṭhas* of the Pasupapata Saivas, situated in the Telugu country during that period. As these institutions continued to flourish till the end of the Kakatiya dynasty, the information provided in this epigraph is quite relevant and useful for the present study.

The Shitabkhan's Warangal inscription dated A.D. 1504-36 informs us about the desecration and the destruction of the Hindu temples situated especially in the Warangal fort by Muslim rulers and their revival by Shitabkhan alias Sitapati.

Similarly, the inscriptions found at Srisailam, Simhachalam, Ahobilam, and Tirumalai–Tirupati are a mine of information regarding the various aspects of the life of the Hindu temples and *Maṭhas* of the period. Tirupati alone has about a thousand epigraphs of the period and one of them dated 1546 A. D. actually gives very interesting information about the annual budget of the temple of Vithala of that place.[37]

Literary Sources

The contemporary source literature can be divided into three sub-categories—the Telugu and the Tamil literature, the Muslim chronicles and the Traveller's accounts, and the *Kaifiyats*.

Telugu and Tamil Literature

Telugu and Tamil literature contain some useful information for the subject. For example *Sripaṅḍitārādhya Charitramu,* a Telugu treatise was written by the Veerasaiva poet Palkurki Somanatha, a contemporary of Kakatiya Prataparudra II (A.D. 1280-1323), at the instance of the Asankyata Mahesvarulu, the Saiva religious community incharge of the management of the Mallikarjuna temple of Srisailam. Besides referring to the various religious sects and schools of the period, its author gives a description of Srisailam, of its Sivaratri festival, of the pilgrims and the various kinds of entertainment programmes provided on the night of Sivaratri when the pilgrims observed the holy of Vigil. *Krīḍābhirāmamu,* one of the rare Telugu literary works belonging to the category of *Veedhinatakamu* and whose author Vinukonda Vallabharaya belongs either to the end of the 14th century or the beginning of the 15th century, A.D., was staged by actors in the temple festivals at Mopuru. Besides depicting the religious, social and economic conditions of the people in the city of Warangal during the period of Kakatiya Prataparuda II, it refers to the existence of religious institutions belonging to various religious persuasions including those of Islam and Buddhism in that city. It describes the various activities connected with the temples. The description of the fair held a Srikakulam on the occasion of the festival of the local God, the prevalence of prostitution and the disreputable behaviour of the young widows in that fair, is useful for the subject. *Siddēśvara Charitra (Kakatiya Rajula Charitra—Pratapa Charitra)*, A Telugu work by Kasa Sarvappa belonging to the 17th century, A.D. gives valuable information about the religious and social life of the Kakatiya period and furnishes certain interesting details regarding the policy of the Kakatiya government towards the religious institutions such as the temples and the *Agrahāras*. It also indicates the relative strength of the temples belonging to various Hindu sects.

Sri Kāśi Khanḍamu, a Telugu work by Srinatha (first half of the 15th century A.D.), while referring to the personal religion of the author's patron King Veerabhadrareddi of Rajahmahendravaram, describes the flourishing condition of the *Agrahāras* of the period. It also refers to the *Sanivarotsavas* (periodical festivals), the dancing of the Temple dancers in native style and the sixty four (*Chatushashti*) *Natyakutas* in the Saiva temple of Draksharamamu (Godavari dt.). Srinatha, in his *Śivarātri Mahatmyamu*, another Telugu work written at the instance of Sri Santa Bhikshavritti, the pontiff of Bhikshavritti *Maṭha* of Srisailam and dedicated to Muppalapu Mummadi Santayya who was the chief servant (*Mulabhrityudu)* of the above pontiff, refers to the trustees of the Mallikarjuna temple of Srisailam, its damsels, musicians etc. He also describes the various entertainments and religious discussions at the place. Similarly, *Āmuktamālyada*, a Telugu work by Krirhnadeva Raya of Vijayanagara (A.D. 1509-29) contains the reflections of that monarch on polity. Especially his views with regard to the temple administration are corroborated by the contemporary epigraphic evidence.

Sri Sannidi Guruparaṁparai, a Tamil sectarian work, (ed. K. Anantacharya, Madras, 1914) is a small biography of the pontiffs of the Ahobila *Maṭha* belonging to the *Vadagalai* Srivaishnava sect. It begins with Sri Adivan Sathakopa Jiyar, the founder of that *Maṭha* and ends with Sriranga Sathakopa Yati, the 42nd pontiff. It contains many interesting details about the establishment of that *Maṭha,* period of their pontificate, their various literary and religious activities.

Muslim Chronicles and Other Works

Khazainul Futuh and *Nūh Siphir* by Amir Khusrau[38], *Tarīkh-i-Ferōzshāhi* by Ziauddin Barni[39], *Gulshan-i-Ibrahimi,* generally called *Tarīkh-i-Ferishta* by Muhammad Qasim Hindu Shah, surnamed Ferishta[40], *Burhān-i-Mathir* by Syed-Ali-bin-Azizul-lah Tabataba[41], *Tarīkh-i-Sultan Muhammad Qutbshah*, popularly known as *Tarīkh-e-Qutbshahi* by an anonymous hirtorian[42], are some of the important contemporary chronicles, Though they deal mainly with the political history of the Muslim dynasties of the period, they refer to the policy followed by the Muslim rulers towards the Hindus and the Hindu religious institutions in Andhra Desa. They also furnish some information about the building of the Mosques, and the activities of the Muslim saints. This information, though of stray nature, is useful for the reconstruction of the history of the religious institutions in Andhra Desa. In the case of the last three mentioned works, their English translations as well as their Persian texts have been followed. But in the case of the first three, only their English translations have been followed.

Besides these, there are a few Persian and Urdu works belonging to the period of Asafjahis of Hyderabad, which also contain some information useful for the reconstruction of the history of Muslim religious institutions. *Tārīkh-i-Zafarah,* a Persian work complied in the year A.D. 1871-72, by Girdharilal Ahqar[43], gives a short account of different Mosques and other religious buildings built by the Kings of Golkonda in the Hyderabad city and its suburbs. *Tuzuk-E-Qutbshahi* complied by an anonymous author is another Persian work of the period which contains some information about some of the *Ashurkhanas* and Mosques of the Qutbshahi period. Its author was a contemporary of Asaf Jah IV (19th century A.D.). The manuscript copy of this work, which I have referred to, is preserved in the Salar Jung Library[44]. Similarly, *Mahbub-i-dhil-manam Tadhkira Auliya-i-Dakkani* (an account of saints), a work in Urdu complied in 1331 A.H. (beginning of the 20th century) by Abdul Jabbar Khan Malkapuri is another important source for the subject.[45] It furnishes an account of some of the Sufi saints like Baba Sarfuddin of Hyderabad, Syed Shah Jamal Warangali and Baba Fakruddin of Penugonda. It gives many details about their missionary and intellectual activities. The author states that he based his work on about 153 manuscripts and books, which he mentions by name. Some of them are found in Oriental Manuscripts Library and Salarjung Library, Hyderabad. But most of them were swept away in the Musi Flood of 1909.

Farmans: The *Farmans* are another important source of information for the subject. A *Farman* is a mandate or an order issued by a Muslim monarch. They record various types of grants made to individuals, religious institutions, the functionaries of those institutions and the like. The *Farmans* of this period generally contain, a religious superscription, the seal or the sign manual of the monarch, the name of the administrative authorities entrusted with the execution of the *Farman*, a brief history of the case or the reason which necessitated the issue of *Farman*, the date and the Parwanagai officers under whose *Parawanagi* the *Farmans* were issued.

I have consulted the original Bahmani and Qutbshahi *Farmans* belonging to the Hazrat Bande Nawaz Collection preserved in State Archives, A.P. Hyderabad. These are in Persian language. In this collection, there are very few Bahmani *Farmans* and about fifteen Qutbshahi *Farmans* which are relevant to the subject. As most of them are damaged, it is difficult to get their complete text. But they contain references to the various functionaries of the Muslim religious institutions, the names of the donars, the administrative officials incharge of their execution etc., which are useful for the subject.

Travellers' Accounts: The accounts of the foreigners, who visited the Telugu country during the period under study, also contain some information which is useful for the subject. The most important of this category are the accounts or 'Relations' left by the Dutchman Schoerer, the Englishman Methwold and tne Anonymous Author. The author of the third account who has not mentioned his name appears to be a Dutch Official who served the Dutch factory at Nizampatnam. All the three authors lived in the Telugu country and visited its chief towns during the period between A.D. 1608 to 1632. Their accounts are published under the title *Relations of Golkonda in the Early Seventeenth Century A.D. 1608-22,* (ed. W.H. Moreland, London, 1931). These 'Relations' contain an eye-witness account of the life in the Telugu country and especially in its Coastal districts. They give a trustworthy account of the social and religious life of the people belonging to both Hindus (Gentles) and Muslims, their sects, castes, their religious institutions, fairs and festivals. They help us to know the state of the religious institutions at the beginning of the 17th century A.D. which marks the end of the Hindu rule and the climax of the Muslim political power in the Telugu country.

Kaifiyats: Kaifiyats also known collectively as Mackenzie collections of Manuscripts are another important source of information for the subject. Besides giving a narrative of the political history of the period, they throw a flood of light on the religious, social and economic conditions of the country which is, to a great extent, accurate and reliable. Besides, the texts of a number of inscriptions, both lithic and copper-plate, contained in them, most of which are published in the epigraphical journals by this time, provide a trustworthy information for the subject. Especially, the information furnished by these records about the conditions of the religious institutions belonging to the Brahmanical religion in the Rayalaseema and Coastal Andhra districts after the fall of the Vijayanagara and the Gajapati rule and during their occupation by the Qutbshahi army, is of valuable help for the subject. Mackenzie Manuscripts contain details useful for the subject far the Rayalasema and to some extent the Coastal districts. For Telengana region, we do not get much information except for a few places like Warangal.

The copy of the Mackenzie Manuscripts, which I consulted is that of Sahitya Academy, A.P. Government, Hyderabad. It contains a few scribal errors which I have corrected whenever necessary, after comparing it with the (microfilm) copy of the State Archives, A.P. Government. Where ever the information from State Archieve's copy is used it is mentioned in brackets.

2

Religious Institutions:
A General History

The general history of each category of the religious institutions, the Temple, the *Maṭha,* the *Agrāhara*, the Mosque, the *Khānqāh,* the *Dargāh* and the *Āshūrkhana,* and the fluctuations in their fortunes throughout the period under study are traced in this chapter.

THE HINDU TEMPLE

During the Kakatiya period innumerable Temples were built all over the Telugu country. Kakatiya Kings and their subordinates were great Temple builders. The rise and spread of the devotional religious sects like Veerasaivism and Srivaishnavism, inculcated an intensive love and devotion to a personal god as the means of salvation. Besides, there prevailed a condition of general economic prosperity in the area under the Kakatiyas as a result of the stable political order. These are some of the factors which gave impetus to the Temple building activity during the period. A great amount of public money went into the Temple-building and upkeep during the period.

Temples under Kakatiya Prataparudra II and Ganga Narasimha II

At the beginning of the 14th century A.D., when the Telugu country was under Kakatiya Prataparudra II and Eastern Ganga ruler

Narasimha II, the Hindu Temples were in a flourishing condition. They held a monopoly of the patronage of the State and its subjects. Their prosperity and activities are amply indicated in the inscriptions and the literature available. For example, *Pratāpa Charitra* states that, Prataparudra II spent, every year, one crore of coins[1] for the upkeep of the grandeur of the Temples of Ekasilanagara (Warangal, his capital) itself, besides spending another three crores for the maintenance of Saiva and Vaishnava Temples situated at places like Srisailam, Kalahasti, Kolipaka, Vemulavada, Kanchi, Tirupati, Mangalagiri, Bhadrachalam and Simhachalam in his Kingdom, and Varanasi, Ramesvaram, Arunachalam, Gokarnam etc., outside. It also states that, this monarch set apart 2,000 villages, besides the amount mentioned above, for the expenses of the Temples.[2] This statement and especially the amount of money mentioned in it may be an exaggeration, but it gives an idea as to how the rulers of the period bestowed large sums of money out of the state exchquer, and a good number of villages on the religious institutions for their maintenance.

Regarding the sect-wise strength of the Temples of this period, when the Kakatiya political power reached its high water mark, the Temples belonging to Saiva religious sects, on the whole, were in a most predominant position as far as their numerical strength, prosperity, popularity and activities are concerned. For example, *Pratapa Charitra* gives the number of Temples belonging to different Hindu sects, situated in the Kingdom of Warangal, in the reign of Pratapa Rudra II as follows: Temples dedicated to Siva – 5,500; Vishnu – 1,300; Maliara Deva – 2,400; Bhairava, Durga and Ganapati – 4,400.[3]

The Temples of Srisailam, Tripurantakam, and Puspagiri in the Rayalaseema region; Hanumakonda, Warangal, Pillamarri, Alampur, and Ramappa in the Telangana region, and the Pancharamas of Coastal Andhra are some of the most influential Temples belonging to Saivism. Especially the Saiva Temple (of Mallikarjuna) of Srisailam (Kurnool dt.) appears to have been the richest Temple of the period. The very fact that, this Temple alone had more than fifty-two villages in its possession in the reign of Kakatiya Prataparudra II,[4] indicates the properity and the popularity of some of the Saiva shrines of the period.

The Temples belonging to Vaishnava sects were, no doubt, quite numerous throughout the Telugu country. They were in an influential position especially at Simhachalam and Srikurmam in the Northern Coastal Andhra region, whose rulers, the Eastern Gangas, were staunch followers of Madhwa sect of Vaishnavism. But their position, on the whole, was only next to that of Saiva Temples.

Impact of Muslim Invasions on the Hindu Temples

Muslim invasion during the period of Prataparudra II affected, to some extent, the fortunes of the Hindu Temples in the Telugu country. In order to reduce the rulers of the country to quick submission and to get the immediate results of their enterprise, the invaders appear to have resorted to all sorts of atrocities. They caused widespread destruction in the country by sacking towns and villages and by plundering and enslaving the people on the army routes and in the suburbs of Warangal city. As these early invasion were motivated by the considerations of wealth and political suzerainty, the wealth of the Hindu Temples in those areas definitely attracted the attention of the invaders. Malik Kafur, who earned the title 'idol-breaking Malik' for having destroyed many Temples of South India including that of Srirangam (Tamilnadu),[5] may not have spared the Temples in the Telugu country. In order to procure wood for erecting defence works, the Muslim army under Malik Kafur seems to have levelled the groves and sacred tress of the Temples situated outside the city of Warangal, in A.D. 1309, when it invested that fort. Amir Khusru, describing this siege, writes:

> The trees were cut with axes and felled, notwithstanding their groans, and the Hindus who worship trees, could not at that time come to the rescue of their idols. So that every cursed tree which was in that capital of idolatry was cut down to the roots.[6]

Even the subsequent Muslim invasions also appear to have been characterised by the destruction of the religious objects of the native Hindus. Amir Khusru, describing the siege of Warangal fort by Khusru Khan, Mubarak Shah Khilji's general, writes in his *Nūh Sipihr*:

> They pursued the enemy to the gates and set every thing on fire. They burnt down all those gardens and groves. That paradise of idol-worshippers became like hell. The fire-worshippers of Bud were in alaram and flocked round their idols...[7]

The Muslim invasions affected the fortunes and activities of the Hindu Temple in the Telugu country indirectly also. As the country, during this period of two decades (1303-23 A.D.), was completely engaged in facing the Muslim invaders who invaded it several times, its rulers and their subjects could not think in terms of spending much money on building the Temples and supporting their activities. Payment of tribute to the Delhi Sultan and the increased military expenditure drained the state exchequer and greatly handicapped the rulers in this matter.[8] This factor explains, to a great extent, the absence of any major Temples which can be attributed to the period of Prataparudra II, the last ruler of the Kakatiya Kingdom. No doubt, there are a number of Temple grants belonging to this period which record the grants of lands, cash etc. for the maintenance of worship of the deities. But, in most cases, they were made to the already existing Temples. Thus, the Temple building activity during this period, was less than that of the preceding period.

The fall of the Hindu Kingdom of the Kakatiyas in the year 1323 A.D. and the consequent Tughluq rule hindred the progress of the Hindu Temple which in Andhra Desa was hitherto unchecked. From the epigraphic evidence, many of them appear to have been destroyed and desecrated and some of them converted into Mosques by the invaders. The Vilasa c.p. grant of Prolayanayaka, which gives a vivid picture of the state of the Telugu country during the period, states in unmistakable terms; that the Brahmans were disallowed to perform their religious rites and rituals and Temples were destroyed and idols were desdecrated and broken.[9] While some of them were completely destroyed, some others were converted into Mosques. The principal Mosque of Rajahmundry (Godavari dt.) and the Deval Mosque of Bodhan (Nizamabad dt.) are some of the important examples of the conversion of the Hindu Temples into the places of Muslim worship during the period.[10] In this great calamity, no discrimination appears to have been made by the new rulers; and the Temples belonging to all religions met with the same fate. The rituals and other activities of many of these Temples came to be stopped. Only the Temples situated in inaccessible places, which were far away from the principal towns, like those of Srisailam, Tirupati, Ahobilam, Simhachalam etc. and the minor Temples, might have escaped the fury of the Muslim rulers. Even these also could not function effectively due to the lack of patronage under the alien government.

Hindu Temples in the Post-Kakatiya Times

The fortunes of the Hindu Temple in Andhra Desa have been revived following the establishment of the various new Hindu Kingdom—Musunuri, Velama, Reddi, Vijayanagara (Sangama dynasty), etc. The rulers of these dynasties revived the worship in many Temples which were descerated under the Tughluq rule. There is also definite epigraphic and literary evidence for the building of new Temples and the extension of liberal patronage to the old Temples by these rulers. For example, an inscription of 1353 A.D. from Korukonda village (E. Godavari dt.) refers to the building of the Temple of God Laxmi Narasimha at that place, under the patronage of Mummadi Nayaka, a subordinate of Musunuri Kingdom of Warangal, and to the grant of two villages to that Temple by the same chief.[11] There are a few Temple epigraphs relating to the Velama dynasty of Telangana also. For example, an epigraph of 1369 A.D. from the village Ainavolu (Warangal dt.) states that Anavota I gifted a village to the Temple of Mailaradeva of that place.[12] Another Velama record belonging to the year 1375 A.D. from Kandikonda village (Warangal dt.) statges that the Velama

Chief Venna (son of Mada I) built a temple for the God Janardana, at that place and granted some land for its maintenance.[13] Another inscription, of the year 1376 A.D. from Umamahesvaram (Mahbubnagar dt.), refers to the building of a *mañtapa* to God Mahesvara of that place, by Mada I.[14] The patronage of the Reddi rulers to the building of the Temples and their maintenance is referred to in the epigraphs and literature of that period. Errapragada, in his *Harivamśamu,* gives evidence to the building of the Temples and revival of religious activity in the Coastal Andrah region by Prolaya Vema Reddi, his patron and the founder of Reddi Kingdom. He writes:

> *Agrahāramulu vidyā tapō vriddhula kichchi yajña kartaluga manache—komarāra cheruvulu guḷḷu pratishthinchi lōka sambhāvyamuluga manache...*[15]

According to 'Iksu grant' (Guntur dt.), Anavema Reddi of Kondavidu endowed a number of Temples, like those of pancharamas, Srisailam, Ahobilam, Kurmachalam and Simhachalam.[16] Similarly, there are a good number of epigraphs belonging to the first dynasty of Vijaynagara which record the patronage of its rulers and their subordinates to the Temples in the Rayalaseema region.[17]

The relative strength and popularity of the Temples belonging to various Hindu sects during the period of the above dynasties is almost the same as that of the Kakatiya period. The founders of these new dynasties, most of whom were originally in the Kaktiya service, showed, in continuation of the Kakatiya court traditions, a special preference to Saivism and its institutions. The Saiva Temples in the Telugu country, during this period, continued, naturally, to be predominant. The epigraphs recording donations to Saiva Temples and their activities are more than those of the Temples of any other Hindu sect. The most important evidence illustrating the supreme position enjoyed by the Saiva Temples of the period is the special claim made by the rulers of all the major dynasties of the period, in their epigraphs, to the meritorious act of constructing steps to the sacred hill of Srisailam, the seat of the famous Saiva shrine of God Mallikarjuna.[18] During this period, the Vaishnava temples, though numerous, continued to occupy the second place of importance. But it is also to be noted that the Temples, especially those belonging to Saivism of this period, in spite of the generous patronage extended to them by the rulers of the above dynasties and their subjects, did not attain their former (pre-Muslim period) position with regard to their prosperity, organisation, rituals and other activities.

Regional Variations in the Fortunes of the Temples in the Post-Kakatiya Period

During the post Kakatiya period we find regional variations in the fortunes of the Hindu Temples. These variations can be seen in their prosperity and activities. For example, the Temples in the Telangana region, during this period, were less prosperous and less active than those of the Coastal Andhra and Rayalaseema region. This is indicated, to same extent by the availability of only a small number of epigraphs from this region recording donations by the rulers and their subjects to the Temples during this period. The frequent Muslim invasions of this region and their devastating impact on its general life is one of the important factors that affected the fortunes of the Hindu Temples. Of the three regions of Andhra Desa, it was the Telangana region, which, because of its proximity to the Bahmani Kingdom in the west, was more exposed to the Muslim invasions and was more politically unstable, during the period. Of course, the western districts of Telangana, as far as Golkonda in the east, formed a part of the Bahmani sultanate almost from the period of its inception. But the remaining area was invaded, during the period of Musunuri dynasty, not less than three times by the Bahmani Sultans.[19] Similarly, it was invaded, during the Velama period, a number of times by the Bahmanis. There were, no doubt, wars between the rulers of this region and their Hindu neighbours, namely the Reddis and Vijayanagara. But it was the wars with the Muslims that had a devastating effect on the region and caused more damage to tis Temples than those waged between Hindu rulers. These Muslim invasions affected the fortunes of the Hindu Temples both directly and indirectly. The Pillamarri inscription of 1357 A.D., which records the reconsecration of the image of God Erakesvara of that place by Erapotalenka, an official under Musunuri Kapayanayaka, states that the Temples was damaged, previously by Sultan Alauddin during the disturbances of that period (on the occasion of the one of his invasion).[20] The heavy expenditure incurred by the rulers of the region, on these wars and the war indemnities, might not have permitted them to spend their money liberally on the Temples. The details of the war indemnity presented to the Bahmani Sultan to purchase peace when Kapaya was defeated in the year 1366 A.D. are given by Ferishta. It included, "three hundred elephants, two hundred valuable horse and thirty three lakhs of Rupees", besides the cession of a part of his dominions.[21]

The Hindu Temples in the Rayalaseema and Coastal Andhra region, during the corresponding period, were in a better position than those of Telangana. This was most probably due to the political stability and the consequent economic prosperity and the congenial religious atmosphere prevailing in these two regions under Vijayanagara and Reddi rule. Many Temples like those of Srisailam, Ahobilam, Tirupati, Simhachalam, Srikurmam, Pancharamas and a host of others of this region continued to be active during this period. This is indicated, to some extent, by the large number of epigraphs available from the Temples in these places.

The regional variations in the fortunes of the Temples in Andhra Desa, which depended, to a great extent, on the corresponding political and religious changes, is more clearly visible from the middle of the 15th century A.D. onwards. Their history, especially in the Telangana and coastal Andhra, took an adverse turn at this juncture. The political situation that arose after the disappearance of the Velama and reddi kingdoms from these two regions was to have serious repercussions on their fortunes.

The Temples in the Telangana region were the worst affected due to these political changes. The Bahmani rule, which replaced that of the Velamas in this region, proved to be of great disadvantage to their growth. Due to lack of patronage and protection under the

Muslim rule their activities received a great setback. Many prominent Temples of the region went into oblivion and were no more heard of, either in the epigraphs or in the literature, during the Bahmani period. In fact, we do not have any Temple epigraphs recording either the activities of the Temples or their patronage by the Muslim state and its subjects. Many of them appear to have been destroyed and the worship in them was stopped. The Warangal fort inscription of 1504 A.D. issued by Shitab Khan (Chittapa Khana) indicates how the important Temples in that erst-while capital of the Kakatiyas suffered desecration in the hands of the Muslims, apparently under the Bahmany rule, and how Shitab Khan, a Hindu rebel, restored them to their former glory. It states:

> For the worship of the gods and Brahmans he reinstalled the images of the god Panchala Raya (Krishna), of the Goddess Kakati, the Laxmi of the Kakatiya Kingdom, and of Siva, the primeval and self-existent lord, removed by the Turushkas (Muslims), in their respective shrines...[22]

Some of the Temples of the period, in the region, appear to have been converted into Mosques by the Muslim rulers. Syed Ali Tabataba, while referring to Ahmad Shah Bahmany's conquest of Warangal, Rajukonda and Devarakonda, states that the Sultan demolished a number of Temples at those places and built Mosques and Muslim schools on their ruins.[23] An epigraph of 1484 A.D. refers to the building of a Mosque on the ruins of a Hindu Temple at Rajkonda (the erstwhile capital of the Velama Kingdom) by Malik-An-Nimat, the Bahmani governor.[24]

The history of Hindu Temple in this region (i.e., Telangana), during the remaining period of study, (till the end of 16th century A.D.) was more of less the same as that of the Bahmani in this region at the beginning of the 16th century A.D., though generally described as benevolent in character, the Hindu Temples could not get any more favourable treatment than what they got under the Bahmanis. In the process of expansion of the Qutbshahi political power in the Telugu country many of its Hindu Temples appear to have been destroyed. While describing the capture of Devarakonda fort (Nalgonda dt.) from a Hindu chief by Sultan Quli, the Anonymous historian of Golkonda states that ''the Hindu palaces and Temples (in the fort of Devarakonda), by the Kings' (Sultan Qulis') orders were consumed to ashes, and Mosques built in their stead.''[25] The same historian states in another context, that Sultan Quli demolished one thousand Temples in his Kingdom and constructed Mosques in their place.[26] According to the general tendency of the age they might have considered it meritorious to destroy the Temples and build Mosques in their place. The decline of these in institutions of the region is also proved by the complete absence of positive evidence either for the state patronage or for any activities of these institutions.

Another important factor, which contributed to the decline of the Temples, for that matter, any other Hindu institutions, under the Bahmani and Qutbshahi rule, is the emergence of Islam as the state religion and its institutions with the state support. Hindu religious institutions which monopolised the state patronage under the Hindu rule had to face, now, unequal competition for the same with the Muslim institutions. This, to a great extent, explains the absence of any major Temple in this region.

The fortunes of the Hindu Temples in the Coastal Andhra region were also affected, to some extent, by the political changes that took place in the middle of the 15th century A.D. This region, from the fall of the Reddi Kingdoms till the battle of Rakshasi Tangade in 1565, had changed hands, frequently, between the three major powers of the South i.e., Gajapatis, Bahmanis and Vijayanagara. During the period of political instability characterized by the frequent wars between those three powers, the Temples could not get continuous support either from the rulers or their subjects. The Vijayanagar and the Gajapati rulers who were Brahmanical rulers extended, no doubt, their liberal patronage to the Temples of the region. But their activities suffered a setback under the Bahmani rule (in the last quarter of the 15th century A.D.). Some of them became the victims of the religious fanaticism of the Muslim rulers. The worst fate suffered by some of the temples in the fort of Kondapalli (Krishna dt.) in the year 1477-78 A.D., when it was recaptured by the Bahmani Sultan from a rebellious Hindu officer, is described by Ferishta. He writes:

> The King (Muhammad III) having gone to view the fort, brcke down an idolatrous Temple, and killed some Brahmins, who officiated at it, with his own hands, as a point of religion. He then gave orders for a Mosque to be erected on the foundation of the Temple . . . and Commanded the Khoṭba to be read in his name . . .[27]

The position of the Hindu Temples in the Rayalaseema region during the corresponding period (from the middle of the 15th century till the battle of Rakahasi Temgadi in 1565 A.D.) was better compared to that of the Temples in the other two regions. The absolute security enjoyed by this region under Vijayanagara empire during this period and the states' liberal patronage enabled its temples to become prosperous and active. In fact it is this region, which supplies the bulk of the Temple epigraphs of the period which also amply attest to the prosperity and the activities of these institutions. Many new Temples were also built and additions were made to a number of existing Temples in this region during the period. The important Saiva and Vaishnava Temples built this region under the Vijayanagara patronage, and especially in the 16th century A.D., are the Veerabhadraswami Temple at Lepakshi (Anantapur dt.) built by Virupanna, an official under Achuta Raya, the Ramalingesvara and Chintala-Venkatramana Temples at Tadpatri (Anantapur dt.), the Raghunatha Temple in the fort of Gandikota, built by its chiefs and the Temple of Kaḷyana Venkatesvara at Mangapuram (near Tirupati, Chittoor dt.). The noted additional structures made during this period are the *Gōpuram* of the Kalhasti Saiva Temple (Krishnarayas' period) and the *Kalyana Mantapa* of Jaladisvara Temple at Vellor (Chittoor dt.).[28]

One important fact to be noted in the history of Hindu Temples in Andhra Desa, during the period under study, is the sect-wise fluctuations in their fortunes. As noted earlier, the Temples belonging to the Saiva sects were in a predominant position during the first part of the period, that is, from the beginning of the 14th century A.D. to the Velama and Reddi Kingdoms and the decline of the Sangama dynasty of Vijayanagara empire, the Saiva Temples of the country lost their staunch patrons, and began to decline from the middle of the 15th century onwards. Under the Saluva and Tuluva dynasties of Vijayanagara and the Suryavamsi Gajapatis of Orissa, whose rulers were staunch Vaishnavites, the Vaishnave Temples, especially in the Rayalaseema and Coastal Andhra regions, gained the upper hand. Though the Temples of all Hindu sects were it was patronized by these rulers it was the Vaishnava Temples and especially those which were under the control of the Srivaishnavas and Madhwsa, that got their preferential treatment. The Vaishnava shrines of Tirupati and Ahobilam in the Rayalaseema and Simhachalam and Srikurmam in the North Coastal Andhra became very important religious centers of the period. The sweeping influence of Srivaishnavism and Madhwism in these regions also contributed to the progress of the Vaishnava Temples. This period, especially the last-quarter of the 15th century A.D. and the first three-quarters of the 16th century A.D., can be described as the golden age of not only Vaishnavism but also its Temples as far as their physical size, prosperity, popularity and activities are concerned, in Andhra Desa. The epigraphs belonging to the Temple of Tirupati provide the best evidence to illustrate this fact. It is the Saluva and the Tuluva dynasties of Vijayanagara, that are represented by nearly two-thirds of the total inscriptions of the place, indicating the enormous increase in its daily and periodical rituals and various other activities.[29] During this period (A.D.1509-68) alone, that temple received 115 villages (of the total 150) which made it the richest Temple in the Telugu country.[30] The size of the body of its functionaries also increased naturally to its maximum size during this period.

DECLINE OF GAJAPATI AND VIJAYANAGARA POWERS AND THE HINDU TEMPLE

The fortunes of the Hindu Temples in Andhra Desa received another great setback with the decline of the political power of the Gajapatis and Vijayanagara. The decline of the Gajapati rule after the death of prataparudra Gajapati in 1538 and the consequent expansion of the qutbshahi rule into the Telugu districts of Gajapati dominions (north of river Krishna) affected the fortunes of the Hindu Temples in that region, very severely. Some Muslim governors, appointed over the region by the Qutbshahi government, destroyed some of the Temples of the region and deprived them of their source of income. An epigraph of 1599 A.D. from Srikurmam (Srikakulam dt.) clearly states that Amina Malka (Amin-ul-Mulk, an official under Muhammad Quli Qutb Shah), while returning from a campaign against the rebels, Mukunda Bahubalendra and Vidhyadhara, destroyed the Temple of the God Srikurmanatha of that place and built a Mosque.[31] Similarly, an epigraph of 1604 A.D. from Simhachalam (Vizag dt.) Clearly states that, after the decline of the Gajapati rule over the region, the worship in the Temple of God Narasimha of the place came to a stand-still; there was practically no worship for a period of 40 years afterwards (1565 to 1604 A.D.); and it was revived by Asvaraya, a Hindu official of the Qutbshahi government in the year '1605 A.D., who granted a village for its maintenance.[32]

The Temples in the South Coastal Andhra and Rayalaseema regions also met with the same fate when the hold of the Vijayanagara empire over these regions was weakened following the battle of Raksasi Tangadi. The political disorder in the region, which followed that battle and the consequent expansion of the Muslim power i.e., the Qutbshahis, contributed greatly to the decline of the Temples. Many of them suffered desecration, destruction and confiscation of properties in the hands of the rulers. Many local records and *Kaifiyats* from these regions speak of the ill fate suffered by the Temples in the hands of the Muslim rulers, who occupied those places after their victory in the battle of 1565 A.D. The *Kaifiyat* of Ahobilam clearly states that the famous Vaishnava Temple of ahobilam (Kurnool dt.) was sacked by the Muslim ruler jewels and golden vessels taken away, immediately after the battle of Rakshasi Tangadi.[33]

The local Hindu chieftains, in order to increase their own power, not only joined hands with the Muslim invaders against their Hindu overlords the Vijayanagara rulers, but some of them did not even hesitate to cooperate with the Muslim rulers in the plundering of the Hindu religious institutions. An epigraph of 1584 A.D. from Ahobilam, states that Ahobilam Temple was sacked in the year 1579 A.D. by Ibrahim Qutbshahi in alliance with the Hande Chiefs, who were Hindus.[34] The epigraph further states that the Qutbshahi occupation of that place lasted fox six years when the worship in that temple was completely stopped.

In some cases, the construction of the Temples, which was going on at the time of war, was stopped. According to Gudipudi *Kaifiyat* and Veleru *Kaifiyat* (both from South Coastal Andhra), some of the Hindu Temples of those places, which were under construction at the time of Qutbshahi conquest, could not be completed due to the interference by Amin-Malka.[35] They further record that he destroyed a number of Hindu Temples in that area and built mosques and *Darghās*, apparently with the same material. In most cases the lands and other properties of these institutions were confiscated. This resulted in a complete paralisation of their activities. The *Kairfiyat* of Pedapudi (Guntur dt.) State that the Qutbshahi government (*Turakānyam*) which was established in this region after the fall of Vijayanagara rule, destroyed the Temples, built Mosques over them and confiscated all *Inām* or *Srōtrīya* lands.[36] Sometimes, the Hindus, fearing the desecration of the sacred images by the conquerors, used to bury them underground with the hope of restoring them after the fury was over. Uppalapadu *Kaifiyat* (Guntur dt.) states that the idols of the local Temple were kept underground by the Temple priest to save them from destruction in the hands of Amin-ul-Mulk, who destroyed those Temples and carried away their material to be used for the building of a Mosque and a *Dargāh*.[37] The anonymous historian of Golkonda refers to the destruction of the idols in the Temples at Kalahasti (Chittoor dt.) by Etibarkhan, Muhammad Quli Qutbshah's general, when he occupied that place.[38] Sometimes, even the Hindu officials of the Qutbshahi government imitated their Muslim colleagues in sacking the helpless Hindu Temples. According to the anonymous Historian of Goldonda, Murahari Rao a Maratha General under Ibrahim

Qutbshahi, sacked a famous Hindu Temple near Adoni of its idols made of gold and silver and studded with rubies, and brought to Golkonda in the year 1578 A.D.[39]

It appears thus, that the fortunes of the Hindu Temples in Andhra Desa were greatly affected by the decline of the Hindu political power. The Qutbshahi rule, especially in the process of its expansion, proved to be of great disadvantage to their progress. Some of the Muslim officers like Amin-ul-Mulk, appointed to rule the newly occupied territories, proved to be fanatics and indulged in acts of vandalism. They destroyed some of the Temples in those areas and confiscated their properties. The Qutbshahi kings, who were generally known for their liberal religious policy, might not have directly encouraged the iconoclastic activity on the part of their officials. They were benevolent, to some extent, in permitting at least some of their Hindu officials like Asva Rao to extend patronage and revive worship in those Temples. But that patronage was quite inadequate to maintain their former glory. For instance, the Simhachalam Temple, which had about 10 villages in its possession before the Muslim occupation of the region, had now, after the revival of worship by Asva Rao, to content itself with the income of only one village. It is quite reasonable to presume that, the fate meted out to this major Temple might have befallen many of the minor Temple of that region also. Thus, lack of patronage to the activities of these religious institutions when much of the Telugu country came under the Muslim rule and when the economic wealth was no longer exclusively in the hands of the Hindu Rulers, resulted in their decline. Antony Schorer observes:

> The Gentus also have their churches, called Pagodas, scattered over the country but since it is ruled mainly by the Moslems, many of these are in ruins. Their priests or teachers are called Brahmins, and are very clever... I have never seen the worship practiced in their churches...[40]

Another Dutch employee who was stationed at the Dutch factory of Nizampatam during the same period (A.D. 1608-

1614), and whose name is not given, also gives a similar account about the condition of the temples in the neighbourhood. He writes:

> ...but it may be conjectured that owing to war many things have been lost, and many ancient monuments demolished, especially in places where any Moslems live.
>
> ...The brahmans hold in Honour some of their Temples, called by them pagodas, but not in such great numbers, or with so many ceremonies, as in the Gentu country where the Muslims have no authority. He further states:
>
> In the Gentu Country (in a Hindu state), they (Prostitutes) have to come regularly twice a day to dance in the Temples, in return for which they receive some annual gratification. In the country of the Moslems, who do not accept this practice, there is no custom of dancing in the Pagodas (Temples), but ever year in the month os April the prostitutes of the whole Kingdom have to travel to Bagnagar (Hyderabad) wither they are summoned by a Maldaar, to dance in celebration of the death of the first Muslim king, a thing which seems to be very strange...[42]

These observations indicate, to a great extent, how the fortunes and activities of the Hindu Temple were affected under the Muslim rule during this period.

The decline of the Hindu Temples in the Post-Vijayanagara period is also indicated by the reduction in the strength of their trust-boards and the absence of any land grants. For example, the total number of *Sathānattar* of the Venkatesvara Temple of Tirumalai-Tirupati, which was twelve during the period under review, was only six in 1638 A.D. and was reduced to four by 1684 A.D. Similarly, this Temple did not receive any endowment, either of land or of cash, after the year 1638 A.D. when it came under the Qutbshahi rule.[43]

THE MATHA

The credit for organizing the Hindu monasteries, for the first time, in the cenobitic form, that is, as a corporate body with a fixed residence, goes to Sankaracharya, the great Advaita teacher of the 9th century A.D.[44] For the perpetuation of the invigorated Vedic Brahmanism and for the spread of his Advaitic doctrines, he organized the Hindu ascetics into ten orders known as *Dasanamis*.[45] He established five monasteries at different corners of India (Sringeri, Kanchi, Dwaraka, Puri and Badarinath), having their spiritual jurisdiction over the different regions of India. Each of these *Maṭhas* was presided over by one of his chief disciples, and the above said ten orders of monks have been distributed among these monasteries.[46] The followers of other Hindu religious sects of India appear to have established their *Maṭhas* on the lines of Sankara-*Maṭhas*.

The history of Hindu *Maṭhas*, as far as Andhra Desa is concerned, can be traced from the period of Sankaracharya. Of course, none of the original Sankara's Advaita *Maṭhas* was situated in Andhra Deas. But, with Karnataka, Tamil and Malayalam Countries, the Telugu country was placed under the jurisdiction of the Sringeri *Maṭha*.[47] An Advaita *Maṭha* appears to have functioned at Puspagiri (Cuddapah dt.) in Andhra Desa, as a branch of Sringeri *Maṭha*, during the period under study.[48] But it is not known when this branch was Established.

It can be definitely stated that the Kalamukha and the Pasupatha Saiva teachers were the first to establish their *Maṭhas* in the Telugu country. A copper plate grant of Eastern Chalukyan King Ammaraja II (c.a. 945-79 A.D.) from Tadikonda village, refers to a *Maṭha* attached to the Samastha-Bhuvanasraya Temple of Bezawada consisting of three cells and its pontiff Prabhurasi, belonging to the Kalamukha sect.[49] An inscription from Mahadevi-Mangalam village (Chittoor dt.) belonging to the 9th regnal year of Rajendra Chola (1070-1110 A.D.) mentions a Pasupatha *Maṭha* connected with the temple of Arinjesvara and its pontiff Lakulisvara Pandita.[50] By the 11th century A.D., Srisailam, the famous Saiva center in Kurnool district, appears to have become the seat of a number of Saiva *Maṭhas*. The Kazipet inscription of 1090 A.D., of Kakatiya Kng Beta II, refers to the Mallikarjuna Sila-*Maṭha* of Srisailam and its pontiff Kalmukha Ramesvara Pandita, who was also the spiritual preceptor of Kakatiya Prola I and beta II.[51] An epigraph of 1106 A.D. from Kolanupaka (Nalgonda dt.) refers to one Somesvara-*Maṭha*, attached to the Temple of Traipurusha Deva, situated in the Bhuvanagiri fort (Bongir, Nalgonda dt.), receiving agrant from Paramara Jagaddeva, a subordinate of western Chaukyas of Kalyani.[52] This appears to have been a Pasupata *Maṭha*.

In the meantime, the Veerasaivas, especially the followers of Basavesvara of Karnataka, also entered the field and established their *Maṭhas* in Andhra Desa. A number of Veera Saiva *Maṭhas* are said to have been established at Srisailam. Especially, the Basavanna *Maṭha* and the Bhikshavritti *Maṭha* of Srisailam and the Saranga *Maṭha* of Alampur, which are referred to in the epigraphs of the period under study, appear to have been established during the Kakatiya period. As the area covered by the present Kurnool and Mahboobnagar districts because of its proximity to Karnataka was directly exposed to the influence of Veerasaivism from that area, the Veerasaivas must have concentrated their monastic activities in this part of Andhra Desa. The *Kaifiyat* of Nivarti Sangam states that 'Jangala *Maṭham*' was established at the village of 'Yadamatham' (Earramatham village in Kurnool dt.) by the two Jangama brothers—Santa Bhiksha Vritti and Veera Bhiksha Vritti.[53] These Jangama brothers, as their names indicate, were the members of the Bhikshavritti *Maṭha* of Srisailam. The above mentioned Jangala *Maṭha* at Yadamatham village was probably established as its branch.

The most important *Maṭhas* of the Kaktiya period were the Golaki *Maṭhas*. They were associated with the name of the famous Pasupata Saiva teacher Visvesvara Sivacharya, the spiritual preceptor of Kakatiya Ganapatideva and also a contemporary of Rudrama Devi, his successor. He established Golaki *Maṭhas* at various places of the Telugu country namely Mandram and Bhattiprolu (Guntur dt.), Tripurantakam (Kurnool dt.) Puspagiri (Cuddapah dt.), Gangapuram (Mahboobnagar dt.)[54] and Chandravalli (Karimnagar dt.).[55] The activities of the Golaki *Maṭha* situated at Mandaram, which was granted two villages for its maintenance by Queen Rudramadevi, are described at length in the Malkapuram inscription.[56] These Golaki Institutions continued to flourish in Andhra Desa till the fall of the Kakatiya dynasty in the year 1323 A.D. an epigraph of 1292 A.D. from the village Devarakota (Cuddapah dt.) mentions the Puspagiri *Maṭha* and its pontiff (*Samsthānīkulu*) Somasivacharya.[57] From his name, he definitely appears to have belonged to the line of the Golaki teachers.

Vaishnavas, belonging to the Srivaishnava and Madhwa sects, also commenced their monastic activities in Andhra Desa very early and established their *Maṭhas*. Ramanuja, the great Srivaishnava *Acharya* is believed to have founded 700 *Maṭhas* for the propagation of his religion.[58] Some of them appear to have been situated in Telugu Desa. The Jiyyangar *Maṭham* at Tirupati, the activities of which are recorded in the Inscriptions of the Vijayanagara period, is believed to have been founded by Ramanujacharya when he visited that place in 1057 A.D.[59] Towards the end of the 13th century A.D., the Madhwa teacher Narahari Tirtha established a Dvaita *Maṭham* at Simhachalam probably attached to the shrine of god Narasimha.[60] This *Maṭha* came to be known as Narahari *Maṭham*. Tirumalai-Tirupati (Chittoor dt.) was the seat of a number of Vaishnava *Maṭhas* belonging to both the northern and southern school of Srivaishnavism, during this period. There are epigraphic references to the existence of Tirumali Seyappiran *Maṭham*[61] Perarulalan- *Maṭham*, Tiruvenkatanathan *Maṭham* and Tiruvaliparappinan *Maṭham*,[62] at that place.

It appears, from the evidence available that the *Maṭhas* belonging the Saiva sects were, on the whole, in a predominant position throughout the Telugu country at the beginning of the 14th century A.D. the influential Vaishnava *Maṭhas* of the period were situated only at Tirumalai-Tirupati and Simhachalam. Most of the *Maṭhas* of this period were situated at important religious centers, and in most cases, were attached to the Temples belonging to their respective religious sects. They were also fairly distributed over the three regions of Andhra Desa. Patronized by the monarchs and their rich subjects, they became very influential and rich institutions, possessing a large number of landed estates, buildings and other sources of income.

The Muslim invasions in the first quarter of the 14th century A.D. and the subsequent Muslim rule in the Telugu country, which greatly affected the Hindu religious activity, appear to have affected the fortunes of the Hindu *Maṭhas* also. In view of the evidence to the destruction of the Temples by the Muslims of this period, as referred to in connection with the history of Hindu Temple, and in view of the fact that most of the *Maṭhas* of the period were attached to the Temples, it can be inferred that some of them were directly affected by the Muslim invasions and Muslim rule. The lack of patronage under the new government also must have contributed, indirectly, to the Paralysation of their activities.

There was a revival in the fortunes of the Hindu *Maṭhas* in Andhra Desa when the Hindu political and the Hindu religious activity were revived under Musunuri, Vilama, Reddi and Vijayanagara Kingdoms. Many of the old *Maṭhas*, situated at places like Srisailam, Sangamesvaram, Puspagiri, Alampur, Tirupati, Simhachalam, which were inactive during the Tughluq period, became once again active now and continued to function during the remaining period under study. A few new *Maṭhas* were also established during this period. The Activities of both the old and the new *Maṭhas* are recorded in the contemporary epigraphs and literature.

In the Telangana region, we do not have any evidence for the existence of the *Maṭhas* and their activities during the post-Kakatya period covered by the present study. However, there are one or two vague references to a few Saiva *Maṭhas* only at Alampur (Mahaboobnagar dt.). Hence, the history of Hindu *Maṭhas* in Andhra Desa during this period (from the end of Tughluq period till the end of the 16th century A.D.), is more or less the history of Hindu *Maṭhas* of only the Rayalaseema and the coastal Andhra regions. Between Rayalaseema and coastal Andhra, it is the former that had *Maṭhas* more in number and more influential than those in the latter. Coastal Andhra had only one or two *Maṭhas*, situated at places like Simhachalam and Srikurmam in its northern parts.

In these two regions (Rayalaseema and coastal Andhra) also, there is no evidence for the establishment of new Saiva *Maṭhas* during this period. There is evidence only to the functioning of the old Saiva *Maṭhas*, which were already existing at places like Srisalilam and Puspagiri. All the new *Maṭhas* that were established during this period in Andhra Desa belonged to Srivaishnava and Madhwa sub-sects of Vaishnavism only. The addition of the new *Maṭhas* to the list of those already existing considerably strengthened the position of Vaishnava mathas, on the whole.

Two Dvaita *Maṭhas*, one at Simhachalam (Vizag dt.) and another at Srikurmam (Srikakulam dt.) were established in the middle of the 14th century A.D., by Narasimha Bharati, a Madhwa teacher who was the *Bhoga-Pariksha* of Narasimha Temple of the place.[63] Especially, Tirumalai-Tirupati (Chittoor dt.) and Ahobilam (Kurnool dt.) became the seats of very influential Vaishnava *Maṭhas*, of this period. In the year 1338-39 A.D., two *Tengalai* Srivaishnava *Maṭhas*, one at Tirupati and another at Tirumalai, were built by a certain Immadi Rahuttarayan-Madappan-Singaya-Dannayaka, an important official under the local Yadava chief.[64] Adivan Sathakopa Jiyyar, the head of the *Vadagalai* school of Srivaishnavism, founded a *Maṭha* popularly known as Ahobila *Maṭha* at Ahobilam in the year 1456 A.D. He presided over that institution for sixty years from 1456 to 1515 A.D.[65] The same teacher established another *Maṭha* known as van Sathkopa *Maṭham* at Tirumalai-Tirupati.[66] The latter functioned as the branch of the former. Vyasa Tirtha, the head of the Madhwa-sub-sect of Vaishnavism, built a *Maṭha* known as Vyasaraya *Maṭha* at Tirumalai-Tirupati and another *Maṭha* at Vijayanagara city, during the period of Krishnadeve Raya. The old Jiyyar *Maṭham* or Jiyyangar *Maṭham* established by Ramanujacharya, the famous Srivaishnava Acharya, in 1057 A.D., continued to function at Tirumalai-Tirupati during the entire period under study. We come across in the inscriptions of the period, from that place, the names of Mullai Tiruvenkata Jiyar, Emperumanar Jiyar, Ramanuja Jiyar, Anusandanam Tiruvenkata Jiyar, Emperumanar Jiyar, Vada-Tiruvenkata Jiyar, Yatiraja Jiyar, Vanamali-Jiyar, and Annan

Ramanuja Jiyar, the pontiffs who presided over that *Maṭha* in succession.[67] Another *Maṭha* known as Alagiya Manavala *Maṭha* presided over by the junior Jiyar of the above *Maṭha*, appears to have functic ned as its branch.[68]

The period of one century-the last quarter of the 15th century and the first three quarters of the 16th century-when the Saluva and Tuluva monarchs were on the Vijayanagara throne, can be described as the golden age of the Vaishnava *Maṭhas*. These *Maṭhas*, belonging to Srivaishnava and Madhwa sub-sects, became very active and influential institutions during this period. They became the nerve centres of their respective religious sects and helped their propagation in the Telugu country.

Two factors-the predominantly influential position held by the Vaishnava sects in the Telugu country, and the royal patronage-contributed greatly to the growth in influence and prosperity of the Vaishnava *Mathas* of the period. During this period, the Srivaishnavism and Madhwism reached the climax of their growth and popularity in the area. The leaders of these sects, most of whom also happened to be the founders and pontiffs of the above mentioned *Maṭhas*, wielded great influence over the contemporary monarchs and their principal subjects. The latter extended liberal patronage to these teachers and their institutions. The *Vadagalai* Srivaishnava *Maṭha* of Ahobilam and its branch at Tirumalai-Tirupati, Enjoyed the patronage of Saluve Narasimha Raya of Vijayanagara. Allasani Peddana, the poet–laureate of Krishnadeva Raya's court, was a spiritual disciple of the founder of this *Maṭha*. This poet donated the village Kokatam, renamed as 'Sathakopapuram' to the Srivaishnavas, probably, under the influence of his spiritual master.[69] Vedanta Sathakopa Jiyyar, the fifth pontiff of Ahobila *Maṭha*, is mentioned as the spiritual preceptor of the Nandyala chiefs who were Vijayanagara subordinates.[70] Similarly, Kandadai Ramanujayyanagar, the pontiff of the Jiyyanagar *Maṭham* (*Tengalai*) at Tirumalai-Tirupati, wielded great influence over Saluva Narasimharaya. The latter extended liberal patronage to that *Maṭha* and the Temple of God Venkatesvara of that place.[71] The pontiffs of the Jiyyangar *Maṭham* gained a lot of influence in the management of the Temple of Srvinkatesvara. They acted as its superintendents (*Kōyil Kēlvi*) and the managers of other minor Temples and flower gardens (Nandavanam) of the place.[72] They were also on the *Sthānattar*, (Trust board) of that Temple. Similarly, the pontiffs of the *Vadagalai Maṭha* at Ahobilam played a significant role in the management of the affairs of the Narasimha Temple of that place. Vyasa Tirtha, the founder of the Vysaaraya *Maṭha* at Tirumalai, and the leader of Madhwa School were the spiritual preceptor of Krishnadeva Raya[73] and a towering religious personage of the period.

The decline of the political power of the Gajpatia and Vijayanagara and the subsequent Expansion of the Qutbshahi rule over Coastal Andhra and Rayalaseema regions in the second half of the 16th century A.D., affected the fortunes of the Hindu *Maṭhas* in these regions. Since many of them were attached to the Temples, and their fortunes were linked with those of the Temple, it is quite natural that they were also affected along with the latter. The confiscation of the properties of the Temples, like those of Simhachalam and Ahobilam, and the stoppage of worship in them for several years by the Muslim rulers, as already referred to in connection with the history of Hindu Temple, was bound to affect the working of the *Maṭhas* situated in their precincts. When the political power and the economic wealth were no longer in the hands of the Hindu rulers, these institutions, like the Temples, declined gradually in the Telugu country.

THE AGRAHARA

Agrahāras of the period under study in the Telugu country, besides being great Centres of learning, were also important centers of religious activity. These were no doubt, created by the rulers and granted to the Brahmans for the promotion of learning. The learning in which the *Agrāharikas* were expected to be proficient, was also secular in a few cases. An inscription of Allaya Vema Reddi of Rajamundry Kingdom sates that the Brahman occupants of the *Agrahāra* village Alladareddi Vema Varamu, created by that monarch, were well-versed in logic, grammar and Mimamsa, besides Vedas and *Śāśtras.*[74] Similarly, Krishnadeva Raya, the famous Vijayanagara monarch, granted the village Koppula as *Sarvagrahāra* to a certain Chinna Timmanna for his skill in playing the game of chess with that monarch himself.[75] But the instances of this type are rare.

On the other hand, the learning promoted in the *Agrahāras*, in great many cases, was religious. The Donees of these villages were expected, usually, to have been well-versed in Vedas, *Śaśtras* etc. For instance, the Ikshugrama grant of Anavema Reddi states that, the monarch granted the village Ikshugrama to the Brahmans well-versed in the Vedas and *Śaśtras.*[76] Similarly, according to an epigraph of 1515 A. D. from Amaravati (Guntur dt.), Krishhnadeva Raya of Vijayanagara granted two villages, Nidumanuru and Valluru as *Srvamānya* to 108 Brahmans who were proficient in the four Vedas (*Chaturvēda Vidya Pāragulu*), on the occasion of his visit to Amaravati.[77] The Vedic learning was mainly theological or religious in its character and came to be associated, during the period under study, mainly with the Vedic religion or the *Sanātana Dharma*, one of the many systems of the so called Hinduism.

That, the *Agrahāras* were created and granted some times to the people belonging to a particular religious sect for the promotion of that sectarian religion, also indicates the religious character of these institutions. An inscription of 1544 A.D. from Markapur (Kurnool dt.) records the grant of the village Taranupadu alias Raghupatirajapuram, along with eight hamlets, to a number of Srivaishnavas and a Vaishnava Temple.[78] A certain Venkatadri, the donee of an *Agrahāra* village from Sadasiva Raya, is described in the Revundi grant of that monarch as a Vaishnavite whose mind was always wandering over the lotus feet of the lord Padmanabha (Vishnu) and also as a great scholar in Vaishnavite scriptures and *Nigamas* and *Āgamas.*[79] Similarly, Anavema Reddi of Kondavidu kingdom granted, according to an inscription, Vemavarm village as *Sarvāgrahāra* to Duggirala Ramalingam and Mulasthanam Somalingam who were proficient in Saiva *Āgamas* (*Āgama Śaiva sāstra dharma ḳarma pāragulu*) and who performed the six acts or duties enjoined on Brahmans (*Ṣaṭkarma-niratulu*).[80]

Moreover, the residents of these *Agahāra* villages were expected to be proficient, in many cases, not only in learning but also in performing various types of (Vedic) sacrifices. *Ṣaṭkarmaniratulu*, the qualification ascribed to the donees of the *Agrahāras* as mentioned in the Anavema Reddi's grant and several other grants stands for the six acts or duties enjoined on the Brahmans, namely *Yajanamu*, *Yājanamu*, *Adhyayanamu*, *Ādyāpanamu*, *Dānamu* and *Pratigrahamu* (sacrifice, assistance at the sacrifices of others, study of the Vedas, instruction in the Vedas, performance of a gift). The first two of the above six duties, i.e. the performance of the sacrifices and the assistance at the sacrifices of others, enjoined on them, clearly suggest that the Brahman donees of the *Agrahāra* villages were expected to perform sacrifices, which, again, were associated with the old Vedic religion. Similarly, Ranganatha Dikshita and Siva Dikshita, the two *Purōhits* of Krishnadeva Raya and the recipients of the two *Agrahāra* villages from him, are described in the Amaravati inscription of 1515 A.D. as *Sarva Kratu sarvatōmukha vājipēyi* (who performed all kinds of sacrifices etc.)[81] Errapregada, the court-poet of Prolaya Vema Reddi, cleary indicates, in his *Harivamśamu*, the sacrificial activity in the *Agrahāra* villages granted by that ruler. He writes: *Agrahāramulu Vidyātapō viprula kichchi yagna kartaluga manache*, (by granting *Agrahrāras* to Brahmans well-versed in learning and asceticism Prolaya Vema made them the performers of the sacrifices).[82] The sacrificial and intellectual activities of the *Agrahāras* contributed greatly to the promotion of Hindu religion, especially Advita, Saiva and Vaishnava sects.

The history of the institution of the *Agrahāra* during the period of study is quite fluctuating. Its fortunes, like those of the Temple and the *Maṭha* had many ups and downs, depending on the changing political fortunes of the ruling Hindu dynasties, during the period of the Kakatiyas, the *Agrahāras* in the Telugu country appear to have been in prosperous condition. It was due to the liberal patronage extended by the state towards their maintenance. *Pratapachāritram* states that there were four thousand *Agrahāras* in Possession of the Brahmans in the Telugu country during the reign of Prataparudra II.[83] This figure may be an exaggeration, but it indicates the keen interest taken by the government in maintaining these centres of religious learning.

The fortunes of the *Agrahāras* in the Telugu country appears to have been seriously affected by a series of political changes like the Mohammedan invasions, the consequent fall of the Kakatiya kingdom and the establishment of the Muslim rule in the first quarter of the 14th century A.D. the Muslim rulers confiscated the villages belonging to Brahmans, which were bestowed on them in the preceding period. Vilasa grant clearly states 'all the *Agrahāras* that had long been in the enjoyment of the most learned were taken away.[84] After the liberation from Muslim yoke, the new Hindu rulers appear to have attempted to revive these institutions. Prolaya Nayaka of the Musunuri dynasty claims, in an inscription, that he set the Vedic sacrifices which had been stopped during the Muslim rule, in motion,[85] presumably in the *Agrahāras*. Puvvada Grant of prolaya Vema Reddi also states that the monarch restored the old *Agrahāras*, which had been granted earlier and granted fresh *Agrahāras*.[86] This clearly indicates the confiscation of *Agrahāras* by the Muslim rulers.

In fact, they made it their first duty to re-grant old *Agrahāras* and grant new ones. Prolaya Vema Reddi the founder of the Reddi Kingdom is said to have granted 44 *Agrahāras* to the Vedic Brahmans.[87] The same ruler is described in an epigraph of 1345 A.D. from Amaravati as the one who granted a number of *Agrahāras* on the banks of the rivers Brahmakundi, Krishna and Godavari and in the country situated between them.[88] Similarly, the other rulers of the Reddi dynasty and the Vijayanagara empire granted a number of *Agrahāras*.

The prosperity and the intense religious activity in the Brahmana *Agrahāras*, especially in the coastal Andhra during the Reddi period, is described by Srinatha, the Telugu poet of the 15th century A.D. in his *Kāśikhandamu*. While describing the greatness of his patron king Allaya Vema Reddi of Rajahmundry Kingdom, he writes that due to the liberal patronage of that ruler who was ruling the Kingdom on behalf of his brother Veerabhadra Reddi, the Brahmans in the *Agrahāra* villages were so content and prosperous that they learnt to wear rings set with rubies on their fingers in the place of the sacrificial grass (*kuśa*), to use musk in the place of ordinary river-mud (*Gaṅga-Mattiya*) for markin their forehead, and to put on pearl necklaces etc., while gold and silver rolled in confusion in their homes.[89]

The *Agrahāras*, like the other Hindu religious institutions in Andhra Desa, received a great setback in their fortunes with the decline of the Hindu political rule. Especially the fall of Gajapati and Vijayanagara empires which was followed by the expansion of the Qutbshahis in the coastal Andhra and the Rayalaseema regions, led to their decline. Taking advantage of the political chaos prevailing in the country during this period, the petty Hindu local chiefs, some times, sacked the *Agrahāras* of their wealth. The *Kaifiyat* of Perusomula (Anantapur dt,) sates that during the period of political disorder which followed the battle of Raksasi Tangadi, Mottra Jakka, a *polēgar* of boy caste, sacked and burnt down the Agrahara of Jaggaraju Samudram.[90] In the wake of the Qutbshahi expansion also, a number of *Agrahāras* were confiscated. The *Kaifiyat* of Pedapudi (Guntur dt.) states that the Qutbshahi government (*Turakānyam*), which was established in that region after the fall of the Vijayanagara rule and which confiscated all *Inām* and *Srotriya* lands also confiscated the Pedapudi *Agrahāra.*[91] The Qutbshahi rulers, who are known for their religious toleration, extended their patronage, of course in a limited manner to these religious institution after the consolidation of their power. For example, an epigraph of 1586-87 A.D. from Masayapeta village (Nellore dt.) records the grant of a village as *Agrahāra* to several Brahmans by a Mohammedan official Lalkhan (Lalu Khanu) for the religious merit of Muhammad Quli Qutb shah.[92] But this type of grants are very few, and the limited patronage could not help these institutions to recover their former glory.

THE MOSQUE

The history of the Mosque in Andhra Desa can be traced from the pre-Muslim period of its history. The existence of Mosques at some places is indicated by the epigraphic and literary evidence. The construction of mosque in the year 1293 A.D. at Penugonda (Anantapur dt.) by Baba Fakhruddin, a Sufi saint, is referred to in an inscription from that place.[93] This Mosque was probably meant for the use of the followers of the above-mentioned saint. Similarly, *Krīḍābhirāmamu* of the 15th century A.D. refers to the existence of a Mosque (*Turukala-maseedu*) in the city of Warangal during the of Kakatiya patina Rudra II.[94]

The establishment of the Tughluq rule after the fall of the Kakatiya Kingdom in 1323 A.D., and the consequent state support extended to the Islam appear to have given a lot of impetus to the Mosque-building activity in the Telugu country. The new rulers built their Mosques at various places in the conquered country for the use of their Muslim subjects and also the Muslim Officers appointed for various positions. Delhi sultan constructed a Mosque in the city of Warangal, the capital of the defunct Kakatiya Kingdom, which was renamed as Sultanpur.[95] A Mosque was raised in the year 1324 A.D. at Rajahmundry by an official under Ghiasuddin Tughluq.[96] This appears to be the earliest extant Mosque in the Telugu Country. A Mosque was built by Muhammad Bin Tughluq at Bodhan (Nizamabad dt.) when he first conquered the Telugu country.[97] Thus, it appears that the establishment of the prayer-houses in the newly conquered country became one of the first chosen Tasks of the Muslim rulers. Thecae institutions built at various places having Muslim colonies or settlements, must have acted as great centers of their religious, social and political life during the early period of their rule.

These few Mosques, established during the brief Muslim rule, must have continued to function in the country even when it became independent under the Hindu rule. The rulers of the new Hindu Kingdoms, especially the Musunuri and Velama Kingdoms, in view of their friendly relations with the Neighbouring Bahmai Kingdom, would not have interfered with the activities of the Muslim religious institutions in their dominions.

The gradual expansion of the Bahmani rule into the Telugu country, after the fall of the Velama and Reddi Kingdoms, gave a spurt to the progress of Muslim institutions in this part of the country. During this period, Islam became the state religion. Almost all the important towns in the conquered country, came to have Mosques endowed by the state. Syed Ali Tabataba refers to the building of mosques by Ahmad shah Bahmani at Warangal, Rajukonda and Devarakonda after their conquest.[98] In the year 1460 A.D. during the reign of Humayun Shah, Jami Mosque was built at Pargi (Mahbubnagar dt.).[99] An inscription of 1484 A.D. refers to the building of Mosque at Rajkonda (the erst-while capital of the Velama Kingdom).[100] Another epigraph, from Gudur (Krishna dt.) records the construction of a Mosque at that place by a Bahmani official in the year 1497 A.D.[101]

In the Telugu districts (mainly the Rayalaseema and the Coastal Andhra region) which were under the Vijayanagara rule, also, a few Mosques were built, apparently with the patronage of that Hindu state. The policy of the Vijayanagara monarchs to enlist the Muslims in their service, commenced by Dearaya II and continued by his successors, contributed to the growth of Muslim religious institutions in their dominions. There are References in the contemporary records to the establishment of prayer-houses for the Muslims in the Telugu districts of Vijayanagara empire. A Mosque was built in the year 1425 A.D. at Masulipatam (Krishna dt.) under the auspices of the Vijayanagara monarch (Devaraya II) for the use of the Muslim soldiers enlisted in the Hindu army in its fight with the Bahmani army.[102] A Persian record from the village Kottakota (Chittoor dt.) refers to the building of the 'Jumma Masjid' at that place in the year 1494 A.D.[103] Situated, as it was, in the heart of the Vijayanagara dominions, this Mosque must have been built with the patronage of that Hindu state. The existence of mosques meant for the use of Muslim officers and Soldiers in the city of Vijayanagara is attested to by the reference to them by Ferishta.[104]

The establishment of the Qutbshahi Kingdom of Golkonda at the beginning of the 16th century A.D., marks an important stage in the history of the Mosques in the Telugu country. The Mosques during this period became very prosperous and influential religious institutions. They are very large in size compared to those of the preceding period and catered to the needs of a large number of people. This is indicated by the references, in the contemporary epigraphs and literature, to the building of innumerable Mosques at Golkonda and other principal towns during this period, and the architecture of the extant Mosques attributed to this dynasty. Most of these mosques were endowed by the state, and came to have a good number of functionaries.

Tarīkh-i-Qutbshāhī states that Sultan Quli, the first Qutbshahi ruler, built a thousand Mosques in his dominions.[105] One important Mosque, built by Sultan Quli, is the Masjid-i-Safa which is also known as Jami-Masjid. It is the earliest extant Qutbshahi Mosque and is situated near Balahissar entrance gate in Golkonda fort.[106] According to the author of *Taḍhkiratal-Muluk*, Ibrahim Qutbshahi had built a Mosque in each town and village of his dominions and appointed teachers and servants in them.[107] Some of the extant Mosques of the reign of Ibrahim Qutbshah are: the Mustafa Khan's *Masjid* built in 1561 A.D. and situated in Golkonda fort [108] and the Mosque situated on the Moula Ali hill erected by the same Sultan.[109] A Persian record from the village Gazinagar (Nalgonda dt.) belonging to the year 1576-77 A.D. states that the Mosque of that place was built in the name of Ibrahim Qutbshahi.[110]

During the period of Muhammad Quli Qutbshahi, some of the important Mosques of the Qutbshahi period were built. The Ashrafi-*Masjid* (c. 1589 A.D.) and Chini-Masjid (1589 A.D.), both situated in the Golkonda fort, owe their construction to the reign of this Sultan.[111] One of the grand and wellkonwn Mosques of the Qutbshahi period built before the end of the period under review is the Jami-Masjid (1597 A.D.) situated near Charminar. It was the first sacred building built by Muhammad Quli Qutbshah in the new city of Hydeabad.[112] The Charminar built by the Sultan in the year 1597 A.D. also contained a Mosque.[113] Another Mosque belonging to this period is that of Mughalpura (Hyderabad) built by Dilir Khan, a Qutbshani officer in the year 1597-1600 A.D.[114]

The *Dār-us-Shifa* (Unani hospital and medical college) built during the reign of Muhammad Quli Qutbshah (situated near modern Salarjung museum, Hyderabad) also has a Mosque of this period attached to it. According to the inscription fixed on its entrance gate, it was constructed in the year 1597 A.D. Similarly, the tombs in the royal cemetery of the Qutbshahis also come to have Mosques bilt as adjuncts to them. These tomb-Mosques were built, probably, in commemoration of the royal persons to whom the tombs belonged and were used for the recitation of the Koran for the spiritual welfare of the deceased.

It is to be noted in this connection, that some of the Mosques in Andhra Desa belonging both to the early and the later periods of the Muslim rule, were built either on the foundations of the Hindu Temples or with the materials that came from the destroyed Hindu Temples. The Mosque at Rajahmundry, built during the reign of Ghiyasuddin Tughluq in 1324 A.D., was originally a Hindu Temple converted into a Muslim prayer house.[115] Another noted example of conversion of a Hindu Temple into a Mosque is that of Deval Mosque at Bodhan (Nizamabad dt.), converted during the period of Muhammad bin Tughluq.[116] The very name of this particular Mosque further supports this fact.

This practice of conversion seems to have been continued, in some cases atleast, throughout the Muslim period. That even towards the end of the 15th century A.D., the spoils of the native Hindu Temple supplied the materials for the construction of the Muslim prayer houses is indicated in an inscription of 1484 A.D.[117] It refers to the building of a Mosque on the ruins of a Hindu Temple at Raj Konda (Nalgonda dt.). According to *Tarīkh-i-Qutbshāhī*, Sultan Quli, the founder of the Qutbshahi dynasty, built a thousand Mosques on the ruins of the Hindu Temples which he had destroyed in his dominions. [118] this practice, which was adopted in some cases in the early days of the Muslin rule, continued to be followed even towards the end of the 16th century A.D. As some of these places where the Temples were converted into Mosques, formed the integral parts of the Qutb Shih Kingdom almost from its inception, those acts cannot be described as acts of pure political revenge, which usually followed the conquests of places afresh by the Mohammedans. On the other hand, they seem to have been acts of religious fanaticism on the part of a few individuals. These acts were, probably, intended to impress the local people with the superiority of Islam and expose the helplessness of the Hindu gods to protect either themselves or their devotees.

The gradual decline of the Hindu empire of Vijayanagara after the battle of Rakshasi Tangadi and the gradual extension of the Muslim rule under the Qutbshahis over the remaining Telugu districts (southern coastal Andhra and Rayalaseema) appears to have greatly strengthened the institution of the Mosque in the region by bringing new areas under its jurisdiction. The *Kaifiyats* and local records from the Rayalaseema and the coastal Andhra regions, many of which speak of the destruction of the temples there by the some of the Muslim officials, also refer to the building of Mosques at these places. This has been discussed, at length, in connection with the history of the Temple already.

The change in the political power in favour of the Muslims appears to have greatly contributed to the prosperity and grandeur of the Mosques. And it continued to be in the same influential position for nearly two more centuries. The continuous Muslim rule, in spite of the dynastic changes, ensured the continuity in the fortunes of this institution.

THE KHANQAH

The monasticism in Islam was invariably associated with the mystic movement known as Sūfi movement, which was based on the doctrine of direct and intimate union of the individual soul with God. It mainly aimed, as similar movements in other religions did, at the preservation and spread of the religion i.e. Islam, and became its most vital spiritual force. The establishment of the monasteries or hospices, where the Sūfi saints of various orders lived, became an essential feature of the Muslim religious life. The early Sūfi *Khānqāhs*, whose origin in the Muslim world is traced as early as to the eighth century, were private in character. They became important centres of the corporate life of the mystics only from the twelfth and the thirteenth centuries onwards.[119] Especially, the late medieval period (c. a. 1250-1500 A.D.) when these hospices of the Sufi mystics spread and became popular all over the Muslim world, is considered as the convent era.[120] In India also, the Muslim monasticism was associated with the Sūfis. In the wake of the Muslim conquest a number of Sūfi saints entered India and established their *Khānqāhs* at different places for the propagation of their tenets. On the eve of the transfer of capital to Daulatabad by Muhammad din Tughluq, some two thousand *Ribats* and *Khānqāhs* are said to have been functioning in Delhi alone.[121]

It is difficult to know as to when exactly the Muslim monastic tradition entered Andhra Desa. There is evidence, on doubt, to show the activities of a number of saints belonging to the various Sūfi orders in the Telugu country like that of Baba Sharfuddin (Ob. 1287 A. D.) and his brother Baba Shahabuddin (ob. 1291 A.D.), both belonging to the Suhrawardi Sūfi order, at a place near modern Hyderabad; of Baba Fakruddin of Penugonds (Anantapur dt.) (Ob. 1294-95. A.D.), and of Kadi Ziauddin Multani of Tughluq period at the village Urs (Warangal dt.)[122] Though there is no definite evidence, it can be inferred, in view of the invariable association of the monastic traditions with the sufi movement in other parts of the Muslim world during this period, that the above mentioned saints also established their *Khānqāhs* at the places of their activity. This inference is strengthened by a reference, in a Persian record of 1673-74 A.D. from Penugonda, to the existence of the '*Khānqāh* of Baba Fakruddin' of Penugonda, and an endowment for its maintenance.[123] It is quite apparent that it was established by Baba Fakruddin, one of the above mentioned saints, before his death which occurred in the year A.D. 1294-95.[124]

There is also no definite evidence to the establishment of the monasteries by the Sufi saints in the Telugu country during the period of Tughluqs, Bahmanis, and even the early Qutbshahis.[125] There is only some meager evidence indicating the existence of the *Khānqāhs* in the later half of the 16th century A.D. in the Telugu country.

Hussain shah Wali, a descendant in the eighth degree of Hazarat Khaza Geșu Daraz of Gulbaraga of Bahmani period, came to Hyderabad in the reign of Ibrahim Qutbshah (1550-80 A.D.). This sultan is said to have honoured the saint and also gave him his daughter in marriage.[126] Syed Shah Raju, I, a brother of this saint was in receipt of a *Jāgir* and a monthly allowance from Sultan Muhammad Quli, the next Sultan.[127] Probably, these two mystic brothers built monastery of their own and the above mentioned *Jāgir* was granted towards its maintenance. This inference is strengthened by the reference to the existence of a *Khānqāh* of Shah Raju II, near Hyderabad. Shah Raju II was the son of Shah Raju I and a nephew of Hussain Shah Wali of Ibrahim Qutbshah's period.[128] Shah Raju II was the spiritual preceptor of Abul Hasan Qutbshah (1672-87 A.D.). This last Qutbshahi ruler, who himself was originally a recluse of the *Khānqāh* of that saint,[129] is believed to have been helped by the same saint to get the throne.

Abdul Jabbar Khan Malkapuri refers to the existence of a *Khānqāh* at the village Urs near modern Warangal, established by a saint known as Syed Shah Jamal Baghdadi Warangli in the last quarter of the Sixteenth century A.D.[130] This saint was a descendant of Abdul Qadri Jilani and belonged to the Qadiri order of the Sūfi saints. He came from Baghdad and it appears that he established a *Khānqāh* at the above village. After his death in 1590 A.D., he was succeeded, as the *Kalīfa* of that *Khānqāh*, by his son shah Moinuddin Hassan.[131]

Thus, the activities of only a few of the *Khānqāhs* of the Qutbshahi period in the Telugu country are known from the contemporary records. This indicates, to some extent, their gradual decline by this time. This might be due to the fact that this period belonged to the age of the general decline of the institution of *Khānqāh* in India and elsewhere. Moreover, the place of the *Khānqāh*, as a religious institution, appears to have been gradually taken over, during this period in Andhra Desa by another institution known as *Dargāh*. So, the result was that very few *Khānqāhs* of the period under study survived after the 16th century A.D., whereas some of the *Darghās* of the period continued to function to the present day.

THE DARGAH

It appears that, many of the renowned Sūfi saints of the period in Andhra Desa come to have tomb-shrines built by their disciples, these shrines became, in the course of time, important centres of worship and pilgrimage for not only their spiritual disciples but even to laymen. They played a significant role in the religious life of the people, irrespective of their creed, caste and race.

The *Dargāh* of Baba Sharfuddin situated on a hillock in the Barkas locality, Hyderabad, appears to be one of the earliest *Darghās* of Andhra Desa. Baba Sharfuddin came from Iraq and conducted missionary activity at that place. When he died in the year 1287 A.D. his disciples built a tomb on his relics. The *Urs* (death anniversary) used to be attended, in the subsequent period by thousands of people every year.[132]

Similarly the *Dargāh* of Kadi Ziauddin Multani and the *Dargāh* of Syed Shah Jamal Bagdad Warangali, both situated in the village of urs near modern Warangal, and where *Urs* festivals are celebrated even now, also belonged to this period. The saint of the former is said to have accompanied the army of Muhammad bin Tughluq in one of his wars waged with Prataparudra II of Warangal and died in fighting. The name of the place 'Kazipet' (situated in the neighbourhood of the above village) is said to have been derived from his name.[133] Syed Shah Jamal belonging to the *Qādirī* order of the Sūfi saints, built a *Khānqāh* and died there in the year 1590 A.D.[134]

The *Dargāh* of Baba Fakhruddin of Penugonda (Anantapur dt.) who died in the year 1294-95 A.D. is referred to in a Persian record of 1673-74 A.D. from that place.[135] This shrine, popularly known as Babayya *Dargēh* of Penugonda, became in the subsequent period, an important Muslim religious institution. It appears to have been revered by both Muslims and Hindus alike. Being situated in the center of the Hindu empire, it received the patronage of many Vijayanagara monarchs. Vira Narasimha, Sadasiva, Venkata II and Vendata III of that empire gave several (*hōra*) Villages for its maintenance.[136]

Similarly, the, *Dargāh* of Galib Saheb at Rajkonda (Nalgonda dt.) used to draw, until very recently, over 10,000 devotees on the occasion of its urs held every year.[137] This *Dargāh* is believed, according to a tradition, to have been built in commemoration of a victory of this saint who died fighting against the last Hindu ruler of that place.[138]

At the Shah Ali pasha *Dargāh*, established in the 14th century A.D. at Alampur (Mahbubnagar dt.), the urs is conducted even now in the month of *Jalikāt*.[139] Similarly, a number of tombs of the Sūfi saints of Hyderabad, belonging especially to the later Qutbshahi period became shrines of great religious importance.[140] Some of the inducements to visit these shrines by the people of this period were the desires for having children, recover from sickness, preservation from any grievous calamity and danger or any other event exciting grateful feelings. The Muslims belonging to both the upper classes and the common masses, used to vow, especially in times of crises, to offer some thing to a particular shrine, if the desires were fulfilled. These shrines, like all other religious institutions were patronized by the rulers and their subjects alike. The present practice of celebrating the *Urs* festivals of some of these shrines and making a pilgrimage to them, among the Muslims and non-Muslims, is a continuation of the same of the period under study.

THE ASHURKHANA

The origin and the early history of the institution of *Āshūrkhāna* in other parts of the Muslim world are not known. It is also not known whether any of them were set up in the Telugu country during the period of the early Qutbshahis i.e. Sultan Quli and Jamshid Quli. The *Āshūrkhāna* that figure during the Period under study naturally belong to the later half of the 16th century A.D. covering the reign of Ibrahim Qutubshah and his successor Muhammad Quli Qutbshah. They number about half a dozen, and are situated mainly in and around the city of modern Hyderabad.

All the *Āshūrkhānas* of the period under review, no doubt, have *Ālams* but one *Āshūrkhāna* of this period, situated to Maula Ali, contains the impression of Hazrat Ali's hand on stone. [141] And the Alams of many of these Ashurkhanas contained the relics associated with life of Imams. An account of the Ashurkhanas of this period is given below:

Maula Ali Āshūrkhāna: The earliest Ashurkhana known to have been set up in the Telugu country is that of Maula Ali, situated near Malkajgiri, about 10 miles away from the old Hyderabad city. It was built in the year 1576 A.D. (986 A.H.) to house the impression of Hazrat Ali's right hand, which is believed to have been found on a rock on the Maula Ali hillock by Yakhut, an official of Ibrahim Qutbshah. [142]

Āshūrkhāna-e-Nāl-e-Mubārak: This is another *Āshūrkhāna* built during the reign of Ibrahim Qutbshah. It is situated now, near Shahi Mahal located near the (eastern) Charkaman (old Hyderabad). This *Āshūrkhāna* got its name from the *Nāl* (cresent–like iron piece of the helmet of imam Hussain broken during the battle of Karbala) contained in its *Ālam*. It was brought from Karbala by certain Sayyaids, Nir Miran and Nurul Hada, and was given to a d*ervish* of Bijapur. It was obtained by Ibrahim Qutbshah, who received it with honours, got it fixed to an *Ālam* and housed it at some place in Golkonda fort.[143] In the reign of Muhanmmad Quli Qutbshahi, it was brought from there and housed in the *Āshūrkhāna* built at the present place.[144]

Bāgh-e-Hazrt: Bagh-e-Hazrat is another *Āshūrkhāna* belonging to the period of Ibrahim Qutbshah. It is situated inside the Salarjung palace, Hyderabad. The *Ālam* housed in it contains a piece of the iron coat of Hazrat Abdul Fazal Abbas. It was brought from Karbal by Mir Miran and Nurul Hada, the same Sayyid brothers mentioned above, during the reign of Ibrahim Qutbshah.[145]

Hussāini Ālam of Golkonda: This *Āshūrkhāna* is situated on the road leading from Fathe Darwaza to Balahissar Darwaza inside the fort of Gokonda. The *Ālam* in this building was set up in the year 1592 A.D. by Muhammad Quli Qutbshah, whose name along with those of the 14 imams is inscribed on it. [146]

Bādshāhi Āshūrkhāna: Situated at Pattargatti (Old Hyderabad) was the first *Āshūrkhāna* set in the new city of Hyderabad, built by

Muhammad Quli qutbshah. It was built at a cost of Rs. 66,000.[147] it appears from the inscriptions engraved over the central niche of the *Āshūrkhāna* that its construction continued from A.D. 1592 to 1596.[148] Mir Muhammad Mumin, a Shia divine from Iran, who was the Qutbshahi *Wazier*, played a crucial role in its construction.[149]

Hussāini Ālam (new): this *Āshūrkhāna,* situated in the lane of the same name (Old Hyderabad) contains the *Ālam* of Imam Hussain, who attained martyrdom in the battle of Karbala. It was brought from Karbala by a certain Ali Aga, which was made the caretaker (*Mujāver*) of that *Āshūrkhāna.*[150]

It appears that the setting up of *Āshūrkhānas* and the performance of Muharram festival connected with them were important features of the religious life of the Muslims belonging especially to the Shia sect. The Qutbshahi rulers, who were staunch Shias, appear to have encouraged their establishment, and extended liberal patronage for their maintenance with a view to popularize the Shia sect in the country. Many of the *Āshūrkhānas*, mentioned above, were granted lands and allowances for their upkeep, by the state. Muhammad Quli Qutbshah is said to have spent sixty thousand *Hūns* towards the payment of the employees of the *Āshūrkhānas* and their other expenses. Every year he used to spend another four lakh *Hūns*, which was the annual revenue of the city of Hyderabad, in feeding the *Syeds* and the *Ulema* during the Muharram festival connected with the *Āshūrkhānas* . Another twelve thousand *Hūns* were distributed to the needy and the poor on the same occasion every year.[151] These institutions became very popular in the seventeenth century A.D. when a number of them were set up in the city of Hyderabad and in other towns and villages where Muslims lived.

3

Organization and Functionaries

While the preceding chapter has dealt with the history of the religious institutions in general, the present chapter attempts to give an account of the organization and the functionaries of each category of the religious institutions. The types among the functionaries, their powers, duties and service conditions will be discussed here.

Temple

For managing its affairs, to conduct its various rituals and services and to look after its properties, the Temple had an organizations consisting of a body of functionaries. This body was known variously as *Niyōgālavāru*[1] and *Śrikāryaparulu.*[2] Its size was in consonance with the size of the temple, its properties and the number of rituals and services conducted in it.

The size and the number of the categories of personnel of some of the major Temples belonging to the first half of the period under study are indicated by the contemporary evidence. Two inscriptions from Tripurantakam (Kurnool dt.) dated 1290 A.D. and 1312 A.D. respectively, refer to the staff of the Temple of God Tripurantakesvara of that place as *Bahattariniyōgālavāru* and *Debbāyirenduniyōgālavāru.*[3] Similarly, an epigraph of 1320 A.D. from Umamahesvaram (Mahbubnagar dt.) refers to the body of the functionaries of the Umamahesvara Temple of that place as

Debbayirendu Niyōgālavāru.[4] Finally, *Śivarātrimahatmyamu,* a Telugu work written about 1440 A.D. by poet Srinatha also refers to the existence of *Bāhattari Niyōgamu* in the Mallikarjuna Temple of Srisailam (Kurnool dt.) These two terms *Bahāttari Niyōgalavāru* and *Debbāirendu Niyōgālāvaru* mean the staff of seventy-two categories. This clearly suggests that the functionaries of these Temples, especially belonging to the Kakatiya period, were organized on the model of the administrative system of the contemporary state, which also had similar number of categories of officials.[6] This system continued to prevail in some of the Temples like that of Srisailam till the middle of the 15th century A.D. It is also to be noted that the designation of most of the Temple staff during the entire period under study closely resembled that of the staff of the contemporary Hindu royal palace.

The functionaries of the Temple can be classified, for the convenience of the study, into the following three major categories, each consisting again of various sub-categories, on the basis of the nature of the functions performed by them. (1) The first category includes managerial staff, engaged in supervisory and administrative functions. (2) The second category consists of priestly functionaries, connected with the rituals and other religious services. (3) And the third category includes the non-priestly attendants performing miscellaneous services connected with the various aspects of the day-to-day routine religious duties of the Temple. A detailed account of these functionaries is given in the following pages.

The Managerial Staff

The first category, that is, the managerial staff consisted mainly of the members of the board of trustees, the Temple superintendent, the Temple treasury, and the Temple accountants. Because of their managerial functions they occupied a privileged top position in the hierarchy of Temple administration.

The Members of the Board of Trustees: The Hindu Temple, during this period in Andhra Desa, whether it was large or small and irrespective of its sectarian affiliations, had a board of trustees to supervise its management. The terms *Samsthānikulu, Sthānikulu, Sthānamvāru, Sthānattār,* etc. were used in the inscriptions to denote the trust-boards of the Temples. Their composition and strength varied from time to time and from Temple to Temple depending on the latter's background, size and resources.

An inscription of 1390 A.D. from Tirumalai-Tirupati indicates the composition and the strength of the Board of Trustees (*Sthanāttār*) of the Venkatesvara Temple.[7] The scared food (*prasādam*) allotted (after deducting the donor's share) to the *Sthānattār,* according to this grant, was divided into twelve shares and was distributed among them as – 4 *nirvāham* for the Tirupati Srivaishnavas, 3 *nirvāham* for the *Sabhaiyar* of Tiruchchukanur, 1 *nirvāham* for the *Nambimār,* 2 *nirvāham* for the *Kōyil-kelkum-Jiyars,* and 2 *nirvāham* for the *Koyil-kanakku Tiruninra-ur-Udaiyar,* indicating the total strength of the *Sthānattār* as twelve. Out of the 12 members of this *Sthānattār,* 7 members (4 members of the Srivaishnva community of Tirupati and 3 members of the *Sabhaiyār,* the village assembly of Tiruchchukanur) were apparently laymen.[8] The remaining 5 members consisting of 1 *Nambimār* (priest), 2 *Kōyil-Kelkum-Jiyars* (the Temple-superintendants who were the *Jiyars* of the local Srivaishnava *Maṭha* of *Tengalai* sect) and 2 *Kōyil-kanakku* (Temple accountant) were the regular Temple functionaries. The strength and the composition of the Board of Trustees of Tirupati Temple remained the same from 1390 A.D. to the end of the period under study.[9]

The composition and the strength of the trust-boards of a few more Temples of the period are indicated in the contemporary epigraphs. According to an epigraph of 1515 A.D. from the village Devagudi (Cuddapah dt.), the Board of Trustees (*Sthānamvaru*) of the Temple of Talakantidevi consisted of six members who were *Jiyas.*[10] An inscription of 1544 A.D. from the village Peddadudyala (Cuddapah dt.) also gives the number of the *Sthānikas* of the local Temple as six.[11] But an epigraph of 1560 A.D. from the village Kurmai (Chittoor dt.) states that the number of the *Sthanikas* of the Varadaraja Temple of that place was only four.[12] An inscription of 1406-07 A.D. from Petleru village (Nellore dt.) records that only one *Sthānapati* was appointed over the management of a newly renovated Siva Temple of that place.[13]

It cannot be definitely stated that the strength of all the above mentioned trust-boards remained static throughout the period under consideration. As the office of the board of trustees of some of the Temples was held as a hereditary right by certain families, it is quite likely that, it tended to be divided into a number of shares within a few generations, and they were held by all the descendants of the original office holders. After the death of a particular *Sthānika,* the claim to his office appears to have been regarded as a joint right and divided equally among all his sons, who became *Sthānikas* in their fathers' place. Consequently, the multiplication of this type continued. An inscription of 1552 A.D. from Bhairasamudram village (Anantapur dt.) clearly states that the two *Sthānikas* of the Tiruvengalanatha Temple of that place were the two sons of Chennamayya.[14] This enables us to infer that this office held by one person in one generation came to be divided between the two sons, in the next generation.

In the case of some Temple-trust-boards of the period whose members were ascetics and celibates, the question of increase in their strength did not arise at all. For instance, an epigraph of 1556 A.D. states that Aubalaraja, an official under Sadasiva Raya of Vijayanagara, appointed Ramanujayyangaru as the *Sathanika* of a certain newly built Alwar Temple and enjoined him to manage it in perpetuity through the succession of his disciples.[15] In such cases, only one disciple, generally, succeeded his master at the time of each succession.

The Temple-trust-boards appear to have been headed, in general, by a President known in some cases, as *Sthānachārya* and in some as *Sthānapati.*[16] The reference to two types of Temple dignitaries–one *Sthānāchārya* (the Presiding member of the trust-board) and the other *Sthānamvāru* (four or five ordinary members of the trust-board), separately, with their specific names as the trustees of the Chennakesava Temple of Marakapuram (Cuddapah dt.), in an inscription of that place, belonging to the year 1552 A.D.[17] supports the above hypothesis. This is further confirmed by a reference, in an epigraph of 1554 A.D. from Ahobilam (Kurnool dt.) to these two types of members of trust-board, *Sthānāchārya* and *Sthānikulu* as belonging to the Temple of God Narasimha of Ahobilam.[18] But in the case of Srikuramam and Simhachalam Temples, situated in the Ganga-Gajapati dominions, the presiding member of their trust-boards[19] appear to have been designated as *Sthā napati.* This is indicated in an epigraph of 1309 A.D.[20] and several other epigraphs from Srikuramam Temple, and also in an epigraph of 1353 A.D. from Simhachalam Temple,[21] which make reference to this office. *Sthānapati-muḍra* (Secretary or Seal-bearer of the *Sthānapti*) and *Sthānapati-Vehōralu* (the executive of the *Sthānapati* referred to in an epigraph of 1309 A.D. from Srikuramm, 22 also imply the presiding status of *Sthānapati.*

An inscription of 1408 A.D. from the village Tamballa (Chittor dt.) refers to six *Sthānapatulu* of the local Mallikarjuna Temple, having six chares in the office.[23] It also states that those six major shares were further divided as sub-shares iṇ the next generation. But this epigraph does not indicate whether the term *Sthānapatulu,* referred to in it, was used to denote the office of the presiding members of the Trust-board of that Temple or its ordinary members.

An interesting inscription of 1299 A.D. from the village Alampur (Mahbubnagar dt.) refers to a certain Pedamula Maldevaraju as the *Mahāsthānāḍhipati* of the Temple of Brahmesvara of that place.[24] Several epigraphs of Kalyani Chalukyan period, from the same place, ranging from 1078 A.D. to 1112 A.D. also contain references to this functionary *Mahāsthānāḍhipati* of the same Temple as receiving and making grants on behalf of that Temple.[25] But they do not make any references to the existence of other trust-board members. It appears that this particular temple was managed by a single trustee.

The Functions of the members of the Trust-Board: The members of the board of trustees had superior authority in all matters, religious and secular, pertaining to the Temple. On behalf of the Temple, they received all the grants and took the responsibility of executing them. An epigraph 1554 A.D. from Ahobilam refers to Parankusa Sathakopa Jiyyanagar, the pontiff of the local Srivaisnava

Vadagalai–Maṭha and the *Sthānāchārya* of the Temple of God Narasimha of that place, entering into an agreement, alongwith the *Sthānikas* of the temple with a doncr to fulfil the conditions of a grant made to the temple.[26] Their important duty was to see that the daily rituals and services in the temple and its periodical festivals were conducted in accordance with the injunctions of the religious texts.

They had control over all matters concerning the Temple staff, i.e., their appointments, allowances etc. An inscription of 1559 A.D. from Kurmayi village (Chittoor dt.) states that the *Sthānikas* of the Varadaraja Temple of that place granted some lands to the Temple priest (*Archaka*) as *Archana Vritti.*[27] They managed the lands and other properties of the Temple and protected them from encroachments and thefts. They supervised the collection of revenue due to the Temple. The repairs and renovation of the Temple buildings, the construction of new ones and the extension of the old ones, and the repairs of Temple jewellery were undertaken under the supervision of the *Sthānikas.*[28]

The trust-boards acted as the main link between the Temple and the government, and all written orders to the Temple were addressed to the *Sthānikas.* An epigraph of 1482 A.D. from Tirupati states that, a *Rāyasam* (written order) sent by the Vijayanagara monarch Saluva Narasimha with instruction to execute a grant, was addressed to the *Sthānattār* of Venkatesvara Temple of that place.[29] They also sometimes made representation to the rulers requesting them to provide more income to their Temple. The *Sthānikas* of Mukti Ramesvaram Temple of Ramaesvaram (Cuddaph dt.) made a representation to Krishnadeva Raya, who visited that place, stating that existing provision was not sufficient for the proper conduct of the services of their Temple, and got one more village granted by that monarch.[30]

Temple Superintendent: Some of the Temples had a Superintendent among their functionaries. This official of the Venkatesvara Temple of Tirumalai–Tirupati was known as *Kōyil Kelvi.*[31] (Junior temple superintendent). Thee offices were held by the senior and the junior pontiffs of the local Jiyyangar (*Tengalai*)

Maṭham.[32] Both of them were included in the *Sthānattār* of the Temple. They supervised the religious rituals and services in the Temple.

The Temple-treasury and its officials: The treasury was an important Temple office which transacted all money matters pertaining to it. Almost every Temple having some resources appears to have had a treasury. It was known variously as *Sribhāndāram,*[33] *Bokkasa–bhāndāram,*[34] etc. The money, jewellery and other precious articles belonging to the Temples were kept in its treasury.

The officer who headed the office of the Temple-treasury was known as *Bhāndāri,* and he had his own subordinate staff. An inscription of 1532 A.D. from Kalahasti refers to the *Bhāndāri* of the local Siva Temple.[35] Another epigraph of 1389 A.D. from Simhachalam (Vizag dt.) also makes reference to the *Bhāndāri,* presumably the head of the treasury of the Temple of God Narasimha of that place.[36]

The treasury of the Kalahasti Temple (Chittoor dt.) appears to have had more than one superintendent (*Bhandāri*). This is indicated by an inscription of Achyuta Raya's period from that place.[37] It refers to an agreement among the *Bhandāris* of that Temple–treasury for the execution of a grant and for the proper utilization of the money of that grant. Another epigraph from the same place (Kalahasti) belonging to the year 1567 A.D. states that the *Bhandāris* of the treasury of Tirukkalatti–Udaiya–Nayanar (Siva) Temple granted certain privileges to Venkatappa Nayakkar for keeping watch on the Temple.[38] From the information provided in these two grants it can be inferred that the treasury of the Kalahasti Temple performed, sometimes, the functions of the trustees also.

The *Sribhandāram* of Tirupati Temple, beside keeping the money and costly ornaments, appears to have maintained a store of various materials like clothes, camphor, incense, and cloves, needed for various religious services in the Temple. The Temple grants normally stipulate that the *Sribhandāram* should supply all the articles needed for the performance of the various services instituted by the donars.[39]

The Venkatesvara Temple of Tirupati used to have, besides the *Sribhandāram* (ordinary Temple treasury), a golden treasury known as *Pōr Pandāram (Por Phandāram),* where the gold and silver jewels of the Temple were kept. The importance of this *Por Bhandāram* is indicated by the fact that an important Srivaishnava teacher Kandadai Ramanujayyanagar was appointed as its *Kartār* (guardian) by the Vijayanagara emperor Saluva Narasimha.[40]

Public Works Treasury: The Temple of Srivenkatesvara of Tirupati, appears to have maintained besides *Sribhandāram* and *Por Bhandāram,* a public works-treasury, known as *Tiruppani Bhandarāttār.* This department was in-charge of works of construction and repair of the buildings of the Temple. An inscription of 1482 A.D. from Tirupati states that *Pillai Tiruppani Bhandarāttār* (the officer of the Public works Treasury) was authorized by the *Sthānattār* to accept a village as a *Tiruvidaiyāttam Tiruppanipuram* (a village which was granted to the Temple and whose income is devoted to the construction of the Temple buildings and repairs), and to utilize the income from that village for the construction of the *Gōpurams* (towers) at Tirupati and Tirumalai in the name of the royal donor Saluva Narasimha.[41] Another epigraph from the same place belonging to the year 1468 A.D. also refers to similar functions performed by the *Tiruppani-Bhandāram* of Venkatesvara Temple.[42] So it appears that, the *Tiruppani-Bhandāram* of Tirupati Temple was entrusted also with the works of managing the villages and lands whose income was to be utilized exclusively for the Temple repairs and construction.

Temple Accountants: Many Temples of the period appear to have maintained their own accountants. They are referred to variously as *Srikaranamu, Lēkha Saṁprati, Karanamu,* etc. in the Temple epigraphs, which also indicate the nature of functions performed by them.

According to an inscription of the year 1552-53 A.D. from Udayagiri.[43] Timmaya Deva, the Vijayanagara provincial governor of Udayagiriraja, while making a grant of the income of several villages to the Ranagraya Temple of Udayagiri, enjoined that the Temple accountant (*Dēvuni gudilo lēkha saṁprati*) should collect the contributions and maintain the accounts of the Temple. Another epigraph from Penugonda (Anantapur dt.) states that Chavaram Chenappanayudu, a Vijayanagara official, built a Temple at that place and appointed at the time of its consecration a certain Juturi Aparasu as *Karnam* to maintain its accounts (*Padidharasthvaśyālu Vrāsētaṅduku*).[44]

In the inscriptions from Simhachalam[45] and Srikurmam[46] two types of Temple accountants i.e., *Srikaranam* and *Koshtakaranam* are mentioned. While the *Srikaranam* was, probably, in-charge of maintaining the accounts of the monetary income and expenditure of the Temple, the *Kōṣhtakaranam,* maintained the accounts of the Temple stores. And it was probably the latter's duty to supply the various articles needed for worship in the Temple in accordance with the orders issued by the Temple management. In the case of Simhachalam Temple, its accountants are also referred to, in an inscription from that place simply as *Lēkhakulu.*[47]

Especially, the major Temples like that of Tirupati, appear to have maintained a number of accountants in their service. More than twelve accountants, as belonging to the Temple of Venkatesvara, are referred to in the inscriptions of that Temple belonging to the single year of A.D. 1494.[48] Similarly, another epigraph from the same place belonging to the year 1546 A.D. refers to 13 accountants of the same Temple making a grant.[49] From this, it can be inferred that the office of the accountants of this Temple was a very big establishment. The *Srikarana Maṅtapam* referred to in a inscription of that place of the year 1494 A.D.[50] which records the provision made by one of the Temple accountants for a halt and the propitiation of the deity at that place (*Srikarana mandapam*), appears to be the office of the Temple accountants.

The *Srikarana mantapa* or the accounts office of Tirupati Venkatesvara Temple, which, thus, had a number of accountants, appears to have been headed by a Chief Accounts Officer. And the temple–accountant (*Tiru-ninra-ur-udaiyār*), who is referred to at the end of the most of the epigraphs from that place as being in-charge of drafting the Temple grants,[51] must have been the Chief or Head Accounts Officer of the Temple. Being the Chief-Temple-

Accountant, one of his duties was, probably, to compose the inscriptions of that Temple. It is also to be remembered that, the accountants of this Temple were represented in the Trust-board (*Sthānattār*) of that Temple by two members. This is known from an epigraph of 1380 A.D., which refers to the allotment of two shares to them out of the 12 shares of sacred food meant for the twelve member *Sthānattār.*[52]

Some of the inscription from Tirupati furnish interesting information about the preparation and presentation of the accounts of the Temple of Srivenkatesvara, by its accountants. The day on which the annual accounts of the Temple were written afresh (closing of the old accounts), and the accounts for the new year were opened by the accountants of the Temple was known as *Ādi-ayanam* day. The inscription of 1994 A.D. from Tirupati[53] refers to the day of the *Tirukkārtikai* Temple festival as the day of the commencement of the new year accounts (*Ādiayanam day*). This *Tirukkārtikāi* festival took place, it appears, on the first day of the dark-fortnight of the month of *Kārtikai* of the Tamil year. It is interesting to note that, this is similar to the commencement of the new year accounts by many merchants of the present day Andhra Desa, on the first day of the dark-fortnight of the month of *Kārtīka* of Telugu calendar year, which also corresponds with the *Deepāvali* festival. The presentation of the yearly accounts of the Srivenkatesvara Temple of Tirupati on the 9th day of the Annual *Brahmōtsavam* (*Tirukkōdi-Tirunāl*), in the presence of the (Processional) deity when he was seated in a *darbār* (*Āsthānam*) in front of the Temple granary in the course of his procession in the streets, is referred to in the inscription of 1493 A.D., from that place.[54]

The Priestly Functionaries

The Temple priests known as *Archakas* and some times *Pūjāris* come under the second category of the Temple functionaries. Their main function, as their designation suggests, was to conduct worship and various other religious rituals in the Temples. The *Archaka* was an essential part of the establishment of all Temples including those of the minor deities and female village deities. Of course, the number of *Archakas* varied from Temple to Temple according to their resources and the number of rituals conducted in them.

In the major Temples, which normally maintained more than one priest (*Archaka*) there was a head priest, and the remaining were his assistants who helped him. This officiating priest or the head priest in the Vaishnava Temples, especially at Tirupati, Simhachalam and Srikurmam, appear to have been called *Nambi* or *Nambimar.*[55] The *Samārādhakas,* who are referred to besides the *Nambis,* in the inscription of 1350 A.D. from Simhachalam,[56] appear to have been the assistant priests who were under the head priest in the Temple of Narasimha of that place. The *Tiruvārādhakulu* refers to, in an epigraph of 1563 A.D. from Pedda Ahobilam, as belonging to the Temple of God Narasimha of that place, probably, belong to this category.[57] They must have assisted the officiating priest by way of providing him with water and other *Archana* material and preparing *Naivēdya* etc.

The *Archakas* and especially the officiating *Archakas* were usually appointed from the families belonging to that particular religious sect to which the Temple also belonged. They were to be great scholars,[58] and well-versed in the religious texts. The *Archakas* of the Vaishnava Temples during this period were invariably Brahmans by caste. But some of the Saiva Temples and especially those of Veera Saiva sect and of some of the female deities, had non-Brahman priests. An inscription of 1301-11 A.D. from Kocherlakota village (Nellore dt.) states that Deveri-Nayanigaru, a subordinate of Kakatiya Pratapa Rudra II, appointed a certain Dalamu Varadanna and Tammalla Peddi, presumably non-Brahmans, as the priests in the Siva Temple, newly constructed by him.[59] The *Archaka* of the Temple of Sangamesvara of Animela (Kurnool dt.) is also referred to, in an inscription from that place belonging to the period of Achyutadeva Raya, as a Jangama by caste.[60] That some of the Siva Temples in the Telugu country had Tammalas as their officiating priests during the period of Krishnadeva Raya is known from an interesting episode connected with the visit of that monarch to the Pushpagiri Temple and narrated in the *Kaifiyat* of Hanumadgundam.[61] The *Kaifiyat* states that Krishnaraya was very much annoyed when he found that the *Archakas* in the Saiva Temple of that place (Pushpagiri) were of Tammala caste. He, according to the same source, made arrangements immediately for the appointments of Brahmans for the chanting of the *Vedas* etc. during the Temple festivals of that place. This practice of appointing non-Brahmans, like Tammalas, Jangamas, Balijas etc., as *Archakas,* appear to have been prevalent in the Saiva Temples which were under the management of the Veerasaiva community. This practice, which was in consonance with the teaching of the great Veerasaiva teacher Basava, continues to be followed, even now, in some of the Saiva Temples at places like Hanamakonda and Srisailam.

The *Archaka,* particularly the head-priest, appears to have been invariably associated with the management of the Temple. In many cases, he was a member of the board of trustees. It is to be remembered that the head priest (*Naṁbimār*) of the Venkatesvara Temple of Tirupati was one of the 12 *Sthānattār* of that Temple. In Temples of moderate size, it appears, sometimes the endowments were entrusted to the Temple priest, who undertook to execute them, i.e. to perform the services for which the endowments were made. According to an inscription of 1321 A.D. from Magallu village (W. Godavari dt.) the donor entrusted some land for a food offering to God, and it is stipulated in it that the *Pūjāri* was to run that service.[62] An inscription of 1526 A.D. from Undavalli (Guntur dt.) also states that *Pūjāri* Peda Lingayya was given the authority to perform the Temple services like *Śōdasha-upachāras* and *Angaranga-bhoga* in the Temple of Bhaskaresvara of the place, by certain Settis, who built the Temple and endowed it with lands.[63] Thus, the above two instances show that, the Temple *Pūjāris* also performed the functions of the trustees besides performing their basic functions, that is, doing *Archana* to the deities.

The officiating priest was the key person who played a crucial role on the ceremonial side of the Temple life. This key position appears to have been misused, sometimes, by the Temple *Archakas* who were tempted to commit thefts of the Temple jewellery and ornaments. Nambi Sirrappaiyan, the *Archaka* of the Sri Venkatesvara Temple of Tirupati is said to have committed theft of jewels of that Temple for which he was punished with the confiscation of his houses and house-sites by an order of Saluva Narasimha Raya.[64]

The Non-Priestly Attendants

The third category of the Temple functionaries comprised the numerous non-priestly personnel, attending to miscellaneous functions. The terms such as *Ūdigālavāru, Nibaṅdha Kāṅdru, Koluvulāvaru,* and *Kaṅdācharamvāru* are used in the Temple inscriptions to denote this staff. They were both men and women. A list of them as they figure in the contemporary Temple epigraphs is given in the following Table number I to indicate the nature of the work performed by them.

Some of the employees like dancers, singers, musicians, conchshell blowers, water-men, florist, flutist and drummers, included in the third category, were directly connected with the performance of the day-to-day rituals in the Temples. But the others, comprising the artisans, gardeners, cooks, washer-men etc. performed menial services and were not directly connected with the religious services.

The Temple Artisans: The artisans known as *Paṅchānamvāru*[65] or *Paṅchādulu*[66] (viz. masons, carpenters, goldsmiths, blacksmiths and braziers) maintained by the Hindu Temples, attended to the various needes of the Temple, such as construction and repairs of buildings and Temple cars, supply of vessels, making and repairing of ornaments. They were attached to the Temples on hereditary basis, and their services were remunerative.

The Temple artisans, besides being provided with tax-free lands, and some times with shares in the Temple sacred-food, were entitled to certain privileges. One such privilege enjoyed by the Temple artisans of this period is that they were entitled to accompany the God, by mounting His chariot, when He (God) was taken out in procession in the streets of the village or town during the festival days of the Temple. An inscription of Vijayanagara period from the village Siddhavatam (Cuddapah dt.)[67] refers to such privilege of the Temple carpenters and smiths (*Vaḍla-karamala vāru*) who were entitled to mount the car of the God in procession with their traditional dress and implements during the festival of God Raghunatha of the place. This epigraph records further that their privilege was reconfirmed by the provincial governor, when they made a representation saying that it was denied to them by the local Balijas.

In some of the Vaishnava Temples, the protection of the endowments by the artisans, along with that of Srivaishnava community was sought by the donors. The inscription of 1321 A.D. and several others of the Ganga and Gajapati periods from Srikurmam and Simhachalam refer to such stipulation of the protection by the artisans (*Pañchādirakṣha*) of the service of a perpetual lamp and other services instituted by the devotees in those temples.[68] These instance would indicate their close association with the management of those Temples.

The female functionaries of the Hindu Temple: The Temples employed a number of women who served in various capacities, as dancers, singers, musicians and menial servants. Various terms such as *Raṅga bhōgamvāru, Bhōgamvāru, Dēvadāsi, Patri,* and *Sāni* were used to denote the women employed in the service of God. The women employed in Saiva Temples, and especially of Veera Saivas, appear to have been known as *Dēvara Basavi* or *Basavulu.* They are referred to in an inscription of 1518 A.D.[69]

The basic services for which the women were employed by the Temples were dancing, singing and music which were an essential part of the Temple worship. The employment of women for these purposes was a common feature of the Temple life of this period. Even the Temples of female deities are no exception in this matter. An epigraph of 1515 A.D. from Amaravati refers to the *Sānis* serving in the Temple of Madhurapuri Madhavidevi of that place.[70] The female dancers of the Temples seem to have been proficient in these traditional arts, and were trained specially for that purpose. It some of the Temples, dance-masters were appointed to train them in these arts. Dance-masters (*Naṭṭuvārs*) are referred

Table 1

Sl. No.	Designation	Place	Date A.D.	Source
1.	*Simhālitya* (Songstress)	Srikurmam	1290	*SII.* V, no. 1150
2.	*Dhūpaparichārakulu* (Persons employed in Connection with the offerings of incense to the deity)	–do–	1292	*Ibid.* no. 1214
3.	*Vonikārudu* (Person employed to remove plants on the top of the Temple)	Simhachalam	1296	*SII* VI, no. 868
4.	*Talāri* (Temple Watchman)	–do–	1297	*SII*, IV, no. 161
5.	*Divyala Maigāpu Kondikārlu* (Persons who look after the upkeep of the torches and lights in the Temple)	Srikurmam	1309	*SII* V, no. 1214
6.	*Kaivāri* (the panegyrist or the person who sings hymns in praise of God)	–do–	1309	*Ibid.*
7.	*Bōdiga* (Temple watchman at the main	Simhachalam	1314	*SII.* VI, no. 1136
	gate or *dharmadvaram*)	Srikurmam	1325	*SII.* V, no. 1226
8.	*Koṅdikāruḍu* (conch-blower)			
9.	*Khaṅḍaḍhara* (the person who holds the sword)	–do–	1332	*Ibid.* no. 12919
10.	Person for holding sacred umbrella (*Gōḍuvupaṭṭanu*)	Simhachalam	1339	*SII.* VI, no.939

table contd.

Sl. No.	*Designation*	*Place*	*Date A.D.*	*Source*
11.	*Maṅgala geetālu pāḍutaku sānulu* (women for singing sacred songs)	–do–	”	*Ibid.*
12.	*Ottukāṇdru* (persons playing on Veena)	–do–	1349	*Ibid.* no. 955
13.	*Sutigāḍu* (drone player)	–do–	”	*Ibid.*
14.	A person for fanning God with *Ālavattamu* (a circular fan made of cloth)	–do–	”	*SII.* VI, no. 933
15.	*Thōṅta peṭṭedi Dāsarulu* (Dāsaris who cultivated flower gardens)	–do–	”	*Ibid.* no. 932
16.	Persons for supplying *Tirumañjanam* (items like incence, spices, perfumes etc.)	–do–	”	*Ibid.*
17.	*Dvāra–nāyaka* (the guardian of the inner Temple)	Srikurmam	1353	*SII.* V, no. 1205
18.	*Tōṅta–basuvu (poovulu techchē)* (gardener)	Simhachalam	1383	*SII.* VI, no. 972
19.	Persons for grinding sandal-wood into paste or powder (*Chaṅdanamurāyanu*)	–do–	1396	*Ibid.* no. 1035
20.	Women for fanning the deity with whisk (*Viñjāmaramu paṭṭanu*)	–do–	”	*Ibid.*
21.	Women for holding the mirror before the deity & decorating the Temple floor with rice-flour (*addamu paṭṭanu, muggu peṭṭanu*)	–do–	”	*Ibid.*

table contd.

Sl. No.	Designation	Place	Date A.D.	Source
22.	Men for the supply of milk	–do–	,,	*Ibid.*
23.	Men for grinding the pulses (*Pappu nūrū*)	–do–	,,	*SII.* VI, no. 1035
24.	Men for supplying oil for the perpetual lamp	–do–	,,	*Ibid.*
25.	*Tōṅta-baṅtu* (gardener) (E. Godavari dt.)	Bhimavaram	1434	*SII,* V, no. 34
26.	*Masōya-battu* (mason) (Krishna dt.)	Yenikapadu Century	15th	*SII,* X. no. 740
27.	*Ghaṅta Veeranna kāṅdu* (bell-man)	–do–	,,	*Ibid.*
28.	*Puspāla-vāru* (men for supplying flowers)	–do–	,,	*Ibid.*
29.	*Saṅku-vaṅdu* (the man who blew conch-shell)	–do–	,,	*Ibid.*
30.	*Divya-teeṅdu* (men for holding or lighting the lamps)	–do–	,,	*Ibid.*
31.	Bearers of *Vahanams* (vehicles)	Tirumalai-Tirupati	1496	*TTDE,* II. no. 135
32.	*Pachchadi–K–Kārār* (distributors of offered *prasādam*)	–do–	,,	*Ibid.*
33.	*Tiruveṅkata–Pichchan* (lamp lighters)	–do–	,,	*Ibid.*
34.	*Vinnapam Sēyvār* (persons who seek permission to commence the different religious functions)	–do–	,,	*Ibid.*
35.	*Tevaiyal* (Temple-cooks)	–do–	,,	*Ibid.*

table contd.

Sl. No.	Designation	Place	Date A.D.	Source
36.	*Siṅgamuraiyan* (suppliers of fire-wood)	–do–	,,	*Ibid.*
37.	*Tiruvettu vagai* (proclaimer)	–do–	,,	*Ibid.*
38.	*Tiruppaniyal* (workman)	–do–	,,	*Ibid.*
39.	*Naṭṭuvār* (dance-master)	–do–	,,	*Ibid.*
40.	*Muṭṭukkārār* (time-keeper)	–do–	,,	*Ibid.*
41.	*Emperumānadiyar* (Temple-damsels)	–do–	,,	*Ibid.*
42.	*Dōla-nagasvara-kārar* (drummers & pipers)	–do–	,,	*Ibid.*
43.	*Paḍuvar* (Songsters)	–do–	,,	*Ibid.*
44.	*Pani murāi* (craftsman-artisan)	–do–	,,	*Ibid.*
45.	*Tiruvidhi munaiyar* (street-sweeper)	–do–	,,	*Ibid.*
46.	*Sippiyar* (*Silpi* or engraver)	–do–	,,	*Ibid.*
47.	*Vāsal-kollār* (watchman, smith)	–do–	,,	*Ibid.*
48.	*Uvachchan* (drummer)	–do–	,,	*Ibid.*
49.	*Koyilādiś* (temple door-keeper) of the *Tirumalai-Periya Gōpuram*	–do–	1546	*TTDE*, V, no. 70
50.	Bearers of various articles of stores	–do–	,,	*Ibid.* no. 89
51.	*Paduvāykkarar* (the keeper of the article of stores)	–do–	,,	*Ibid.*

table contd.

Sl. No.	*Designation*	*Place*	*Date A.D.*	*Source*
52.	*Kaikkōlar* (temple servants)	–do–	"	*Ibid.*
53.	*Talaiyāris* (night watchman)	–do–	"	*Ibid.*
54.	Suppliers of weapons for securing fuels	–do–	"	*Ibid.*
55.	*Tiruppani-pillai* (temple repairers)	–do–	"	*Ibid.*
56.	Officer in *Rāmānuja-kūtam*	–do–	"	*Ibid.*
57.	*Mahotus*	–do–	"	*Ibid.*
58.	Pipers and *Vādyakkārar*	–do–	"	*Ibid.*
59.	*Pani-murai* (suppliers of baskets)	–do–	"	*Ibid.*
60.	*Nivaṅdakkārar* (*vahanam* bearers)	–do–	"	*Ibid.*
61.	Garland-suppliers	Tirumalai-Tirupati	1546	*TTDE*, V, no. 89
62.	Persons engaged in water-shed	–do–	1496	*Ibid.*
63.	Persons engaged in *Vēdapārāyanam* service	–do–	1546	*Ibid.* no. 90
64.	*Kaṅgānippān* (Supervisor)	–do–	"	*Ibid.*
65.	*Kummara svarūpam* (potters)	–do–	"	*Ibid.*
66.	*Mēgai Svarūpam* (brass vessel suppliers)	–do–	"	*Ibid.*
67.	Carpenter (for the decoration of *maṅtapam*)	–do–	"	*Ibid.*
68.	Servants for the construction of *Pandal*	–do–	"	*Ibid.*
69.	Store-keepers	–do–	1550	*TTDE*, V, no. 125
70.	Persons (Srivaishnavas) for reciting *Vedas*	–do–	"	*Ibid.*
71.	Persons for bringing water	–do–	"	*Ibid.*
72.	Persons for cleaning and decorating dining *mantapa* in the *Rāmānuja-Kūtamu*	–do–	"	*Ibid.*
73.	*Adhikāri* (Superintendent of *Rāmānuja-Kūtam* in Tirupatu)	–do–	"	*Ibid.*

to in an inscription of 1496 A.D. from Tirupati.[71] An inscription of 1349 A.D. from Srikurmam refers to the appointment of one dance master and two dancing girls in the Srikurmesvara Temple by Gangadevi, the queen of the Ganga King Narasimha III.[72] The *Abhinavabharatachārya Chappannambēya-kāra Todaramallu Raṅganātha vāgyakārudu,* referred to in an inscription of 1421 A.D. from Simhachalam as being granted a share in the sacred food by the *Bhōgapariksha* of Narasimha Temple,[78] was quite probably a dance teacher of that Temple.

Almost every Temple appears to have had a dance-hall known as *Nātyamaṅtapa* or *Raṅgamaṅtapa* attached to it in front of the sanctorum (*Garbhagriha*), where the Temple dancers entertained they deity as well as the devotees with singing and dancing. Many of the grants, recording the endowments to the Temples, stipulate for providing *Raṅga-bhōga* (dancing and singing) besides the *Aṅga-bhōga* to the deities. An inscription from Chodavaram (Vizag dt.), which appears to belong to Gajapati period, refers to the existence of a *Nātya Sriśāla* (dance hall) attached to the Temple of God Vallabharaya of that place where the god was entertained with dancing and singing (*Nīrtya-Gitādulu*).[74] Similarly, an inscription of 1381 A.D. from Draksharamam (Godavari dt.) refers to the construction of a *Nātyamaṅtapa* attached to the Bhimesvara Temple of that place.[75]

Some of the Temple women appear to have been well-versed in both vocal and instrumental music. An inscription of 1359 A.D. from Simhachalam refers to the *Sanis* who were employed to sing the *Nāma-saṅkīrtana* (recital of the sacred name of God) at the time of offering the sacred incense (*Dhūpa*) to the God Narasimha of the place.[76] Another epigraph of 1299 A.D. from the same place (Simhachalam) refers to the singing by the Temple women of the sacred songs (*maṅgalageetālu*) at the time of offering the sacred light to the God Narasimha.[77] Two women were employed to play the Veena and other instruments in the presence of God Narasimha, according to another inscription of 1349 A.D. from Simhachalam.[78]

Some of the Temple dancers appears to have known acting also. They staged dramas in the Temple precincts. An interesting

Temple record of Krishnadeva Raya's period, from the village Cheruvu Belagallu (Kurnool dt.) refers to the gift of some land to a *Patri* (Temple dancer), a daughter of Nattuva Timmayya, and another male dancer Nattuva Nagayya both of whom were connected with the drama *Tāyikuṅda Nāṭaka.*[79] As the Temple of Jalasayana or Jalasingadeva is mentioned in this grant, it is quite probable that this drama was staged in that Temple in commemoration of its festival.

Someties, women who were well-versed in dancing and singing were deputed to serve the Temples, by royal donors. An inscription of 1531 A.D. from Tirupati states that Muddu Kuppayi, who was originally attached to the palace of Achyutadeva Raya was ordered by the King to proceed to Tirupati and render service in the Temple of God Venkatesa. Her grandfather, Ranjakam Srirangaraja was the master of the drama troupe of *Nātakaśala* attached to the Vijayanagara royal palace.[80] Several other functions performed by the women employees of Temples are refererred to in the epigraphs of the period. An inscription of 1382 A.D. from Simhachalam refers to the service of *Chāmara-sēva* i.e., the service of fanning the deity with whisk, by two *Sanis.*[81] Another epigraph from the same place refers to the services of *Addamupaṭṭanu,* i.e., holding the mirror to the deity, and *Muggupeṭṭanu,* i.e., decorating the Temple floor with rice powder, performed by a woman in the local Temple.[82] That the women employees had a voice in the management of the affairs of some of the Temples belonging to Kakatiya Prataparuda II's period is indicated in an epigraph of 1292 A.D. from the village Peddakallepalle (Krishna dt.)[83] It stipulates that the service of perpetual lamp instituted by a donor in the local Temple was to be maintained and protected by the *Sānimunnūru* along with the *Sthānamvāru* of that Temple. Besides getting their usual allowances, tax-free lands, and shares in the Temple sacred food, the Temple dancers enjoyed certain other privileges like accompanying the God in the chariot during the car-festival. It is prescribed by the donor in a Temple grant of the period from Udayagiri (Nellore dt.) that the Temple dancers (*Naṭṭuvār*) alongwith other servants of the Temple of Ranga-nayakulu were to be inside the car at the time of chariot-festival (*Rathōtsava*).[84] Some of the Temple dancers were very much honoured and were conferred with certain privileges by the Temple authorities for their devotion to duty. Tiru Venkata Manikkam, the dancer in the Temple of Sri Venkateswara of Tirupati during the period of Achyutaraya of Vijayanagara, was permitted by the Temple authorities to use a palanquin for her conveyance.[85] This is a rare privilege conferred on a Temple dancer.

The inscriptions of the period do not give us any idea of the private life, the caste and the social status of the female employees of the Temple. The terms like *Bhōgam-varu, Lañja,* and *Vēsya* were used in some of the inscriptions of the period to denote these women.[86] But it is difficult to say whether these terms carried any derogatory sense in which they are used and understood today. Even the use of the Sufix '*Sāni*' at the end of the names of these Temple women in the inscriptions, also does not indicate their social status because of its use as suffix to the names of the married and respectable women during this period. Of course, some of the inscriptions of the period give us to understand that some of the Temple women led a married life and had children. An inscription of 1391 A.D. from Bezawada states that Bhogam Namburi Annasani, the dancer of Bezawada Mallikarjuna Temple, had a daughter-in-law.[87] indicating married life in her family. This is also confirmed by a number of epigraphs from Simhachalam and Srikurmam.[88] They refer to two types of women employees—*saṁpradāyamuvāru* and *Sānulu*— as serving the Temples of those places. The women belonging to the first category remained unmarried and were attached to the first category remained unmarried and were attached to the Temples, and those of the second category were married. They led an independent life but were employed by the Temples on a part-time basis.[89]

Caste–Orientation in Temple Services: Certain communities appear to have been specialized in performing some of the Temple services. They were very much preferred for these services. To begin with, the priestly functions in Hindu Temple were performed invariably by the Brahman community. But in some of the Saiva Temples, especially belonging to the Veera Saiva sect, the non-brahmans like the Jangamas, the Tammalas and the Balijas were employed as priests. For some of the menial services such as cooking, supplying flowers, lighting the lamps etc. in both Saiva and Vaishnava Temples, people belonging to Tammala, Dasari, and Satani castes were specially engaged.

In the Vaishnava Temples, the Dasaris and Sattada Srivaishnavas (Satanis) were employed for cultivating flower gardens (*Nandavanams*) and supplying flowers. At Tirumala Tirupati, some of the flower-gardens belonging to the Temple of Sri Venkatesvara were, no doubt, managed by the *Jiyars* of the local *Tengalai Maṭham,* who were Brahmans. But it was the Sattada Srivaishnavas (Satanis) who were actually engaged to cultivate them and supply the flowers and garlands to the Temple.[90] These Sattada Srivaishnavas served the Temple in other capacities also. They supplied various items like spices, perfumes and incense for the *Tirumañjanam* (holy bath) of the Lord every day, and chanted the *Prabhañdas* of the *Alvārs* in the presence of God.[91] They were sometimes appointed as cooks in the Temples. This is referred to in an inscription of 1556 A.D.[92] Some of these services in the Temples of Simhachalam and Srikurmam appear to have been performed by men belonging to the Dasari community. An inscription of 1314 A.D. from Simhachalam refers to these men who supplied garlands to that Temple as *Tirumāla Peṭṭedi Dāsarulu.*[93] An inscription of 1345 A.D. from Srikuramam also refers to these Dasaris (*Tōñta-dāsarulu*) as performing the service of supplying flowers everyday to the Temple of Srikurmaswami.[94] A reference in the Kamalapuram *Kaifiyat*[95] to *Sankirtana* Vobala Dasari belonging to a certain Chennakesvara Temple, suggests the employment of Dasaris for reciting the sacred names of God.

Is Saiva Temples, the people of Tammala community rendered the services of cooking, keeping lamps, supplying water, flowers, leaves etc. It is not known as to when this custom of supplying all these items to these Temples by this particular community came into existence. A few inscriptions of the period, especially of Vijayanagar, record the exemption of these people from some of these menial services to the Temples. An inscription of 1523 A.D.

from Nitturu village (Anantapur dt.)[96] records that the Tammalas were exempted by a Vijayanagara official from the service of *Vīstarākula vetti,* that is, supplying leaves (in which *Prasādam* and food were served) to the Temple of Nilakantha of the place. The official asked them to supply water for the god's *Abhiśēkha* instead. Another epigraph of 1546 A.D. from Kakulamiduturu village (Kurnoold dt.) states that Konayadeva, a subordinate of Vijayanagara empire exempted the Tammalas from the service of supplying water and cooking in the local Veerabhadra Temple, and asked them to supply flowers and garlands to the deity, and to keep lamps in the Temples instead.[97]

The same is the case with the music services in the Temples. As the rituals conducted in the Hindu Temple had to be accompanied by the music, almost all of them appear to have maintained a band of musicians, who played a variety of instruments like *Sonnāyi, Nāgasvaram* (Pipes), *Dōlu, Maddela* (drums) etc. To play these instruments, usually the people of the Barber community (*Maṅgala*) were employed. An inscription of 1550 A.D. from Veludurti village (Cuddapah dt.) refers to the Barber Chinnoju who performed *Dōlu-Nāgasvaram* service (music on drum and pipe) in the Temple of Chennaraya of that place.[98]

Service Conditions and Remuneration of the Temple Functionaries: Most of the Temple functionaries, who were enumerated under all the three categories mentioned above were full-time employees and received remuneration for their services. They appear to have been paid regular salaries both in cash and kind.

The donors, while endowing the Temples with villages and lands, usually made provision, by giving lands and cash payments, for the maintenance of the Temple staff. An inscription of 1560 A.D. from Amaravati village (Guntur dt.), which records the grant of a village by a Vijayanagara subordinate to the Temple of Goddess Madhavidevi of that place, states further that half of that villages was for the maintenance of worship in that Temple and the remaining half for the *Archakas, Sthānikas* and *Sānis* of that Temple.[99] These lands granted to the Temple staff, in most cases, were tax-free (*Sarvamānya*). An epigraph of 1544 A.D. from Nittur (Anantapur dt.) records the gift of some land as *Śrōtrīyam* to the *Sthānkas* of the local Temple by a certain Tirumalayya of Jakkampundi.[100] This will be illustrated with more evidence in the chapter, 'Relations with the State'.

The Temple functionaries appear to have got, besides the land grants, in most cases, a share in the *Prasādam.* The donors, while making a grant for a particular service in the Temple in their name, usually made a special provision for feeding the men connected with that particular service, by granting a share (which was usually one fourth of the total food offered by the donor to the deity). For example, when Aubala Timmarajayya, a Vijayanagara official, instituted certain services including food offering in the Temple of Narasimha of Mangalagiri (Guntur dt.) in the year 1558 A.D., he made the stipulation in the grant that one fourth of the consecrated food and one eighth of the spices (sandal paste etc.) should be given as the share of the *Sthāna-prāpti.*[101] And if their share was not sufficient, the donors purchased the sacred food from the Temple's share, and made arrangement for its distribution among the Temple staff connected with their service. An inscription of 1396 A.D. from Simhachalam which refers to the institution of the service of a food offering (*Bhōgamu-āragimpu*) by Uttamadevi, the queen of the Ganga King Narasimha IV, also records that the donor (Uttamadevi) purchased 17 *Kuṅchālu* of *Prasādam* from *Sri Bhaṅdāram* of God Narasimha by paying 85 *Mādas* and made arrangements for the distribution of the same among the various Temple personnel connected with that particular service.[102]

The Temple staff were entitled, sometimes, to sell their share of the sacred food which was in excess of their needs. This practice existed at Tirumala-Tirupati during the Vijayanagara period.[103]

Finally, there is evidence to show that most of the functionaries of the Temples, other than the honorary office holders, were paid regular salaries in cash, besides the lands and shares in the Temple sacred food, for their maintenance. An epigraph of 1560 A.D.[104] from Markapuram (Cuddapah dt.) gives interesting information that the salary (*Jeetham*) of the various servants (*Kaṅdāchāram-*

vāru) of the Temple of Chennakesava (including the several bands of musicians) who numbered ninety totally, was fixed at 520 *varahas* (gold coin) per annum. From this, it can be inferred that the salaries of the servants of this particular Temple were fixed for a year. Each one of them got on an aveage, at the rate of, approximately, half a *varaha* per month. This also makes it clear that they received this salary in cash, in addition to the other privileges like getting a share in the food and other offerings. But it does not state whether they were paid their salaries once in a year or in monthly instalments.

In some of the inscriptions belonging to the middle of the Sixteenth century A.D. a few details about the salaries paid to the Temple functionaries of that place, are available. For example, an epigraph of 1547 A.D. from Tirupati[105] furnishes the budget estimate for the Temple of Sri Vithalesvara Perumal in Tirupati (a minor shrine managed by the *Sthānattār* of the Temple of Sri Venkatesvara of that place). This budget estimate also contains the details of the salaries paid to the various functionaries of that Temple in the year. Similarly, another epigraph from the same place (Tirupati) belonging to the year 1550 A.D. also furnishes a list of the salaries paid to the various functionaries of the shrine of Nammalvar and the Ramanujakutam, both instituted by Aravidu Kondaraja, a Vijayanagara subordinate.[106] With the help of these two epigraphs, it is possible to know the exact rates of the pay of the only a few of them as indicated in Table 2.

Of course, it is reasonable to presume that these functionaries got shares in the food offerings besides these salaries.

The Temple functionaries appear, sometimes, to have got some extra remuneration (periodical cash payments) if they performed any additional function besides their regular duties in the Temple. The *Nambimār* (*Archakas*) of the Temple of Sri Venkatesvara of Tirupati, during this period, were paid extra remuneration in every festival such as *Tirukkōḍi-Tirunāl* (Annual *Brahmōtsavam*) and *Laxmidēvi Tirunāl,* celebrated in that Temple.[107]

All these Temple employees appear to have held their job on hereditary basis. Their descendants were entitled to succeed to their

Table 2
Information from the Epigraph of 1547 A. D.

Sl. No.	*Designation of Functionary*	*Salary in Rekhai-pon* per year*
1.	The officer in Ramanujakutam	60
2.	The keeper of articles of stores	60
3.	Temple-Repairer or officer in charge of public works (*Tiruppani Pillai*)	10
4.	Temple servants-per head	12
5.	Watchmen (*Talaiyars*)	6
6.	Person engaged in *Vinnapamu* service (performer of the religious functions in the Temple)	11/5

Information from the Epigraph of 1550 A.D.

Sl. No.	*Designation of the Functionary*	*Salary in Rekhai-pon* per year*
1.	(*Adhikāri*) Superintendent of the Ramanujakutam	24
2.	Temple-cooks— per head	12
3.	Servants who arranged articles in the Ramanujakutam	61/4
4.	Watchmen— per head	6
5.	Persons who brought water and cleaned vegetables—per head	5
6.	Persons who clearned and decorated the dining hall in Ramanujakutam	3

[* One *Rekhai-pon* is equivalent to 10 *Panam* and 15 *Panam* is equivalent to one *Varāha*, a Gold-coin equivalent of a *Hon*.]

position either in the case of death or physical incapacity. A copper plate grant of 1406-07 A.D. from Malkonda village (Nellore dt.) clearly states that Maharaja Malla Reddi, a subordinate of Kondaviti Kingdom, granted the hereditary right of worship in the Temple of

Vishnu in several villages to a priest, who was entitled to enjoy it with his sons and grand-sons in perpetuity.[108] The implication of the hereditary appointment is that they were entitled to handover to their successors not only their positions (*Vrittis*) in the Temples but also the privileges like tax-exemption, emoluments etc. attached to the services, and also the right to sell them. And as a result, most of these offices of the Temple, in many cases, tended to be divided into a number of shares and sub-shares in the course of a few generation from the original occupants of those offices. And all the share-holders of a particular office of the Temple enjoyed the endowments and other privileges which that office carried with it. They performed the duties of that office, one after the other, for a fixed number of days, in every month which fell to their share.

That the Temple functionaries were entitled even to sell their share of the *Vrittis* (services) and the endowed land which was carried with the service, to the other functionaries belonging to the same category, if necessary and that they were not prevented from doing so, can be inferred from the inscription of 1410 A.D. from Puspagiri.[109] It records that two *Sthānapatis,* Veerajiyya and Ramajiyya, of the Temple of Ramesvara of the place, sold away their *Vrittis* (shares of service as trustees) in the Temple of Somanatha-Mallinatha Devara and also the land belonging to that service and also their assets like houses, cattle, produce, metals etc. The inscription of 1396 A.D. from the village Devagudi (Cuddapah dt.) which records the sale of a *Vritti* of one day (Service of worship for one day) by a priest of the Talakanti Devi Temple of four days to another priest states that the *Vritti* sold included *Grihārāmakshētras* (houses and fields, etc.), *Dhanādanya* (yield and cash), *Pancha lōhālu* (five kinds of metals) and *Jeevadhanam* (cattle etc.)[110]

Some categories of the Temple employees of the period appear to have been organized, *Sāni* three hundred, the women employees of a Temple at Peddakallepelle village (Krishna dt.) and their association with the management of that Temple is referred to in an epigraph of 1292 A.D. from that place.[111] Similarly, two inscriptions from Simhachalam dated 1427 A.D. and 1441 A.D.

respectively refer to *Sānula Sāmpradāyamu* who were in the service of the Narasimha Temple of the place.[112] From these, it appears that the women employees of some of the Temples of the period, whose strength, in some cases, ran into a large number, formed themselves into professional guilds in order to protect their professional interests. Similarly, the Srivaishnavas and the *Panchādis* (artisans) who were in the service of the Temples of Srikurmam and Simhachalam and were associated with their management, as indicated in a number of inscriptions from these places, also appear to have functioned as professional guilds during this period.[113]

These guilds, usually were corporate bodies and consisted of families and individual members belonging to a particular profession or skill. The leaders or heads of these corporate bodies exercised judicial powers and decided all cases concerning the members. They made rules and regulations of the work and the wages, the working hours, etc. These regulations had the force of law. As the means of lively-hood of these families depended on their knowledge and skill, these traditions and techniques were jealously guarded within the guild and were handed-over from one generation to the other. This accounts for the preservation of most of the traditions and techniques of arts even to this day.

MATHA

The Hindu *Maṭha,* whichever sect it might have belonged to, evolved its own organization for the management of its affairs. It had a number of functionaries to man that organization. It appears to have been organized on monarchical principles. Its *Maṭhādhipathi* or pontiff, around whom the entire organization revolved, occupied the pivotal position in it. An inscription of 1292 A.D. from the village Peddakallepalli (Cuddapah dt.) describes Somasivacharya, the pontiffs of the Puspagiri *Maṭha* (probably of Pasupata sect), as its *Santtānikudu.*[114] The pontiffs of the *Maṭhs* of the Tengalai as well as *Vadagalai* Srivaishnavas were known as '*Jiyar*' or '*Jiyyangār'*. According to Sadhu Subrahmanya Sastry, the pontiff of the Jiyyangar *Maṭham* of Tirupati belonging to the

Tengalai sect of Srivaishnavism, was designated as *Jiyar* or as *Maṭhādhipathi,* the order of monks as '*Siyar*' and finally the individual monks as '*Siyan*'.[115]

The pontiff were absolute masters of the *Maṭhas* and had the superior authority in matters both spiritual and secular pertaining to those institutions. Around the *Maṭhādhipati* gathered, usually, a band of monks, who were his spiritual disciples. They received instruction, from him, in the scriptures of the sect to which the *Maṭha* belonged, and rendered him personal service in accordance with the ancient custom. They were only to assist him and serve him but not to have any say in the management of the affairs of the *Maṭha.* As the pontiff himself would nominate his successor, the monks had no hand even in the selection of the next head of the *Maṭha.*

When a particular *Maṭha,* belonging to a particular religious sect had a number of branches functioning at different places, the pontiff of the central *Maṭha,* or the parent–*Maṭha,* appears to have acted as the supreme pontiff of all the branches. He had some supervisory powers over the functioning of all the branches and their individual pontiffs. This practice can be seen in the case of many *Maṭhas* of this period. As the Sringeri *Maṭha* (situated in modern Karnataka state) had the privilege of having Adi Sankaracharya as its founder-pontiff, all other Advaita *Maṭhas* established by him at different corners of India were regarded as its branches. And its pontiff was regarded as the chief-pontiff of all the Advaita monks belonging to all the branch–*Maṭhas.*[116] This tradition of treating the Sringeri *Maṭha* as the central Advaita *Maṭha* and its pontiff as the chief-pontiff, and all the other Advaita *Maṭhas,* including the one at Puspagiri (Cuddapah dt.)[117] situated in Andhra Desa as its branches, must have continued even during the later period also. Visvesvara Sivacharya, the founder of the various branches of the Golaki *Maṭha* in Andhra Desa during the Kakatiya period, and who appointed the pontiff of the Golaki *Maṭha* at Mandaram village[118] must have appointed the pontiff of all the other branches and acted himself, probably, as some kind of super-pontiff for all of them. It has already been noted that, the Golaki *Maṭhas* of Andhra Desa and South India had their central-*Maṭha* in Dahala country situated in Central India. This parent-*Maṭha* must have claimed some control over them. The subordinate position of the Sarangesvara *Maṭha* situated at Alampur (Mahbubnagar dt.) to the Veerasaiva Basavanna *Maṭha* of Srisailam, the parent–*Maṭha* is indicated by an inscription of 1593 A.D. from Alampur[119] It described Peddakuppu-Sakanthadeva, the pontiff of Sarangesvara *Maṭha* of Alampur as the disciple of Pattada Pramathesvara, the pontiff of Basavanna *Maṭha* of Srigiri (i.e. Srisailam).

The founders of some of the *Maṭhas*, at the time of their establishment laid down certain rules and regulations to be followed in the selection of the pontiff, and also enjoined upon the certain responsibilities. They also made provision for the removal of the irresponsible and incapable pontiffs, presumably by the other members of those institutions. Sankaracharya, while prescribing, in his work *Maṭāmnāya*[120] certain rules and regulation to be followed by the pontiffs of the various Advaita *Maṭhas* founded by him, lays down that if any occupant of that religious seat failed to carry out the duties prescribed for him, he should be removed from his office and a better person installed. Similarly, Visvesvara Sivacharya, the founder of the Pasupata Golaki *Maṭhas* in Andhra Desa, also prescribed certain qualification and rules of conduct for the occupants of the pontificate of the *Maṭha* at Mandaram. He lays down that the pontiff of that religious seat was to be one who was installed by a preceptor of Golaki line, an adept in the mysteries of Saiva faith, well-versed in the Saiva doctrine, the protector of the Saiva *Saṅtana,* pure, resigned, merciful, learned, the foremost among virtuous Brahmans, and a great *Naiśṭhika* teacher. He further lays down that, if the teacher (pontiff) happened to be negligent of his duties or misbehaved otherwise, the whole Saiva community (*Saṅanika*) was empowered to appoint another in his place[121]. The method of selection of pontiffs prescribed by Visvesvara Siva of Golaki *Matha,* appears to have been followed during the period under study.

The *Maṭhādhipatis* were usually nominated by the preceding *Maṭhādhipatis* before their death. This hypothesis is supported by the mode of selection of pontiffs prevailing in the Jiyyangar *Matham* at Tirupati of the period. A certain Yatirjaja *Jiyyar* presided over the Jiyyangar *Maṭha* (*Tengalai* Srivaishnava) at Tirupati as its pontiff (*Jiyyar*) from 1535 A.D. to 1541 A.D. After his death or retirement, he was succeeded to the pontificate of that Matha by Vanamamali Jiyyar who occupied it from 1541 AD to 1545 A.D.[122]. But during the Pontificate of Yatiraja *Jiyyar*, Vanamamalai *Jiyyar* was designated or nominated as the Junior *Jiyyar* of Jiyyangari *Matham* and was made to preside over another *Maṭha*, situated at the same place, known as Alagiya Manavalan *Maṭham*.[123] Most probably, this Alagiya Manavalan *Maṭham* presided over by Vanamamalai *Jiyyar*, before he became the senior pontiff of the Jiyyangar *Maṭham*, was a branch of the latter, and this *Jiyyar* who was junior and second in order of seniority presided over the branch *Maṭha*. So, this explains, to some extent, the principle of succession prevailing in the Jiyyangar *Maṭham*, where the senior pontiff appears to have nominated the senior most among his disciples as the Junior *Jiyyar*, to succeed as the next pontiff. This inference is strengthened by the position held by the *Jiyyars* in the management of Venkatesvara Temple. While Yatiraja *Jiyyar*, the pontiff of the Jiyyangar *Maṭham* was designated as its *Periya-Kōyil Kelvi* (senior Temple superintendent), Vanamamalai *Jiyyar*, the head of the Alagiya Manavalan *Maṭham*, and the prospective pontiff of Jiyyangar *Maṭham* was designated as its *Ilaya-Kōyil-Kelvi* (junior temple superintendent).[124]

This practice of the pontiff of the *Maṭha* appointing his successor as junior pontiff, appears to have been followed in this Jiyyangar *Maṭham* at Tirupati during the entire period under consideration. This practice of appointing the successor over the pontificate by the existing pontiff is followed in the Sringeri *Maṭha* even now. In November, 1974, Sri Vidyatirtha, the 35th pontiff of this *Maṭha* appointed Sri Bharatitirtha as his successor over the pontificate.[125]

In the absence of the senior pontiff, the junior pontiff appears to have managed the affairs of the *Maṭha*. Whenever Chandra Sekhara Bharati (1386-09 A.D.) the pontiff of the Advaita *Maṭha* of Sringeri was on religious tours, which he used to undertake very often, his chief disciple and the would be successor, Narasimha Bharati (1389-1408 A.D.), used to look after the management of that *Maṭha.*[126]

With regard to caste, only Brahmans (as in the case of the Pasupata Saiva Golaki *Maṭha*), appear to have occupied the pontifical seats in all the Hindu *Maṭhas,* except those of the Veera Saivas, where the Jangamas etc. occupied them.

The pontiffs of the *Maṭhas,* to whichever sect they might have belonged, commanded so much respect among the occupants of the *Maṭhas*, besides his followers outside, that very often they were deified after this death and their images were worshipped. The image of Adivan Sathakopa *Jiyar,* the founder of Ahobila *Maṭha* was consecrated at Tirunarayanapuram (Melkote, Karnataka), the village of his birth, by Sriman Narayana *Jiyar*, next pontiff of that *Maṭha.*[127]

Other Functionaries of the Maṭha: No doubt, the Hindu *Sanyāsis,* as their name itself suggests, were bound, as individual members of the *Maṭha,* by vows of poverty. But the *Maṭhas* to which they belonged were wealthy institutions. Due to the generous patronage of the rulers and the ruled (lay disciples), the Hindu *Maṭhas,* like the Hindu Temples, came to accumulate lot of properties in the shape of villages, lands, buildings, money etc. To manage their properties and to assist them in conducting various other activities, the *Maṭhas* engaged a number of persons, who worked under the general supervision of their pontiffs.

An inscription of 1558 A.D. from Pedda Ahobilam (Kurnool dt.) refers to a certain Emberumanar Jiyyangaru as the *Mudrakarta* (seal-bearer) of Srivan Sathakopa Jiyyangar, the pontiff of Ahobila *Maṭha.*[128] It records that he gave an undertaking, along with the agent (*Kāryakarta*) of the Vijayanagara provincial governor, and the trustees of Ahobilam Temple, to execute a grant, to a Temple donor. A certain Ramanuja Jiyyangar is referred to in inscription of 1563 A.D. from Chinna Ahobilam (Kurnool dt.) as the *Mudrakarta* of the same pontiff (Sri Van Sathakopa Jiyyangar).[129] It also records that he gave a similar undertaking as the above, along with the Ahobilam Temple trustees and the agent of the provincial governor, to a temple donor. Yet, another inscription of 1584 A.D. from Chinna Ahobilam,[130] refers to Vakulabharanam *Jiyyar* as the *Kāryakarta* (agent) of Van Sathakopa *Jiyyar* (probably the same pontiff mentioned above) of Ahobila *Maṭha*, granting along with the trustees of the Temple of God Narasimha of the place etc., certain Temple honours to a certain Kondraju Venkataraju.

During this period, even the pontiff of the (Veera Saiva) Bhikshavritti *Maṭha* of Srisailam had their *Kāryakartas* who played a very important role in the management of the affairs of that *Maṭha* and the Temple of Mallikarjuna of that place. The two Jangama brothers—Santa Bhikshavritti and Vira Bhikshavritti—are referred to, in the *Kaifiyat* of Nivarti Sangam, as the *Kāryakartas* of the Baikshavritti *Maṭha.* The *Kaifiyat* further states that they in that capacity, went to the neighbouring villages to collect funds and bring the pilgrims (*Paruṣam*) to the shrine of Mallikarjuna.[131]

It is apparent that, the pontiffs of some of the major Hindu *Maṭhas* had under them the *Mudrakartas* and the *Kāryakartas,* who were like their namesakes maintained by the temporal princes. And they assisted the pontiffs in discharging certain duties, especially connected with the management of the Temple affairs.

Besides these, the *Maṭhas* of the period appear to have employed a number people to conduct their various activities. An inscription, which appears to belong to the Kakatiya period, from Tripurantakam (Kurnool dt.)[132] refers to the *Maṭha-paricharākulu* (menial servants), *Maāha-satramu-vaṅṭala-vāndru* (cooks), *Kāvadivāru* (men for bringing water), *Maṭhamu-tōnta-chēsēvāru* (gardeners), *Maṭhamurātripagalu kāchikoni undedi-vāru* (watchmen) etc. who were in the service of a *Maṭha* of the Sudha Saivas, built near the Temple of God Tripurantaka of the place.

AGRAHARA

The *Agrahāras* during this period, were generally of two types i.e. *Ēka-bhōga* and *Bahu-boga.* If an *Agrahāra* was granted for the sustenance of a single scholar, it was known as *Ēka-bhōga-*

agrahāra. For example, according to an inscription of 1438 A.D. from the village Podili,[133] the village Tippalidevi was granted as *Ēka-bhōga-agrahāra* to a certain Tammanarya by a royal donor. That means, all the lands in that village were to be possessed and enjoyed by that single individual or his family without having any co-sharer. If the donees were several, it was known as *Ghanabhōga* or *Bahu-bhōga-agrahāra.* For example, the Vilasa village granted as *Agrahara* by Prolaya Nayaka in the year 1330 A.D.,[134] was divided into 108 shares and allotted to 108 Brahman scholars. This must have been a *Bahu-bhōga-agrahāra.*

But contrary to this hypothesis, an epigraph of 1586 A.D. from Kanigri.[135] states that Lalu-khan, a Qutbshahi official under Muhammad Quli Qutbshah, granted the village Uppanutula as *Ēka-bhōga-sarvagrahāra,* to three scholars–Markandeya, Somayajulu and Panchagiri Dikshitulu. Here, the village, though granted to three donees, was also described as *Ēka-bhōga-agrahāra.* This seems to be an exceptional case. N. Venkataramanayya is of the opinion that even the *Ēka-bhōga-agrahāras* tended to become *Bahu-bhōga-agrahāras* within a few generations of the original doness.[136]

There is another important feature to be noted in this connection. Whenever an *Agrahāra* was granted to the Brahmans, either as *Ēka-bhōga* or *Bahu-bhōga,* by the rulers, it appears, that the custom was to grant one or more hamlets along with it. As the Brahmans of these *Agrahāras* were engaged completely in intellectual pursuits and sacrificial activity, they themselves could not cultivate their lands, Moreover, it appears, no other people than the Brahmans could live in those villages. So the farmers who cultivated their lands lived in separate hamlets granted and attached to the main *Agrahāra* village for that purpose. These hamlets of the *Agrahāras* were known variously as *Pūṅdi, Pālemu, Grāma-grāsamu, Grāmōpahāramu,* etc.[137] For example, the Nelandanuru *Agrahāra* (Cuddapah dt.) had four *Grāma-grāsapu-pallelu* (hamlets) in the year 1309 A.D., according to an inscription of that year from the same village.[138] Similarly, the Gotur village, referred to in an epigraph of 1540 A.D. from Puspagiri (Cuddapah dt.)[139] as the *Grāma-grāsamu* of Puspagiri *Agrahāra,* must have been a hamlet of that *Agrahāra* where the ryots lived and cultivated the lands of the *Agrahārikas.*

The Brahman *Agraharas* appear to have been autonomous and self-governing villages. The affairs of each of these villages, and especially in the case of the *Bahu-bhōga-agrahāras,* were managed by an assembly known as *Sabha.*[140] This *Sabha* consisted of the shareholders or the prominent occupants of that village known as *Vidvan Mahājanas* or simply as *Mahājanas.* The inscriptions of the period, though refer to the *Sabha* and its members do not give any in formation regarding their powers and functions. But from these references, it appears that (the members of) their assemblies (*Sabha*), used to take all the decision regarding the management of these villages. They acted as the trustees of the Temple situated in those villages and managed their affairs. They decided all civil and criminal cases, collected the taxes, if any, in that village and paid to the government. They acted as the link between their village and the government. It can be stated that the powers and functions of these *Sabhas* were almost similar to those of the village officials in the village belonging to the government (i.e. *Bhandāravāda-grāmas* in Vijayanagara empire). N. Venkataramanayya maintains that these *Sabhas,* besides performing the above functions, also acted as the civil courts and tried cases which were referred to them by the King or his subordinates in the Vijayanagara empire.[141]

In the case of the *Ēka-bhōga-agrahāra,* the individual Brahman scholar, who alone had the ownership right of that village, must have acted as its head and managed its affairs by himself. A grant of 1313 A.D. (from Duvvuru) refers to Lingana Somayaji, the only donee of the Virupakshapura *Agrahāra*, with the surname *Kshētrapālaka.*[142] This was used probably, to denote his headmanship of that *Agrahāra* (*Kshētra*). Similarly, P.V. Parabrahma Sastri, quotes in his work a few epigraphs of the 12th and 13th centuries A.D. belonging to the Kakatiya period referring to the *Prabhu* or *Prabhu-mukhya,* as the head of the Brahmana *Agrahāra* village.[143] Probably, these terms also denote the same meaning as that of *Kshētrapālaka.*

MOSQUE

With the help of the contemporary evidence, which is scanty, it is rather difficult to give a complete picture of the organization and the functionaries of the Mosque of the period under review. In addition to this, considerable information regarding this aspect is available in the records relating to the Qutbshahi Mosques of the 17th century A.D. From this, allowing some developments after 1600 A.D., the basic structure of the management of the Mosques prior to 1600 A.D. can be inferred.

The Mosque, like any other religious institutions of the period, had its own organization and functionaries for the management of its affairs. Like the Hindu Temple, it had trustees, who occupied the top most position in the hierarchy of its functionaries. A *Farmān* of 1615 A.D.[144] (of the Qutbshahi period) records the grant of trusteeship (*Muṭawalli*) of the Mosque, built (at Hyderabad) by Malik Almas, together with a *Sarāi,* of 83 rooms and the open space attached to that Mosque, to a certain Sayyid Muhammad Quadri (son of Sayyid Shah Muhiuddin Quadri, his spiritual master). From this, it appears that the trustees of the Mosques were usually appointed at the time of consecration of the Mosques by the founders themselves. They were appointed on hereditary basis, with the right of succession to that office, given either to the spiritual disciples or to the sons of the occupants of that office. The responsibility of the *Muṭawalli* was to maintain the Mosque, i.e. to manage its affairs, to conduct its services and to supervise the work of the other functionaries.

Another important functionary of the Mosque was the *Imām,* who was the leader of the congregational prayers. A fragmentary inscription of the 16th century A.D. from the village Palat (Mahbubnagar dt.)[145] refers to the *Imām,* of the local Mosque and records the endowment of a village for his maintenance, for the maintenance of his descendants, and also for that of the Mosque. This epigraph indicates that this functionary (*Imām*) was appointed on hereditary basis with the right of succession to that post given to his descendants.

A Persian epigraph of 1681 A.D. from the Mosque of Miyan Mishk (old Hyderabad city) furnishes the following list of functionaries of that Mosque and the amount of salaries paid to each of them per year.[146]

Table 3

Sl. No.	*Designation of the Functionaries*	*Strength*	*Salary per year (in Huns)*
1.	*Muṭawalli* (Trustee or Superintendent of the Mosque)	1	20
2.	*Muadhdhin* (Crier who calles the people to prayers)	1	10
3.	*Farraśh* (The person who spread prayer carpets)	1	6
4.	*Saqqā* (Water carrier	1	6
5.	*Diviti* (torch-bearer	1	7½
6.	*Durbān* (door-keeper)	1	12
7.	*Jarūbkash* (sweeper	2	6
8.	*Navisinda Bahman* (Brahman clerk)	1	8½
9.	*Pullakāri* (Mason for repairing steps)	1	6
10.	*Kisamāl* (The person who applies Shampoo)	2	15
11.	*Māliabkash* (Servent for drawing water)	2	12

This list enables us to know the nature of work performed by the various Mosque-functionaries. The rates of their salaries mentioned in this epigraph also indicate the relative importance of their position in that Mosque. The mention of a Brahman clerk as one of the functionaries of the Mosque is quite interesting. The employment of high caste Hindus in the service of Muslim religious institution was probably due to their skill in accounts–keeping.

And, it is quite reasonable to presume that atleast some of above mentioned functionaries were provided food in the Mosque and were granted lands, besides the cash payment, for their maintenance.

Finally, it is quite reasonable to infer, from the references in the contemporary epigraphs to the conduct of the various services such as food distribution and teaching in the Mosques, that they had in their service a number of menial servants, and teachers, besides the above mentioned personnel.

KHANQAH

The evidence that is forthcoming regarding the organization and the functionaries of the *Khānqāh* of the period in Andhra Desa is too meager to enable us to give a full picture of the same. Some idea of it can be given with the help of the information available about the contemporary *Khānqāhs* of the Western Deccan and Northern India. This attempt would not be unreasonable in view of the fact that, the *Khānqāhs* of Andhra Desa, which mainly belonged to the Chisti, Qadri and Suhrawardi orders of Suifs, inherited their traditions from those areas.

The *Khānqāh*, like the Hindu *Maṭha*, was organized on the basis of monarchical principles. The pontiff generally known as *Shaikh* was at the apex of the organization of the *Khānqāh*.[147] He was also known as *Pīr* sometimes. As the head of the *Khānqāh* he presided over the religious congregations in it, and gave instruction to his disciples. He was the chief administrator of the *Khānqāh* and enjoyed absolute authority over its inmates. In fact, one of the cordinal principles of *Khānqāh* life was the total submission of its members to their master in matters both spiritual and material.[148]

The spiritual disciples of the pontiff, who occupied the *Khānqāh* with him, were known as *Murid*.[149] The *Shaik* used to confer the *Khilāphat* (chief discipleship) on several of his spiritual disciples. Syed Muhammad Hussain Gesu Daraz of Gulbarga, during the period of his pontificate (A.D. 1400-21) conferred *Khilāphat* on altogether forty-two members of his *Khānqāh*. They were his chief disciples and attained very high spiritual and moral position. Many of them organized monastic activity in different parts of Deccan.[150] The senior most *Khalīpha* was the *Shaikhs'* deputy or right-hand man, and acted for the *Shaīkh* in the latters absence. As the deputy of the *Shaīkh,* he must have assisted his master by organizing various activities, both spiritual and material, of the *Khānqāh* and acted as the spokesman of that institution on behalf of his master.

After the death, of the *Pīr,* the chief *Kahlīpha* succeeded to that pontificate, usually nominated by the *Pīr* himself before death. He inherited not only the spiritual powers of his predecessors but also the material wealth of his *Khānqāh.* The symbols of the spiritual inheritance included, among other things, the tunic, and the cap which his predecessor were. G. Yezdani, referring to the *Khānqāh* of Hadrat Shah Abul Faid at Bidar, states that the *Sajjāda* (the present incumbent) of the office of the pontificate of the *Khaāqāh* had the tunic of Hadrat Farid-ud-din Shakar Ganj and the cap of Hadrat Banda Nawaz Gesu Daraz, which "he puts on when he is installed on the carpet of his predecessor."[151]

During the early period of the history of Sūfi *Khānqāhs* in India, the principle of succession to the pontificate in them, appears to have been spiritual and not hereditary. Shaikh Nizamuddin Auliya and Shaikh Nasiruddin Chirag of Delhi and Burhanuddin Gharib of Deccan of the early 14th century A.D. were celibates and after their death, they were succeeded to the pontificate by their spiritual disciples.[152] But some of the pontiffs of the *Khānqāhs* of the period in Deccan, appear to have deviated from this policy and nominated their family members as their successors to be the pontiffs after their death. For example, the famous Chisti saint Gesu Daraz of Gulbarga, unlike his predecessors, was not a celibate, but led married life. He had several children whom he trained in the filed of spiritualism. At the time of his death he is said to have left a will appointing one of his ons as his successor, thus, making the succession to the pontificate in his *Khānqāh* hereditary.[153] After his death there were quarrels among his family members for the succession, resulting in the intervention of the King Ahmad Shah Bahmani.[154] Similarly, Hadrat Shah Abul-Faid of Bidar was succeeded over his pontificate after his death in 1475 A. D. by his second son Kalimullah Hussain. And the latter was succeeded by son Sayyid Shah Atul Hassan in 1487 AD. over the same pontificate[155] This hereditary succession appears to have also prevailed in some of the *Khānqāhs* in Andhra Desa during the Qutb Shahi period. Syed Shah Jamal was succeeded to the pontificate of his *Khānqāh,* established by him at Urs village near Warangal, by his son Moinuddin Hussan, who was his *Khalīfa.*[156] Shah Raju II, the pontiff of the *Khānqāh* at Hyderabad of the period, and the spiritual preceptor of Abul Hasan Tanesha, the last Qutb Shahi ruler is described as the son of Shah Raju I, a contemporary of Ibrahim Qutbshah and his successor Muhammad Quli.[157] It is quite reasonable to infer that Shah Raju II succeeded his father over the pontificate of that *Khānqāh.*

The acceptance and the acquisition of properties to the *Khānqāhs,* during this period, besides the married lives of the pontiffs, appear to be the important factors which led to the hereditary succession in them. Their anxiety to retain the material wealth of the *Khānqāh* within the possession of their own family members must have compelled the pontiffs to manipulate the succession in favour of their descendants. This hereditary succession is alleged to have been one of the factors leading to the decline of the some of the *Khānqāhs* of the period. Especially, in the case of the above mentioned *Khānqāh* of Gesu Daraz of Gulbarga, it is said to have led to many quarrels over the question of succession and finally led to the decline in the prestige of that institution in the eyes of the monarchs and the common people.[158]

In view of the scanty nature of material available, it is very difficult to know about the various employees of the *Khānqāhs* of the period. They must have maintained, in their service, teachers, clerks, cooks, watchmen, sweepers, fire-wood suppliers etc. to render various services.

DARGAH

Direct information relating to the organization of the *Dargāhs* of the period under study in Andhra Desa is scanty. Supplementing this with the material available about the *Dargāhs* in the Western Deccan of the contemporary period, an attempt is made here to give an idea of the general organization of a *Dargāh.*

Each *Dargāh* appears to have had a *Muṭawalli* who was generally a descendant of the saint to whom the *Dargah* belonged. Some times, the saint himself, before his death, appointed the *Muṭawalli* of his tomb. For example, Shaik Muhammad Bin Sirajuddin Junaidi, the Chisti saint of Gulburga (of Muhammad Shah Is' period) appointed his grand-son Shaikh Abul Fadi Junaidi as his successor over the pontificate of his *Khānqāh* (*Sajjādanasheen*) and also as *Muṭawalli* of his tomb through a written will.[159] If the deceased saint had no children, one of his near relatives or chief disciples was appointed as the *Muṭawalli.* Naturally, the post of *Muṭawalli* was held on hereditary basis. The *Muṭawalli* was the owner of the properties (buildings, lands, etc.) of the *Dargāh.* He decided all important matters concerning the affairs of that institution.

The other important functionary of the *Dargāh* was the *Sajjāda* (Manager). Abdul Jabbar Khan Malkapuri refers to the *Sajjada* of the *Dargāh* of Baba Sharfuddin (Ob. 1287 A.D.), situated on a hillock in the Barkas locality, old Hyderabad.[160] *Sajjāda* managed the affairs of the *Dargāh.* He looked after its properties, conducted its annual festival (*Urs*) and supervised the work of the menial servants. The *Sajjāda* was appointed by the *Muṭawalli* of the *Dargāh.* The latter could remove a particular person holding the post of *Sajjāda* and appoint another person in his place. But usually the post of *Sajjāda* was held by the members of the same family on hereditary basis. He received a fixed salary for performing his duties. In the *Dargāhs* of minor importance which had limited income, the *Muṭawalli* himself performed the functions of the *Sajjāda.*

The menial servants of a *Dargāh* generally included the waterman, the sweeper and the man who kept the lamps in the *Dargāh.* These functionaries held their posts on hereditary basis, and had *Inām* lands for their maintenance.

ASHURKHANA

The *Āshūrkhāna* like other religious institutions of the period, had an organization and functionaries to conduct its affairs.

The chief functionary of the *Āshūrkhāna* of the period under study appears to have been the trustee, known as *Muṭawalli.*[161] He was appointed, usually, by the government at the time of the erection of the *Āshūrkhāna* itself. He held that post on hereditary basis. He was, practically, the owner of the properties endowed for the maintenance of the *Āshūrkhāna*. He maintained the *Āshūrkhāna* and also himself with the income derived from its lands, etc.

The *Āshūrkhāna* had a caretaker known as *Mujāver* to look after its maintenance, and to manage its properties. He was appointed by the *Muṭawalli* of the *Āshūrkhāna* who paid his salary and who could also remove him of necessary. Ali Aga was the *Mujāver* of Āshūrkhāna-i-Hussaini Alam, the *Āshūrkhāna* established in the reign of Muhammad Quli Qutbshah, and situated in the lane of the same name, old Hyderabad. Ali Aga himself brought the *Ālam* (standard) of Imam Hussain, housed in this *Āshūrkhāna,* from Karbala. He was appointed as its *Mujāver* by the Sultan.[162] In many cases, the post of *Mujāver* was held on hereditary basis. The above mentioned Ali Aga appears to have succeeded to the post of *Mujāver* of Āshūrkhāna-i-Hussaini-Alam by his descendants. Dara Baig, a grandson of Ali Aga, is said to have made a number of additions to the building of that *Āshūrkhāna.*[163] Only in the capacity of its *Mujāver,* he could have done it. In the *Āshūrkhāna*s of less importance, the *Muṭawalli,* himself performed the functions of the *Mujāver.*

The *Āshūrkhāna*s do not appear to have maintained the menial servants on a regular basis. Only during the days of *Muharram* festival when these institutions were usually kept open, a few menial servants like sweepers, watermen, light-men etc., were appointed on daily wages.

4

Finances

The key to the functioning of any institution lies in its finances and it is on the nature of the management of its finances that the success or the failure of the institution depends. The religious institutions of the period under study, unlike many other institutions whose goal was to maximize the return on investment, endeavoured to promote the spiritual welfare of the society and they were service oriented institutions. The financial aspect of these institutions has been studied in terms of the following three points. Income, Expenditure, and Utilization of surplus income and financial difficulties.

INCOME

The income of the religious institutions of the period, whether they belonged to the Hindu religion or that of Islam, was mobilized from various sources. These can be classified under two main categories: Long-term or fixed assets and Short-term or current assets.

The first category consists of bothe the movable and immovable properties, and include villages, land, buildings, cattle, jewellery and other valuable articles. The second category comprised the proceeds of taxes and tolls, monetary endowments, daily presents and gifts.

The religious institutions were able to acquire these assets mainly from the munificient gifts made by the pious donors at the time of their foundation and subsequently for their upkeep and maintenance of various services instituted in them. These donors came from a wide cross-section of the society and consisted of kings, their consorts, their subordinate officials, such as the provincial and district officials, nobles, corporate bodies such as the guilds of merchants and artisans, communities and private individuals both rich and poor. But the grants made by the kings and their subordinates are more numerous and richer than those of the donors of other categories. The next, in order of importance, are those of the corporate bodies and the private individuals respectively. The grants and gifts were made to the religious institutions by the people usually with the intention of getting religious merit for themselves, for the fulfillment of which donations were made, were of mundane character, such as the birth of a son, marriage of a son or daughter, enjoyment of health, prosperity in profession, the safe termination of a journey, success against the foes, etc.

INCOME FORM LONG-TERM OR FIXED ASSETS

Landed property: It may not wrong to suppose that every religious institution of some size and pretensions, and whatever its religious affiliation, possessed landed property, which was one of the important sources of its income. Of course, the quantum of the property possessed by each institution was dependant on its size and popularity. An idea of this can be formed with the help of the contemporary records.

The more popular and bigger institutions possessed a number of villages and individual plots of cultivable land. For example, at the beginning of the 14th century A.D., when the Telugu country was under the rule of Kakatiya Pratapa Rudra II, the Mallikarjuna Temple of Srisailam possessed more than 52 villages.[1] Similarly, the Temple of Sri Venkatesvara of Tirupati had in its possession 150 villages in the middle of the 16th century A.D.[2] The Temples of medium size and popularity possessed less number of villages. For instance, the Temple of Simhachalam (of god Narasimha) possessed 10 villages at the beginning of the 16th century A.D.[3] Likewise, the temple of God Narasimha of Ahobilam, according to an inscription of the year 1586 A.D. from that place, had 10 villages in its enjoyment. But the minor shrina like those of it village deities might have owned only plots of cultivable lands in the villages owned either by other institutions or the government. The same is the case with the case with the Hindu *Maṭhas*. For example, the *Kaifiyats* of Gollapalli and Gandikota refer to the granting of the village Gollapalli (Cuddapah dt.) and several other villages in the Dravida country to Govinda Bharati Swami, the Poniff of the Puspagiri (Advaita) *Maṭha* in the year 1540 A.D. and 1545 A.D. respectively.[5] And some of the *Maṭhas* might have owned only one village or individual plots of lands.

The same is the case with the Muslim institutions. The Babayya *Dargāh* of Penugonda of the period under study had in its enjoyment more than six villages besides a number of individual plots of cultivable land and gardens granted by the Vijayanagara monarchs.[6] Similarly, the *Khanqāh* of Syed Shah Raju I was in receipt of a *Jāgir* from Sultan Muhammad Quli.[7] And the Mosques of the period had landed estates granted by their founders at the time of their erection and subsequently by the pious donors for their upkeep. It may not be wrong to assume that the larger Mosques, especially those situated at Golkonda and Hyderabad, the capitals of the Qutb Sahi Kingdom, and other important towns, which were meant for the use of the royal personages and officials must have possessed a number of landed estates for their maintenance.

Houses and shops were also granted to the religious institutions. Especially, some of the Muslim institutions of the period possessed this type of property which provided income to them almost on a permanent basis. For example, a Persian epigraph of 1657 A.D. from a Mosque of Qutbshahi period (Salhi Begam's Mosque) in old Hyderabad city, (near Kotla Ali Jah) states that Salih Begam Sayyida, a royal donor, bequeathed several houses and shops to that Mosque for its maintenance.[8]

The primary purpose of the land-endowments, that is, the grant of villages and plots of cultivable lands, was to ensure the permanency of the services for which they were made. They provided a permanent source of income to the institutions and also enabled them to get the necessary foodgrains, fruits, vegetables, flowers, etc. needed for performing various religious services and conducting charities.

These land-endowments besides assuring a permanent income also served other important purposes. They provided a productive place for investing surplus funds of the institutions or the cash derived from the monetary endowments made by devotees for the performance of various services in their name. This enabled them to get an additional income. The waste lands of these villages provided the grazing fields for their cattle. Out of these lands granted to them, they were able to provide lands to their various functionaries in lieu of their services for the people who executed their work. It also enabled them to sell a part of it, if any need arose.

The nature of land-endowments: The land-endowments made to the religious institutions were usually of perpetual character. The donee also became the absolute owner of the land or village granted to it. Especially in the case of the Hindu religious institutions, [9] the land grants were described as to last as long as the Sun and the Moon endure (*ācandrārcasthāyiga*). The lands or villages granted, carried with them the eight kinds of enjoyment[10] and also the right to gift, sell and mortgage (*ashta bhōga tēja swāmyamulu* and *dānādi kraya parivartana.*).

Similarly, the villages and lands granted to the Hindu religious institutions are usually described as *Sarvamānya*. The *Sarvamānya* character of the grants facilitated the exemption of the donees i.e., the religious institutions, from all kinds of government taxes.[11] But contrary to this general assumption, it has been often found that the religious institutions, some times, had to pay certain taxes to the government on their sarvamanya villages and lands.[12]

Lands and cultivation: It appears from the contemporary records that the cultivable lands owned by the religious institutions in their own villages as well as in the government villages, in a majority of cases, were leased to the tenants who were to give them a portion of the produce as the owner's share. The donors, the king or his subordinates, while granting the lands or villages to the religious institutions, also appear to have transferred to the donees even the tenants who were already cultivating the land. The Konkudur plates of Allaya Dodda of 1430 A.D. record that the donor (Allaya Dodda) granted to the Brahmans and temples an *Agrahāra* village, knwon as as Gumpini, with its cultivators and other rights.[13] Simiialy, an epigraph of 1464 A.D. from the village Sayampeta (Warangal dt.), which records gift of Muchcherla and Mandapalli villages to the God Tiruvengalesvara of Macherla, to the 12 *Ayyangars* and to the 12 *Mahājanas*, by a Velama Chief Ravu Dharmanayudu of Recarla family, states that those villages were granted along with their cultivators and all other rights (*Nidhi nikṣhēpa aṣhtabhōga tēja swāmya somētanga...* and *krisivala samētanga).*[14]

Thus, these two epigraphs clearly show that the grant of the village or the land carried with it the cultlvators also. They also suggest that those tenants could not be disturbed and new tenants introduced in their place by the new lord, that is, the donee. The donees also could not cultivate those lands themselves by employing their own servants. So, the same tenants continued to cultivate those lands and paid to the new masters whatever share they used to pay to the previous lord on the produce of the land. Of course, if any new land was brought under cultivation in the endowed villages or if any old tenant left the leased lands, the religious institutions were, probably, free to lease them to new tenants.

In the case of the Brahman *Agrahāras*, the tenants cultivating the lands of the *Agrahārikas* lived in the hamlets attached to the main *Agrahāra* village. In these *Agrahāras*, as noted earlier, nobody except the Brahmans could live. The farmers lived in the hamlets variously known as *Grāmagrāsamu*, *Pūndi*, *Palle*, *Grāmōpaharamu*, etc., granted by the donors along with the *Agrahāra.* For example, the Konkuduru plates of Allaya Dodda of the year 1430 A.D. from the village Kokuduru, (West Godavari dt.) which record the grant of the village Gumpini, surnamed Allada-reddi Doddavaram, as an *Agrahāra* to the Brahmans and Temples, also state that the donor granted, along with that, another village known as Annavaram for subsistence (*Grāma grāsartham*).[15] That the lands owned by the Muslim institutions were leased out to the tenants is known from an inscription of 1681 A.D. from Hyderabad city (from the Mosque of Miyan Mishk). It refers to the grant by a Qutbshahi general, of the income from the produce of lands and gardens leased for cultivation in the village of Atapur, to the Mosque mentioned above.[16]

That the lands owned by some of the Hindu religious institutions of the period were cultivated by those institutions themselves, directly, with their own bullocks and servants, is indicated by an interesting epigraph of 1626 A.D. from Amaravati (Guntur dt.).[17] It clearly states that the male-calves of the cows donated by a certain Handrikam Peddappa were to be utilised for ploughing the fields of the God Amaresvara of the place (*swāmiki kshētralu dunnānu*). This reference gives scope for the inference that this particular Temple cultivated, probably, a part or the whole of its cultivable lands by employing its own bullocks and servants. If that was not the case there was no need for the Temple, to put its own bulls to cultivation.

Flower-gardens and fruit-groves: The flowers were a prime requisite for the decoration of the deities in the Temples in the course of their daily worship as well as during their festivals. Similarly, the vegetables and fruits of different kind were needed for the preparation of various food offerings to the deities. Their perennial supply throughout the year and in sufficient quantities was ensured by the maintenance of groves and gardens (*Tōṁpu, Nandanavanam*) by the Temples in their vicinity, In these gardens and groves, the plants and trees of various types of flowers and fruits were cultivated. The cultivation of plants of red-lotus, aromatic herbs like *Maruvam*, *Davanam* and *Tulasi* in the ponds and flower-gardens of Tirupati Temple are mentioned in the epigraphs from that place.[18] Similarly, an epigraph of 1536 A.D. from Chennur village (Cuddapah dt.) refers to the grove consisting of the trees of mango, jack-fruit, myrobolan, elephant apple, tamarind, plantain and sizigium-jambolaum, fruits, planted on both the sides of the Temple of God Tiruvengalanatha of that place by the donor, Rayasam Vengalappa, a Vijayanagara official.[19] Finally, an epigraph of 1492 A.D. from Tirupati mentions the coconuts, unripe and ripe mangoes, jack-fruit, unripe and ripe-plantains, citron, lemons and other fruits, grown in a grove planted by a donor and donated to the Temple of Sri Venkatesvara.[20] The gardens and groves were planted some times by the devotees and some times by the Temple authorities themselves. No uniform policy appears to have been followed by the institutions in the management and the cultivation of these groves and gardens.

Sometimes, the donors, while granting the groves and gardens to Temples, made a direct provision for the maintenance of the gardeners who cultivated them. An inscription of 1408 A.D. from the village Tirupati (Godavari dt.) states that Mukkantiraju (a brother-in-law of Kataya Vema Reddi), who granted a garden (*Briṅdāvanam*) to the Temple of Sringar Raya of Komaragiripuram, also granted some land for the maintenance of the gardeners who cultivated it.[21] Similarly, an epigraph of Sadasiva Raya's period from the village Chagalamarri (Kurnool dt.) records that certain Kondraju granted some land to the Temple of Ahobilesvara for planting a flower garden and some land for the ten gardeners cultivating it.[22]

Sometimes, the donors who planted the flower-gardens or groves and transferred their possession to the Temples, made also arrangements for the maintenance of the gardeners indirectly. They either deposited some money in the Temple-treasury or granted some land to the Temple for that purpose. And the Temple authorities undertook either to pay the monthly salaries of the gardeners or to issue a quantity of the sacred food every day to them for cultivating the gardens. This practice appears to have been adopted, sometimes, by the authorities of the Sir Venkatesvara Temple of Tirupati, where mostly the Sattada Srivaishnavas were employed for the purpose.[23] Similar system appears to have prevailed in the Temple of Lord Narasimha of Simhachalam where the gardeners (*Tōṅtabantu*) cultivating the Temple gardens were provided *Vrittis* of *Prasādam* (sacred food).[24]

From these and other references in a number of the Temple epigraphs, it is clear that the Temples themselves got their gardens and groves cultivated by employing the gardeners who were provided for their maintenance by the donors either directly or indirectly. In these cases, the entire produce, obviously, went to the Temples.

Besides this, the system of letting the Temple gardens to the tenants on lease basis also appears to have been adopted in some cases during this period. An inscription of 1534-35 A.D. from Kanchipuram refers to the tenants of the Temple gardens and the share of produce which accrued to them.[25]

The share of the religious institutions in the produce of their lands leased out: No uniformity appears to have been observed with regard to the proportion of the produce which the religious institutions claimed as their share from the ryots cultivating their lands. As most of these lands and villages originally (i.e. before their grant) belonged to the government, it is not unreasonable to assume that the institutions (the new owners) got from the tenants whatever the government used to get from them. As in the case of the government lands, the proportion of the produce which the religious institutions got, might have varied with time, place, soil, irrigation facilities and finally with the political set-up. The following few examples will illustrate this.

During the Vijayanagara period, the trustees of the Temple of Vardaraja Swami of Kanchipuram (Tamilnadu), appear to have claimed three-fourths of the produce of the soil as the share of the Temple leaving only one fourth to the cultivator.[26] But an inscription of 1550 A.D., from Chinna Ahobilam (Kurnool dt.) mentions different ratios for grain and fruits. According to it the tenants (4 men) who cultivated the grove of various fruits (areca, mango, plantain, orange, etc.), belonging to the Temple of God Narasimha of Ahobilam and situated in the village of Alamuru, were to get two-thirds of the produce and the remaining one share was to go to the Temple. But in the case of wet land the produce (paddy) was to be shared equally, that is, half of it going to the cultivators (*kāṁpulu*) and the remaining half to the Temple.[27] Viraraghave Charya also seems to be of the opinion that the tenants who cultivated the lands of the Sri Venkatesvara Temple of Tirupati, took half of the produce of the soil (grain) as their share.[28] But contrary to this opinion, Burton Stien, while discussing the tenure system of the villages belonging to the Temple of Tirupati, states that the major share of the produce (*mēlvāram*) went to the Temple and the minor share (*Kudivāram* or *Kulivāram*) went to the cultivator. He further, states that this system was prevalent in the villages belonging to the government before their grant to the Temple and the same system of sharing was retained by the Temple. According to him, the major share (of the Temple) varied between 51 per cent and 75 per cent.[29]

So, it appears that the religious institutions of whatever category got the major share of the produce (grain) from the ryots who cultivated their lands. But in the case of the fruit groves and flower-gardens, the major share went to the tenants cultivating them. The system was intended, probably, to help the cultivator. The trees took more time compared to the crops of grain to give the yield; and in the initial stages the cultivator would get less income.

Of course, in times of famine and other natural calamities, the religious institutions appear to have been considerate to their tenants and reduced their share of the produce in order to help the tenants. An inscription of 1534-35 A.D. from the Tamil country (Kanchipuram, Chinglepet dt.) states that the *Mēlvāram* (the major share belonging to the Temple) on areca, coconuts, mango and other trees grown on the *aTiruvidaiyattam* lands (*sarvamānya* land granted to the Temple) of the Arulala Perumal Temple in Little Kanchipuram, was formerly three-fourths of the yield, the remaining one fourth going to the cultivator; that in a severe drought the above trees withered; that the tenants were asked to plant trees freely and pay up the *Mēlvāram* in the reduced ratio of two-thirds.[30] Similarly, the collection of the share of the religious institutions in the case of the new lands or lands brought under cultivation for the first time, might have been based on progressive rates, to help the cultivator. The government also appears to have adopted this system.

The religious institutions, it is quite reasonable to infer, collected their share of the produce from the tenants, in kind only to meet their daily requirements.

Other income from the Sarvamānya lands: The religious institutions of the period, appear to have been entitled to levy a number of other dues, besides the share in the produce of the soil from the tenants in their *Sarvamānya* villages. N. Venkataramanayya refers to some 11 kinds of taxes (*Tirunāla-kānike*, *Haludu*, *Hostu*, *Grāmavechcha*, *Biti*, *Birāda*, *Sollege*, *Avudu*, *Bēḍige*, *Bējavāri* and *Solage*) which were collected by the Temples from their tenants in the Kannada country during the Vijayanagara period and states that the same number of dues must have been collected by the Temples in other parts of the Vijayanagara empire also.[31] Similarly, the dues from the tenants of the *Agrahāras* to the owners of the land included, besides the share in the produce of the soil, the fines collected in those villages (*Dasāparādhamulanu vichārinchi jarimāna vidhinchutaku*) and free-services (*veṭṭi vēmulu).*[32]

The religious institutions appear to have helped their tenants by various means. Some of the Hindu Temples and *Maṭhas* of the period embarked upon improvement of agriculture in their villages by undertaking the construction of tanks and irrigational canals. Sometimes, they used to get the irrigational works in their villages done by the devotees themselves, on the basis of *Daśavanda* system. Under this system, out of the ten shares of the cultivable land under that particular new irrigational project, nine shares were to go to the owner of the land and the tenth share to the person who carried it out. An inscription of 1554 A.D. from Chinna Ahobilam (Kurnool dt.) states that, in that year, the trustees of the Temple of God Narasimha of that place granted some lands as *Daśavaṅdamānyam* at the rate of one share (*martulu*) for each 10 shares to a certain Avubalaraju for having constructed an irrigation tank in the Temple village.[33] Similarly, and epigraph from the village Nosam (Cuddapah dt.) belonging to the reign of Krishnadeva Raya refers to the construction of an irrigation tank, in the village of Nosam belonging to a *Maṭha*, by a certain Varada Setti, and to the lands granted to him as *Kaṭṭumānya* (same as *Daśavaṅda*), presumably by the authorities, of the *Maṭha*.[34]

Sometimes, the religious institutions invested the money belonging to the monetary endowments for the improvement of the irrigational facilities in their villages. There are number inscriptions from Tirupati which record this type of activities by the *Sthanattār* of that Temple. For instance an of 1476 A.D. from that place states that Sathakopadasar Narasimha Raya Mudaliyar, one of the Srivaishnavas of Tirupati, deposited 1500 *Narpanam*, as capital, in the *Sribhaṅdāram* of the Temple of Sri Venkatesvara for certain food offerings to the God. The *Sthanattār* invested that money for the excavation of channels from tanks in the *Tiruvidaiyāttam* (Temple) villages. They also undertook to perform the service in the name of the donor with the income accruing from that investment.[35]

Sometimes, the devotees themselves got these irrigational works done. There are a number of references to the royal donors as well as private donors financing or executing this type of works in the inscriptions from Tirupati and Srisailam.[36] These an epigraph of 1574 A.D. from Srisailam (Kurnool dt.) states that Dantikanti Lingappanna, the *Kāryakarta* of Ramarajayyadea (son of Tirumala I) repaired the bund across the river Bhogavati in the area belonging to the Temple of Srisailam these fecilities not only brought additional income to the institutions but also helped the tenants cultivating the lands.

The Cattle Wealth: Another important form of wealth possessed by the religious institutions of the period and from which they derived considerable income is cattle. Especially, the Hindu Temples of the period maintained, for their use, a large number of cattle consisting of cows, bulls, buffaloes, sheep, goats etc. An idea of the immense cattle wealth of the Temple of Sri Venkatesvara of Tirupati can be had from the fact that one single donor, Periya Obala Nayakkar Rama Nayakkar, a general under Viranarasimharaya of Vijayanagara, alone presented altoghether

350 cows on three occasions within a period of 30 years (from 1505-1535 A.D.).[37] Most of the cattle were granted to them by the devotees to ensure the maintenance of the services like food offerings and lamps instituted by them in the Temples on a perpetual basis. This type of grants are mentioned in the inscriptions, mostly of the early part of the period under consideration, that is during the 14th and 15th centuries A.D.

In order to ensure the proper breeding of the cattle which would make the above perpetual services doubly sure, the donors many a time, it appears, also granted bulls in addition to cows. For instance, an epigraph of 1291 A.D. from Tripurantakam (Kurnool dt.) refers to the grant of 50 cows and 3 bulls to the Temple of Tripurantaka Mahadeva of that place by Recerla Mummadi Nayaka.[38] Similarly, another epigraph of 1335 A.D. from the same place (Tripurantakam) states that a certain Potireddi Tallaya Reddi presented 100 cows and a bull to the Temple of that place.[39]

In a number of cases, the donors, while donating milch cattle like cows, buffaloes, sheep and goats to the Temples, especially for the lamp-services, entrusted them to private individuals belonging to the shepherd class such as the Gollas and the Boysos. They entered into an agreement with those individuals who bound themselves to supply a fixed quantity of ghee in perpetuity by enjoying the remaining income from the cattle. These agreements were made presumably with the consent of the authorities of the Temple in which the services were instituted. This practice appears to have been very common during the Kakatiya period and there are a number of epigraphs of this period, which record this type of transactions.

Sometimes, the donees, while entrusting the cattle to private individuals, also made provision for their (shepherds') maintenance and for the maintenance of the cattle too. For example, an inscription of 1426 A.D. from Simhachalm (Vizag dt.) states that *Simhādri Bhōgapariksha* Haridasa Sahasa Malludu instituted a food offering to the God Narasimha of that place and kept 20 cattle (*Mōdālu*) in the possession of *Parasu Khilāri* (shepherd) with the stipulation that the latter would supply the necessary curd every day for that service.[40] It further states that the donor dept some gold (*Payindi*) in the possession of that shepherd for his maintenance in lieu of his service. Another epigraph of 1398 A.D. from Simhachalam, which records that a certain Rikudasu Nayudu kept 100 goats in the possession of Potnuri Garaboyudu and provided for the latter's maintenance, stipulates that the shepherd should supply 7 *Tūmus* and 2 *Kuṅchas* of ghee every month for the perpetual lamp instituted by the donor in the Temple of God Narasimha of that place.[41] Similarly an inscription of 1428 A.D. from the same place, (Simhachalam) records that a certain Dharummayi Sahasamalludu kept 110 sheep in the possession of two Golla-brothers, Erraboyindu and Ganga-boyindu, and also granted a field of one *Puṭṭi*-land for their maintenance with the stipulation that they should supply 7 *Tūmus* of ghee at the rate of one *Aḍḍa* per day for the maintenance of the perpetual lamp instituted by him in the Temple of God Narasimha of that place.[42]

In may cases, the cattle granted for the services in the Temples by the donors appear to have been handed over to the Temples themselves. The latter were free to manage them by employing their own servants. Mallana, the chief-minister under Devaraya II, presented 82 heads of cattle including cows and calves to the Temple of Sri Venkatesvara of Tirupati in the year 1409 A.D. for maintaining 3 lamps set up by him.[43] Similarly Kandadai Ramanujayyangar, the Vaishnava preceptor, presented 40 cows to the same Temple in the year 1469 A.D. for supplying curds for a food offering to the God.[44] In these two cases the Temple itself must have managed the cattle through its own servants by paying wages. There are a number of epigraphs during this period recording the remission by the government of the taxes on Temple cattle and the herdsmen who tended them.[45]

Besides ensuring the perpetual supply of ghee and other dairy products to the Temples, the cattle wealth especially the male calves and bulls appear to have served other useful purposes. They were used for transporting goods, carrying water, ploughing the fields, etc. An epigraph of 1626 A.D. from Amaravati (Guntur dt.) clearly states that the cows donated by the donor, Handrikam Peddappa, were meant for supplying ghee for lamps and the male calves for ploughing the fields of the God Amaresvara.[46] The major Hindu Temples of the period appear to have maintained their own transport system consisting of bullock-carts, bulls, etc. for carrying the provisions for their daily use. That the bullocks were sometimes specifically granted for the transport purposes of these institutions by donors, is known from an epigraph of 1553 A.D. from Tirupati.[47] It records the grant of two hundred bulls bearing swan-mark (*Humsa mudra*) by Sadasiv Raya to the Temple of Sri Venkatesvara of the place, for carrying, on the carts, of daily provisions such as food, ghee, oil, vegetables etc. belonging to that Temple. The bullocks were also used by the religious institutions, both Hindu and Muslim, for pulling water from wells and for carrying it for their daily use, Besides cows, bullocks, sheep and goats many temples to the period appear to have maintained elephants for conducting such religious services as waving fans before the God, and taking out the God in procession. An epigraph of 1546 A.D. from Tirupati refers to the mahouts who were in the service of the Temple of Vithalesvara Perumal of that place.[48] And finally, it can be stated that the cattle of these institutions which remained unused, especially the male-calves, he sheep and he-goats, must have been sold.

INCOME FROM SHORT-TERM OR CURRENT ASSETS

Income from taxes and tolls: An important source of income of the religious institutions, next to the income from the landed estates, were the proceeds of the taxes and tolls granted to them by the king and his subordinates. The rulers of the period, apart from granting villages, lands and buildings as *Sarvāmanya*, also allotted the land revenue, that is, the share in the produce of the soil due to the government in its own villages, for various services in the religious institutions. For example, Harihara II of Vijayanagara granted, in the year 1388 A.D., the revenue of the village of Pungodu for conducting a festival in the Temple of Tirumalai.[49] An epigraph of 1409 A.D. from Karshanapalli village (Chittoor dt.) states that a Vijyanagara subordinate Vira Obaladeva Chola gifted a portion of income, accruing to the royal treasury, from certain lands at

Muttukuru in favour of the local Temple.[50] Krishnadev Raya granted a similar income due to the government from a few villages to the Temple of Sri Venkatesvara at Tirupati.[51] In all these cases, the religious institutions were entitled only to the land revenue (hitherto paid to the government) from the tenants. The villages or lands remained, for all other purposes, under the donors control. Even that revenue which was granted to the institution was collected, in many cases, by the government officials or the donor's agent and was paid to the Temple treasury. In the case of Harihara II's grant, mentioned above, the village was kept in the possession of a private individual (Mullai Tiruvenkat *Jiyyar*) who paid the stipulated income every year to the Temple treasury.[52] Similarly, Adaippon Sevvappa Nayaka and Tirumalai Nayaka, the officers under Sadasiva Raya of Vijayanagara, granted the annul income of 70 *Pon* and 80 *Pon* from two villages respectively to the Temple of Sri Venkatesvara of Tirupati for certain offerings. But they retained those villages in their own possession and agreed to deposit that amount every year in the Temple treasury.[53]

The religious institutions of the period derived a considerable income from the tolls collected at certain places and assigned to them by the rulers. For example, Prataparudra II granted, according to an epigraph 1293 A.D., two *Visās* (one-sixteenth part of a *Māḍa*) on every *Māḍa* on the goods, sold in the market in the village of Danaduvolu to the Temple of Sri Pandesvara Mahadevara of that place.[54] Another epigraph, of 1309 A.D. from the village Devagude (Cuddapah dt.) refers to the grant of *Ubhayamārga Śuṅkam* (tolls levied on goods in transit–both ways) at the rate of two *Rūkas* for each village in the Gandikotaseema by Chinnaya, a Kakatiya official, for the service of a perpetual lamp in the Temple of Talkantidev.[55] This type of grants were more numerous during the Vijayanagara period than those of the other dynasties.

The grant of various types of tolls come to our notice during this period. An inscription of 1443 A.D. from Singarayakonda records a grant to the local Narsimha Temple, by all the officials of the 18 sects of all countries and all persons who reside in the 56 countries, of the tolls on various articles of merchandise carried for sale on the road leading to Tirupati on certain days of the Temple festival.[56] An epigraph of 1521 A.D. from the village Mailavaram (Cuddapah dt.) records the grant of *Sthalasuṅkamu* (duties levied on goods to be sold at one place) collected from the village of Renati Nandela for the lamp services in the Temple of Chennakesvara of that place.[57]

Another inscription of Krishnadeva Raya's period from Kondavidu (Guntur dt.) records the grant of tolls levied on various kinds of trade, at various rates in the town of Kondavidu by Nadindla Gopamantri to God Raghunayaka Swami of Kondavidu.[58] Yet another epigraph of 1548 A.D. states that Pasupula Timmayadeva, a Vijayanagara official granted the *Pēṭasuṅkam* (a tax on stalls?) of Andhirajukondur village for a food offering to the God Chennadesava of that village.[59]

The Muslim religious institutions also used to derive some income from the tolls granted to them by the royal donors. A Persian epigraph of 1681 A.D. from Hyderabad city (Mosque of Miyan Mishk) refers to the grant by Malik Mishk, a Qutbshahi general, of the income from the *bāzār* attached to the Mosque, from the stalls on both sides of the *bāzār* and from the market, for the maintenance of certain charities instituted by him in the Mosque.[60]

Besides this, the religious institutions of the period used to get some income from the remissions granted by the government on certain taxes and tolls which they used to pay themselves to the government.[61] Many of the inscriptions which record the collection of these taxes and tolls by the government from the religious institutions also record in some cases their remission by the kings and their subordinate officials in favour of the religious institutions themselves. The remissions were made, sometimes to help them financially, and sometimes, for conducting various services instituted by those royal donors.

That, the government of the day sometimes donated the taxes, due to it on the marriages performed by the people, to the religious institutions, is known from a number of inscriptions and local records. For example, the Ramesvaram *Kaifiyat* states that Saluve Timmarasu, the *Kāryakarta* of Krishnadeve Raya of Vijayanagara and Govindaya and Adeppa Nayudu, the other two officers under him together granted the tax on marriages performed in the *Sīmas* of Penugonda, Siddavattam, Kandanavolu, Gandikota, Pottapi, Chandragiri, Pakanadu, etc. to the Temple of Mukit Ramesvara Swami of Ramesvaram village (Cuddapah dt.)[62]

Income from the grants made by Guilds and Communal Organizations: The epigraphs recording the grant of tolls and a part of profits to the religious institutions and especially to the Temples by the individual merchants as well as their guilds are quite numerous. They belong to the period of almost all the dynasties. For example, the Kondavidu *Kaifiyat* states that in the year 1449 A.D. the members of a merchant guild (*Prithviyābayyāru dēśāla ayyavāli chālumūla mukhyamaina samstha pekkandru*) granted a portion of their profits (*Perike-mūlavīsamu*) on the sale of several articles of merchandise for certain services in the Temple of Srisailam, on the occasion of *Sivaratri* festival.[63] Similarly, an epigraph of 1531 A.D. from the village Animala (Cuddapah dt.) refers to the grant of certain toll-income (*Magama*) on articles of trade, such as cotton, yarn, cloth etc. made by the *Veera-Balanja* merchant guild of Ayyavolu, for the lamp-offerings of God Sangamesvara of that village.[64]

The grants made by the communal organization also brought considerable income to the religious institutions. These organizations, affiliated to different religious sects, granted a portion of their income to the Temples, *Maṭhas* etc. for various religious services. An epigraph of 1310 A.D. from Mated village (Warangal dt.) records the gift of 5 *Visas* in every *Māda* of the tax *Siddhāya* (due to the government) by the people of 18 *Varnas* (castes) of that village for the *Aṅga-raṅga-bhōga* of the Gods Mallesvara and Kesava in the local Temple.[65] Similarly, an epigraph of 1497 A.D. from Amaravati (Guntur dt.) records that the *Paṅchānamvāru* (artisans) of Dharanikota and Amaravti, granted *Paidipannu* (a tax on gold) to God Amaresvara of the place.[66]

Among the communal grants, those of the *Vipravinodins* (Brahman jugglers), *Veeramuṣtis* (village servants) and *Dommaras* (acrobats) are quite numerous during this period. But a majority of them belong to the Vijayanagara period. Of these communities, the *Vipravinodins* appear to have been the followers of Vaishnavism. For, most of their grants were made in favour of the Vaishnava Temples. For example, an inscription of 1550 A.D. from the village Chavuduru (Cuddapah dt.), which records the grant by the *Vipravinodins* of their income (betel-leaves, areca-nuts, clothes, ornaments, śandals, flowers, vehicles, other articles, cash, etc.) due from the Brahmans of Kalamalla village, to the Temple of Kesava of that place, describes that Vaishnava deity as the family deity of that community (*Kulaswāmi*).[67] The *Veeramustis*, on the other hand, appear to have been staunch followers of the Saivite faith. This is indicated in a number of inscriptions. For example, the inscription of 1558 A.D. from Bondalakunta village (Guntur dt.) clearly states that the *Veeramusti* Sivayogi Lingayya and others gifted the *Veeramusti Pannu* due to them from several countries, to the God Visvesvara (a Saiva deity) of that place under the direction of several Saivite communities of Mulkinadu.[68] These *Veeramustis* attached themselves to the *Dēvāngas* (weavers) and merchants and also described themselves as the followers of the Saiva teachers such as the pontiffs of the Bhikshavritti *Maṭha* of Srisailam. They also served the Saiva Temples as guards.[69] But the *Dommaras* appear to have made gifts to both Saiva and Vaishnava deities indicating their affiliation to both. This is indicated in an inscription of 1553 A.D. from the village Valluru (Cuddapah dt.).[70] It registers the gift of the income due to the *Dommaras*, to the Gods Hari, and Hara (both Vaishnava and Saiva deities) of that village. Similarly an epigraph of 1546 A.D. from Bedaduru village (Cuddapah dt.) records the grant by the *Dommaras* of their income from the *Agrahārikas* of that village to the Gods Tiruvengalanatha Swami, Chennakesava (both Vaishnava Gods) and Mahlingam (Saiva god) etc. of the place.[71]

Religious taxes: The religious institutions derived some income from certain religious taxes and contributions collected from the people.

One such tax from which some of the Hindu Temples were benefited is *Mahārāja-prayōjanālu* or *Mahārājatantu*. An epigraph of 1549 A.D. from Jillella village (Cuddapah dt.) states that Chinna Timmaraju Kondayya (Vijayanagara provincil governor) granted the money that was collected for *Mahārāja-prayojanas* from the village Jillella which belonged to the Temple of Narasimha of Ahobilam, to Sri Virabhadra (deity) of that village of the celebration of *Parupu-pārivēṭa*.[72] Similarly, an inscription of 1543 A.D. from a village in Kurnool district refers to the grant of the income accruing from *Mahārāja-prayojanam,* levied from the Ademala village belonging to his *Nāyaṅkara*, to Ankalamma (a female deity) for the celebration of her *Parupu-pāriveta*[73]. This tax was levied by the Vijayanagara government to utilize it on the worship and the festivals of the village deities in order to protect their dominions from wrath of those deities.[74] It appears from the above epigraphs that it was collected from people not only in the villages belonging to government and the feudal nobles (*Amara-Nāyakas*) but also from the villages belonging to the religious institutions. But it is not known, whether this tax mentioned in the epigraphs belonging to a few Telugu areas of the Vijayanagara empire, was collected in the entire country during the period under study.

Besides the above tax, a few more religious contributions appear to have been made by the people for the benefit of the religious institutions. N. Venkatramanayya refers to the taxes-*Ganācāra-tere* (a tax paid to the Jangama or the Lingayat priest by Saivas), *Jiyar-terege* (a tax paid by the Vaishnavites to their Guru) *Maṭhaterege* and *Kūṭa-terege* (taxes paid for the purpose of maintaining the *Maṭha* and Ramanujakuta respectively), *Tēre kānike* (a tax paid for the expenses of the dragging of the car in the festival of God), *Jātre* (a levy raised for celebrating the periodical festival of the village deities), etc.,; prevalent in various parts of the Vijayanagara empire.[75] And it is quite reasonable to presume that most of these religious contributions were collected in the Telugu districts of the Vijayanagara empire also.

It is known from the contemporary evidence that the Hindu religious institutions and especially the Temples and *Maṭhas*, used, to collect religious contributions and funds from the people or devotees by sending their agents to the villages belonging to the area of their spiritual jurisdiction. The *Kaifiyat* of Nivarti Sangam (Kurnool dt.) refers to the tours undertaken by the two Jangama brothers–Santabhikshavritti and Virabhiksavritti, the *Kāryakartas* of Bhikshavritti *Maṭha* of Srisailam, towards the end of the 15th century A.D., to collect funds in the villages of the neighbouring areas and to bring pilgrims (*Pruṣamu*) to the shrine of Srisailam.[76] As the pontiffs of the Bhikshavritti *Maṭha* were incharge of the management of the affairs of the Temple of Mallikarjuna of Srisailam, it is quite reasonable to infer that the agents of this *Maṭha* performed that function on behalf of the temple. The above *Kaifiyat* also gives the interesting information that on behalf of the Srisailam Temple, agents were sent to the villages of the neighbouring districts to bring pilgrims. It is a matter of fact that the visit of more pilgrims brought more revenue to the shrine in the form of gifts and presents to the deity. So, these agents were engaged to move from place to place to bring more and more pilgrims by impressing upon them of the greatness and the sacredness of those shrines and of the religious merit of visiting them. This is similar to the practice of sending *Pāndas* by the temples of Puri for similar purposes, during this period and even in recent times.[77]

Mode of collection of the proceeds of the taxes, tolls and other monetary grants: No uniform policy appears to have existed as far as the mode of collection of the proceeds of all these taxes and tolls granted to the religious institution by the government private organizations and individuals. It has been noted earlier, how in some cases the donors themselves took the responsibility of collecting and depositing that amount with donees. But we, also, gather from the inscriptions that sometimes the recipients themselves were asked to take the responsibility of collecting them. For example, an inscription of 1558 A.D. from the village Chadalavada (Nellore dt.), which records the grant of several taxes and tolls due to the government from that village and several other villages in the *Sīmas* of Addanki and Ammanabrolu, to the Temple of Ranganyakulu of the above mentioned village, clearly states that the trustees (*Sthānamvāru*) of that temple should collect those taxes by giving receipts for the same to the payees and credit the amount in the temple treasury.[78] Similarly, when Sadasiva Raya of Vijayanagara granted as *Sarvamānya* gift, various taxes due to the government from various provinces and districts (*Rājyas* and *Sīmas*) of the empire (including a few from Telugu country) for the conduct of charities instituted by him in the Temple of Tirupati, the trustees (*Sthānattār*) of that temple took the responsibility of collecting those taxes.[79]

In such cases these institutions must have been compelled to employ a number of people for the collection of these taxes from such a wide area as mentioned in the above grants.

The Gifts: another important source of income for the religious institutions of the period were the various gifts of cash, valuable articles, jewellery etc. given by pious devotees.

An inscription of the Reedi period from Simhachalm (Vizag dt.) records that King Virabhadra Reddi granted a golden vessel, pearl-necklaces, a golden fillet, besides a village and a few cows, to the God Narasimha of that place.[80] Like-wise, the gift of numerous jewellery made of gold, precious stones and pearls, vessels of gold and silver to the Temples of Tirupati, Simhachalam, etc., by Krishnadev Raya, on several occasions, when he visited them along with his consorts, are referred to in the epigraphs from those places.[81]

That, sometimes, individuals having no heirs bequeathed their property to the religious institution, is indicated in an epigraph of 1370 A.D. from Chittoor.[82] It states that a certain person, who had no heirs, bequeathed his eight cows to a Temple.

Sometimes, devotees presented looms, oil-mills etc. also to these institutions. For instance, an epigraph of this period from the village Kallur (Nellore dt.) states that a certain Anapotinayudu presented an oil-mill for providing an oil-bath to the deity Gangesvaradeva of that place.[83] However, it is not mentioned how the Temples utilized the oil-mills and looms to get oil or cloth for the stipulated services. It is quite probable that they were rented and from this the temple got the rent in kind.

The *Dargāhs* of the period, used to get considerable income from the offerings in cash and kind made regularly by the devotees with requests for the intercession of the saint or as thanks-giving for benefits received.

In the Muslim states, the government used to grant stipends to the religious institution in their dominions. It is stated, in the statement of revenue and expenditure, of the Golkonda kingdom for the year 1097/1685-86, A.D., given in *Tārīkh-i-Zāfrah*, that the Qutbshahi government spent Rs. 3,97,801 as *Nadhar* (gift or stipend) to Miron Shah Raju (Shah Raju II, the pontiff of a *Khānqāh* at Hyderabad), the preceptor of the Sultan, and Rs. 64, 925 as allowance to Hindu Temples.[84]

EXPENDITURE

The Items of Expenditure

The religious institutions, being service-oriented in character, had to incur a lot of expenditure on the performance of various services. We gather from the inscriptions and other sources that the important items of expenditure of these institutions were—the remuneration of their functionaries, purchasing of various articles for food and various religious services, charities and other social services, construction and conservation of the buildings, and taxes. Due to the meager information available on the subject, it is very difficult to give the exact proportions of the amounts spent on these items.

As far as the Hindu Temples of this period are concerned, we have got, fortunately, an epigraph from Tirumala-Tirupati belonging to the year 1546 A.D.[85] It furnishes the detailed budget-estimate of the Sri Vithalesvara Perumal Temple at Tirupati for the year 1546 A.D. ofcourse this Temple was a minor shrine consecrated and endowed by a certain Devaraya-Bhattar and managed by the *Sthanattār* of the Sri Venkatesvara Temple of that place. And it might have had less number of functionaries and conducted less number of services compared to those of the major and independent Hindu Temples of the period. But still it provides very useful information, on the basis of which a fairly clear idea can be formed about the pattern of the expenditure in terms of the important items and the proportion of the amounts spent on them. The details of the budget of that Temple given below will illustrate this point.

Table 1

Sl. No.	*Item (Wages of Functionaries)*	*Rate per month*	*Expenditure per annum in Rēkhai-pon and Panam*[86]
1.	Servants (bearers of various article of store from tirupati to Tirumalai)	50 *R.P.*	600
2.	The keeper of the articles of stores (*Paduvāykkārar*)	—	10
3.	Temple Servant (*Kaikkalar*)	—	6
4.	Temple-Servants (6 persons)	6 *R.P.*	72
5.	Night Walchmen (*Talaiyāris*)	—	24
6.	Suppliers of weapons for Securing fuel	—	12
7.	Temple Repairers (*Tiruppani Pillai*)	—	10
8.	Officer in Ramanujakutam	—	5
9.	Elephant-keepers (*Mahouts*)	—	6
10.	Examiners	—	5
11.	Watchman (*Talaiyāri*)	—	6
12.	Cultivators of flower-gardens	—	6
13.	Additional sum for the cultivators of the Flower-gardens	—	7-2
14.	*Sahasranāmārchana* (performers)	—	1
15.	Suppliers of flowers	—	3
16.	Pipers and *Vādyakārar*	—	36
17.	Suppliers of baskets (*Panimurai*)	—	36
18.	Fuel Suppliers (*Siṅgamurai*)	—	30-6
19.	Temple accountants	—	60
20.	*Vahanam* bearers (*Nivaṅdakkārar*)	—	60

table contd.

21.	Suppliers of holy-water (*Tirumañjanam*)	—	1
22.	Servants engaged in *Tirumañjanam* Services	—	12-6
23.	Distributors of offered *Prasādam* (*Pachchadi*)	—	1-2
24.	Garland Suppliers	—	2-4
25.	Additional sum for the persons engaged in watershed	—	2-4
26.	Additional sum for the servants engaged in watershed	—	1-6
27.	Suppliers of flowers for worship	—	2-4
28.	Persons engaged in *Vēdapārāyanam* services	—	1-2
29.	Persons engaged in *Vinnapam* Services	—	1-2
		Total	1021-6

Sl. No.	*Item (Expenditure on Article)*	*Rēkhai-Pon and panam per Annum*
1.	(Supplies of) Ghee-12 Jars	60
2.	Gingelly oil –12 pots	12
3.	(Supplies of) various articles of store during the *Purattasi Brahmōtsvam* in the Temple at Tirumalai.	30
4.	Rice	12
5.	Supply of sacred threads (*Pavitram*)	1
6.	Old clothes for *Harti*, evening lights and torches	1-2
7.	Preparation of food offerings (*Paruppuviyāl*)	66
8.	Supply of *chandanom*	16
9.	Curds	1
10.	Preparation of food offering (*Monōhara-pādi*)	25
11.	...(broken)	25
12.	Cash-offering (*Tirumun-kānikkāi*)	6
13.	Butter	6
	Total	261-2
		1021-6
		261-2
	Grand Total Expenditure of the Temple	1282-8

Thus the total amount, earmarked in this budget-estimate, for the various items of expenditure per year in this Temple comes to about 1282 *Rēkhai-pon* and 8 *Panams*. As no surplus amount is shown in it, this amount was probably the total income as well as the total expenditure of that Temple. Out of the total expenditure, the amount spent on the salaries of various functionaries and the wages of various persons engaged for the supply of various items and for the conduct of services is about 1021 *Rēkhai-pon* and 6 *Panams*. And it comes to about 80 per cent of the total amount of the expenditure. The remaining 261 *Rēkhai-pon* and 2 *Panams*, that is 20 per cent of the total amount, was spent on purchasing various articles for food, food-offerings and other religious services.

Similarly, a Persian epigraph of 1681 A.D. from Hyderabad city[87] furnishes a complete list of the various items of expenditure incurred for one year in the Mosque of Miyan Mishk of that place. Of course, the date of this epigraph overlaps the period under study by 81 years, though it belongs to the reign of the last Qutbshahi ruler Abul Hasan Tanesha. The revenue of the Mosque was provided by Miyan Mishk, a Qutbshahi general, who appears to be its builder and the principle donor. So, to give an idea of the proportion of the amount spent on various items of expenditure of a Mosque of the Qutbshahi period, the details of expenditure in the above mentioned Mosque are furnished below:

This epigraph mentions the amount 320 *Huns* as the total income of that Mosque. The total amount of the expenditure, if calculated according to the above list, comes to about 300 *Huns*. The remaining 20 *Huns* was probably the surplus amount left, though not mentioned as such. Out of the amount 300 *Huns* which was the total expenditure, the amount spent on the salaries of the functionaries of the Mosque is about 115 *Huns*, that is, about 34 per cent of the total expenditure. The remaining amount of 184 *Huns*, that is, about 66 per cent was spent on the purchasing of various articles needed for the maintenance of the religious services and the charities in the Mosque and for its conservation.

Table 2

Sl. No.	*Item-functionaries (as salary)*	*(Huns per annum)*
1.	The Superintendent of the Mosque	20
2.	The crier who calls the people to prayers	10
3.	The Spreader of prayer carpets	6
4.	The additional sum	6
5.	Water carrier	6
6.	Torch-bearers	
7.	Door-keeper	12
8.	Two sweepers	6
9.	Brahman clerk	8 1/4
10.	Masons for repairing steps	6
11.	Two shampooers	15
12.	Two *Mālies* for drawing water	12
	Total	114 3/4 or 115
13.	Oil for lamps	1½
14.	Oil for lamps (additional sum)	6
15.	Carpets for the Mosque	2
16.	Kitchen	6 3/4
17.	Conservation & other expenses	12
18.	Establishment of bath & other related expenditure	98
19.	Fuel for the bath	40
20.	Fodder for Oxen, and buckets & ropes	16
21.	Matting and bath-sheets etc.	1
	Total	183 3/4 or 184

Utilization of Surplus Funds and the Financial Difficulties

Under normal circumstances, the income from all the sources appears to have been sufficient for the religious institutions to meet the expenditure incurred by them for conduction various services and for paying the wages of their functionaries. In the case of the more influential and popular institutions, which had more income than expenditure, there must have been left some surplus money also. But this surplus money was not kept idle. They invested this money, sometimes, in acquiring new properties, such as lands, villages, etc., which in return yielded some more revenue. This is indicated in the contemporary epigraphs. An inscription of 1537 A.D. from Lepakshi (Anantapur dt.) records the purchasing of some land by the Temples of Papavinasadeva, Viresvaradeva and Raghunathadeva, from the *Mahajanas* of the *Sarvamānya-Agrahāra Pratāpa Dēvarāyapura.*[88] Similarly, an epigraph of 1539 A.D. from the village Vanipenta (Cuddapah dt.) records the purchasing of the entire *Agrahāra* village Chagalamarri form its owners, Venkatayya and Appayya, the two sons of Nalatatacharya, by the Temple of Chennaraya of Vanipenta for 170 *varāhas.*[89] Sometimes, the religious institutions purchased the properties of their sister-institutions too. This was probably to help them to overcome from their financial difficulties. An instance of this type is found in an inscription of 1537 A.D. from Kalahasti (Chittoor dt.).[90] It states that the Temple of Kalahasti-Udaiya-Naynar purchased a village from Rudra Sivacharya (presumably either the *Sthānāchārya* or priest) of the Temples of Tirumani Gangai Naynar and Nanmuga (Shanmuga?) – Nayanar etc. It further states that the Acharya had to sell the village to liquidate the debts he had incurred in connection with the worship and offerings in those Temples. This was due to the drought during the two preceding years.

But some of the religious institutions ran into financial difficulties due to certain unfavourable circumstances. For example, in times of famine, when they and their functionsries could not get the stipulated income from the lands, they were compelled to resort to borrowing, in order to make the both the ends meet. It has been noted above how some of the Temples of Kalahasi incurred debts due to the drought prevailing in the preceding years, and how they were compelled to sell their village to another temple of the place which was, probably, in a better financial position. Similarly, that, the priests of a Temple mortgaged their share of *Vrittis* on account of famine is known from an inscription of 1298 A.D., from Devagudi (Cuddapah dt.)[91] It registers the release-deed relating to the share of Nala Baira Jiyya, the priest of the Talakantidevi Temple who had sold it formerly on account of the hardships experienced during the famine of the previous three years. The chronic problem of mortgaging lands by the religious institutions, due to their financial difficulties, existing in the southern districts of the Telugu country towards the end of the period of Vijayanagara empire is indicated in an epigraph of 1643 A.D.[92] It states that Hande Siddappa Ramappa Nayaka, a subordinate of Sriranga III of Vijayanagara, issued an order to the farmers of his *Nāyaṅkara* territory of Koikunta-*sima*, declaring that the mortgages of the *Mānya* lands of the Gods and Brahmans in that territory should restore back, free from all charges and together with the documents (*Bhōgya-patramu*), the lands to the mortgagers after twelve years; and that those who disobeyed the order were liable to be fined.

Besides, the religious institutions had to face financial difficulties in times of unfavorable political conditions in the country. This was the case, especially with the Hindu religious institutions during the period of Muslim occupations of the country, when they could not get sufficient financial support either from the rulers or their subjects, and when some of them were, even, deprived of their sources of income. For example, the Temple of Simhachalam, which possessed some ten villages till the middle of the 16th century A.D., was deprived of the same by the Qutbshahi rulers who captured that region from the Gajapatis towards the end of that century.[93] And in the year 1604 A.D., only one village was granted by a Hindu official of the Qutbshahi government for its maintenance.[94] It is quite natural that, due to these hardships, the Temple must have cut short its expenditure, and consequently its various services were affected.

5

Relations with the State

The relations between the Religious institutions and the state were close and continuous and mainly pertained to such aspects as patronage, supervision and control, protection and fiscal regulations.

RELIGIOUS INSTITUTIONS AND STATE PATRONAGE

The chief patron of the religious institutions was the state, most of them owing their foundation, development and maintenance to the latter. No doubt, the private donors, such as, the rich individuals, the professional guilds and the communal groups also extended considerable patronage to these religious institutions. But this only supplemented the state patronage.

The government of the period, whether they belonged to the Hindu state or Muslim state, used to earmark a considerable part of their income, landed property and other valuables for the maintenance of the religious institutions in their dominions. The amount spent on these institutions appears to have been one of the major items of expenditure in the state exchequer. According to *Pratāpa Charitramu,* some four thousand villages, as *Agrahārs*, were in the enjoyment of Brahmans and another two thousand village were in the possession of the Temples during the reign of Pratapa Rudra II, the last Kakatiya monarch of Andhra Deas.[1] In addition to the grant of these villages, Pratapa Rudra II used to spend, every year, four crores of coins[2] (out of the 44 crores of the total income of the Kakatiya Kingdom) for the maintenance of the Temples situated in the capital city, Warangal, and the other Temples situated in other parts of the kingdom and some even outside the kingdoms.[3] An inscription of 1313 A.D. from Srisailam (Kurnool dt.) belonging to the reign of Kakatiya Prataparudra II furnishes a list of more than 52 villages which were in the enjoyment of the famous Saiva shrine of God Mallikarjuna of that place alone at the time of the grant.[4] In view of this fact and also the existence of a large number of Temples belonging to all religious denominations in the kingdom, most of which were patronized by the government, the above statement of *Pratāpa Charitramu* does not appear to be an exaggeration. Prolaya Vema Reddi, the founder of the Reddi kingdom, granted, according to a Sanskrit *Cātu* verse, in all, 44 villages as *Agrahārs* alone.[5] And it is quite reasonable to infer from this that a few hundred villages must have been in the possession of the Temples, *Maṭhas* and Brahmans during the entire period of the Reddis. According the Nuniz, emperor Mallikarjuna of Vijayanagara used to spend one fifth of the state revenue on only the Temples of the empire.[6] It is known from *Rāyavāchakam* that the Vijayanagara government's expenditure on *Dēvādāya, Maṭhapura* and *Brahmadēya* and other *Sarvamānya* endowments in the reign of Veera Narasimha (Tuluva) was 60 lakh *Varāha.*[7] The same *Rāyavāchakamu* says that the expenditure of the Vijayanagara state, at the beginning of the reign of Krishnadeva Raya, on the maintenance of the religious institutions (*Dēvādāya, Sarvamānya* and *Brahmadēya*) alone, accounted for 84,000,00 out of the 10,84,000,00 *Varāhas,* which was the gross total income of the state per annum.[8] Similar details of expenditure incurred by the government in some of the Muslim states of the period are available. A statement of revenue and expenditure of the Golkonda Kingdom for the year 1685-86 A.D. (the year just before its fall) states that Rs. 3,97,801 was given as *Naḍhar* to Miran Shah Raju (Shah Raju II), the Sufi saint and the preceptor of the Sultan, Rs. 6,35,001 as *Inām* to Muslims and orphans, Rs. 64,450 for expenses of *Āshūrkhānas,* Rs. 2.08,901 for *Langar* of two *Imāms.*[9] Thus, it is clear that the governments of the day patronized their religious institutions by spending a considerable part of their revenue on the latter's maintenance.

THE SUPERVISION AND CONTROL OF THE GOVERNMENT

The governments while extending patronage to the religious institutions took considerable interest in the proper functioning and the welfare of these institutions. The management of the day-to-day affairs of the religious institutions was, no doubt, left in the hands of their Trust-boards or governing councils. But the government exercised some control over those bodies and had overall supervision on their functioning.

In Hindu as well as Muslim states, there appears to have been a separate department which was incharge of the religious endowments. The existence of a separate Religious Endowment Department, in the Vijayanagara government, is alluded to in the *Rāyāvachakam*. It refers to a certain *Dharmāsanam Ḍharmayya*, who used to give a daily account of the working of the religious institutions like *Agragāras*, of the empire in the court of Veera Narasimharaya (Tuluva)[10]. This *Dharmāsanam Adhiākri* appears to have been the minister in-charge of the Religious Endowment Department as well as of Law.[11] This department appears to have supervised, through its officials, the functioning of the various religious institutions in the empire and kept with it the original copies of the grants which recorded donations to those institutions.

A similar arrangement, that is, entrusting the charge of the religious endowments to the minister of law, appears to have existed in the other Hindu kingdoms of the period in the Telugu country. A certain *Dharmāsanam Lingambatlu* is referred to in an epigraph of 1430 A.D. from the village Draksaramam (Godavarti dt.) as making grant of some land which he had received from Allada Vema Reddi of Rajamahendravara kingdom, to God Bhimesvara of that place.[12] The reference to this official, similar to that of *Dharmāsanam Ḍharmayya* of *Rāya Vāchakam* mentioned above, makes it possible to infer that the former was a minister in-charge of the administration of justice and religious endowments in the Reddi kingdom of Rajamahendravaram.

In the contemporary Muslim states also, similar departments appear to have been incharge of the religious endowments. In the Bahmani Sultanate, there was a minister in the government known as *Sadrush-Shāriah* who was in charge of religion and endowments besides the administration of justice and law.[13] This post appears to have been usually held by people of great scholarship and acknowledged legal reputation.[14] This minister was one of the highest officials of the government and the highest religious functionary in the state.[15] And the same system must have also prevailed in the Qutbshahi kingdom of Golkonda which was one of the succession states of the Bahmani Sultanate.

The governments, especially in the case of the Hindu state adopted various measures to exercise supervision and control over the management of the religious institutions in the area of their jurisdiction.

The Vijayanagara, the Ganga and the Gajapati governments, some times, adopted the practice of entrusting this work of supervision and control over the religious institutions and especially over the Temples, to its provincial and districts officials. These officials, who were primarily incharge of law and order and revenue matters of their respective areas, were also asked, sometimes, to see that the religious institutions in those areas functioned satisfactorily and the grants made to them by the government were executed. According to *Jammulamadugu Vriṭṭāntamu,* Devaraya II of Vijayanagara, while making a land grant to the Temple of Talakantidevi of Danavulapadu village (Cuddapha dt.), sent orders (*Rayasam*) to a certain Singappa Dannayaka to execute that grant and also to see that the services in that Temple were conducted properly.[16] This official, as his designation *Dannāyaka* suggests, was a military commander and also the provincial governor incharge of maintenance of law and order and revenue collection in his province.

The association of the provincial governor with the administration of some of the major Temples situated in the Telugu districts of the Ganga-Gajapati dominions is indicated in the epigraphs belonging to those Temples. Most of these records registering doniations especially to the Temples of Srikurmam and Simhachalam of this area mention that those donations were made during the authority of such and such a *Kalingaparīkṣa,* the governor of Kailnga province, followed, sometimes, by that of *Bhōgaparīkṣa,* the Temple executive officer. For example, an epigraph of 1371 A.D. from Simhachalam states that during the authority of *Kalingaparīkśa* Dharmadasa Jiyana and that of God Narasimh'a *Bhōgapariksa* Chilama Sahasamalla (*Sri Kaliṅgaparīkṣa Pātra Dharmadāsa Jiyana Aḍhiṣtānamṅdu. Sri Narasimhanāduni Bhōgaparīkṣa Chilama Sāhasamalla Veharna...*), a certain donor made a grant.[17] Similarly, an inscription of 1455 A.D. (of Kapilesvara Gajapati's period) from Srikurmam, which records a donation to the Srikurmesvara Temple by a donor, states that the transaction took place during the authority of *Kaliṅgaparikṣa* Sri Kundalesvara Mahapatra and that of the Temple *Bhōgaparikṣa* Chengamanatha (*Kaliṅgaparikṣa Srikundalesvaramahāpatruni Adhikarana Bhōgaparīksa Cheṅgamanathuni Adhittānamaṅdu*).[18] Examples like this can be multiplied. Some of these epigraphs also refer to the *Kalingapariksa* acting as the executive officer of those Temples. For example, an epigraph of 1376 A.D. from Simhachalam mentions Dharmadasa Jiyana acting both as the *Kalingaparikṣa* and also as the *Bhōgaparīkṣa* of the Temple of Narasimha (*Sri Narasimhanathuni Bhōgaparīkṣa kalingaparīkṣa Pātra Dhārmadāsa Jiyana Adhikāramaṅdu*).[19]

Thus is appears that the *Kalingaparīkṣa,* who was the governor of the province of Kalinga under the Oriya government, had a say in the management of the affairs of the temples situated in his province. Sometimes, he also acted as the executive officer of Temples, probably, in the absence of the latter; and supervised the management of the affairs of the Temples.

The association of the district revenue officials of the Vijayanagara government with the administration of the Temples is indicated in a number of epigraphs of the period. For example, an epigraph of 1532 A.D. from Kalahasti (Chittoor dt.) refers to

Pārupatyamvāru, along with the Temple *Baṅdāri* and *Sthānikas* and others, who were provided with shares in the sacred food of a local Temple.[20] An inscription of 1560 A.D. from Markapur (Kurnool dt.) refers to *Mannevāru,* alongwith the Temple trustees, the *Kāryakarta* of the donor and others conferring the revised rates of remuneration on the employees of the local Temple.[21] Similarly, a Temple epigraph of 1575 A.D. from Kommuru (Guntur dt.) refers to *Pārupatyagāṅdru* alongwith *Adhikāri, Kāryakarta* etc.[22] The *Pārupatyamvāru,* sometimes also known as *Pārupatyagāra, pārupatyagāṅdru, Mannevāru,* and *Suṅkamaniyagāṅdru,* were the revenue officials of the *Sīma* (district), which was the administrative sub-division of the *Rājya* (province) in the Vijayanagara empire. N Venkataramanayya gives the opinion that these *Sima-Pārupatyagār* or *Maniyagār* acted as the executive officers of the Temples and had some supervising powers over their management.[23] The hypothesis is supported, to some extent, by the evidence coming from the Tamil and Canarese regions of the Vijayanagara empire. *Kōyilolugu,* referring to the early rule of Vijayanagara over the Tamil country, states that the Raya and his servants began to administer the *Tiruvidaiyāṭṭam* lands which were *Dēvadānams* (lands of the Temples) in the same way as they administrated the government lands by appointing in Srirangam, their own servants as *Maniyam* and as *Saṃprati.*[24] Likewise an epigraph belonging to the period of Krishnadeva Raya, from Karnataka refers to *Pārupatyagār* having the authority to enquire into the affairs of a particular Temple of that area.[25]

It appears, this system of combining the revenue administration and the work of the supervision of the affairs of the religious institutions in the hands of the same officials, adopted by the Vijayanagara government in the case of some Temples, did not always yield happy and satisfactory results. The provincial or the district revenue officials, sometimes, misappropriated the funds of the religious institutions to make up the losses sustained in the revenue administration. This mismanagement of the Temple revenues affected their normal functioning and necessitated the appointment of special officers for that purpose by the government, atleast, in some cases during the period of Krishnadeva Raya. According to the above mentioned inscription from Karnataka,[26] Krishnadeva Raya issued an order with regard to the management of a particular Temple in Chamarajnagar (Bangalore dt.) as follows:

> All grants are to e taken care of by Allappa, the Agent of the Temple of the God. He will take possession of them, and appointing such Temple servants, as he wishes, will continue the Temple services from time to time, the Parupatyagar has no authority to enquire into the affairs of the Temple. Allappa will be the agent of the Temple and no one else.

Krishnadeva Raya expresses similar views in his work *Āmuktamālyada.*[27] He suggests:

> Do note entrust (the administration of the properties of Temples and others (endowments) to the officers whom you employ to collect the revenue due to you; for, being anxious to collect money, he will make good any, loss caused to the king's revenue from the income (of the Temples and other endowments), and send it to the royal treasury. That is not good. So, appoint a separate officer (for the management of the Temple properties, etc.). If he misappropriates some part of the income, he alone will be ruined.

While making these suggestions, the monarch seems to have had the prevailing condition in his mind.

In the post-Krishnadeva Raya period, we come across a few references, for the first time, in the Temple grants from the Telugu districts of the Vijayanagara empire, to the dignitaries known as *Adhikamvāru*. Four grants belonging to the years 1535 A.D., 1550 A.D., 1554 A.D. and 1554. A.D. consecutively from the village Chinna Ahobilam (Kurnool dt.)[28] refer to this *Adhikamvāru* alongwith the Temple trustees and others as either making grants or giving undertakings to the donors on behalf of the Temple of God Narasimha of that place. The term *Adhikamvāru,* which literally means the superiors, does not appear to have been used here as a synonym for the government revenue officials residing in that place where the religious institution was situated. If that were the case, they would have been mentioned as such specifically with their designations.

Hence, it appears that *Adhikamvāru* were specially appointed by the Vijayanagara government as its representatives, presumably, in line with the new policy initiated by Krishnadeva Raya and were posted at the place of the Temples. They probably belonged to the Religious Endowments Department at the centre and their position was like that of the Temple Executive Officers of the modern period. The above inscriptions also enable us to make the following few inferences in this regard. They participated in the management of the Temple affairs one half of the government. They supervised the work of the trust-boards of the Temples and prevented the mismanagement of their properties and the misappropriation of their revenue. They, along with the trustees, appointed the necessary Temple servants and supervised the payment of their salaries and distribution of food offerings. They also ensured the execution of the grants made by the donors and the proper conducting of the various services in the Temples. And finally, the also settled the disputes, if any, in the Temples affairs.

In the case of Srikurmam and Simhachalam Temples situated in the Telugu districts of the Oriya kingdom also, we come across, in a number epigraphs belonging to the later Eastern Ganga and Gajapati periods from those places, references to a Temple executive officer known as *Bhōgaparīkṣa*. It has been mentioned already how a number of donative inscriptions from those places mention that the donations to those Temples were made during the authority of such and such a *Bhōgaparīkṣa* with the specific mention of his name sometimes alongwith that of *Kaliṅgaparīkṣa.*[29] It appears from these epigraphs that *Bhōgaparīkṣa,* appointed by the government, acted as the Temple executive officer and represented the government on the administration of those Temples. The fact that the *Kaliṅgaparīkṣa.,* the provincial governor, also acted sometimes, as *Bhōgaparīkṣa,* confirms the inference that he was a government official.[30] The *Bhōgaparīkṣa* designee appears to have been liable for quick transfer.[31] The importance of this office is indicated by the fact that it was occupied by men of high political and spiritual attainments.[32]

Agents of the royal donors at the Temples: Besidest the executive officers (*Adhikāmvaru*), there were the agents of the royal donors who also had some say in the management of the Temple affairs. The royal donors, the kings, the provincial governors and other important officials, especially in the Vijayanagara empire, it appears, while making endowments (grants of lands or proceeds of taxes) to the religious institutions, sent their own agents with an order (*Rāyasamu*) to the place of the recipient of the grant. The duty of these agents was to see that all the stipulations of the grants made by their masters were fulfilled. They had to give the physical possession of the land to the donee if it was a land-grant. In the case of the grant of the proceeds of the taxes and tolls or remission of the same, they had to see that those financial benefits reached the donee. And finally, they had to see that all the religious services for which the grants were made were performed as stipulated by the donors. These agents are mentioned in the Temple epigraphs variously as *Adhikāri, Kāryakarta* and *Muḍrakarta.* Their participation in the Temple management is indicated in these epigraphs. For instance, a Telugu epigraph of 1521 A.D. from Kanchipuram (Tamilnadu) refers to a certain Narayya as the *Adhikāri* under Sripatayya, a *Rāyasam* (writer) of Krishnadeva Raya.[33] It states that *Adhikāri* Narayya executed the provisions of the endowment made by his master Sripatayya to a Temple of that place. Similarly, an inscription of 1535 A.D. from Chinna Ahobilam (Kurnool dt.) refers to Vithalam Timmarasu as the *Adhikāri* under Chinna Tirumala Rajayya (a Vijayanagara provincial governor).[34] According to this record, the *Adhikāri* (agent) alongwith the *Adhikamvāru* (executive officers as concluded above) and the Temple trustees executed an endowment made by a donor to the Temple of God Narasimha of the place. As these two dignitaries, *Adhikāri* and *Adhikamvāru,* are mentioned side by side in the epigraph as participating in the management of the Temple affairs, it is clear that the former was different from the latter. So, here the term *Ahikāri* is used to denote the agent of a royal donor. Whereas the term *Adhikamvāru* stands for a state representative, that is, the counter-part of the modern Temple executive officer.

Similarly, the *Kāryakartas* (personal secretaries)[35] of the royal donors were sent to execute grants on their behalf. Their participation in the Temple management is indicated in the epigraphs. When *Mahamandalesvara* Nandela Aubaladevamaharaja made, by an order, the lands belonging to the gods and Brahmans in the Tangeda *Seema* into *Sarvamānya* (tax-free), according to an inscription of 1545 A.D. from Tangeda (Guntur dt.), his *Kāryakarta* Papineni executed it by inscribing that order on stone (*Śilāśāśnamu Vēyiṅchināru).* The participation of the *Kāryakarta* of the royal donors in the management of the Temple affairs is clearly indicated in an inscription of 1560 A.D. from Markapur (Cuddapah dt.).[36] It records that Kadarinathappa, the *Kāryakarta* of *Mahamandalesvara* Siddharaju Timmaraju, along with the *Rachakaranamu,* the *Mannevāru,* and the Temple trustees, conferred the revised rates of remuneration upon the servants of the Temple of that place.

The *Mudrakartas* (Officer in-charge of seal) were also present at the Temples, executing the grants made by their masters and participating in the Temple management. According to an epigraph of 1502 A.D. from Markapur (Cuddapha dt.), Muunangi Mallappa, who was the *Mudrakarta* of Madraju Nagappa (a Vijayanagara government official) along with the trustees of the Temple of Chennakesvara of that place gave a grant to the Temple farmers.[37] The participation of *Mudrakarta* in the administration of the Temples during the Vijayanagara period is indicated in the *Rayavachakam* also. Replying to the enquiries made by Veera Narasimha Raya (Tuluva), in the daily routine of his court proceedings, the *Ayyaṅgārs* and the *Ārādhyas* state that the Vaishnava and Saiva shrines in the empire were in a flourishing condition due to the proper care taken by the *Mudrakartas* stationed at those places.[38]

Thus, it appears from all this evidence, that the *Adhikamvāru* were some kind of Temple executive officers belonging, probably, to the religious endowment department of government in the Vijayanagara empire and were kept at the place of the religious institutions on a permanent basis to supervise their affairs. The *Adhikāris*, the *Kāryakartas* and the *Mudrakartaqs* were the agents of the royal donors (kings and the other important officials) sent to the place of the religious institution for a time, till the grants made by them were executed. During their stay at that place they also participated in the management of the affairs of the religious institutions. And the presence of all these officials at the Temple and their involvement in the Temple management ensured their proper administration.

But it cannot be stated, however, that revenue officials of the government, in the case of the Vijayanagara empire, have completely ceased to have any connection with the management of the religious institutions. One of the above mentioned inscriptions from Markapur, (Cuddaphad dt.) belonging to the year 1560 A.D.[39], states that the *Rāchakaranam* (the royal household accountant) and the *Mannevāru* (*Manyagār* or *Pārupatyagār* or tax-collector of the *Sīmas*) along with the *Kāryakarta* (agent of the provincial governor) and the Temple-trustees conferred the revised rates of wages on the servants of the local Temple, indicating their participation in its administration. The participation of even the government village revenue officials in the management of the Temple affairs is indicated in an epigraph of 1529 A.D. from Siddavatam (Cuddaphad dt.).[40] It states that Chittaya Papayya, the *Ūrakaranam* of that village, made, along with the *Sthanikas* and the *Adhikāri*, a land grant to a mason, on behalf of the Temple of Kesava of that place for its repairs.

Thus, the state exercised control and supervisory powers over the management of the affairs of the religious institutions by various means. But it must be remembered, at the same time, that the state control over them was not so much as to infringe on their autonomy and disturb them in their free functioning. In the case of the *Agrahāras* one of the conditions incorporated, usually in the grant itself, was that they were not to be entered by the government officials and soldiers (*Accatta Bhaṭṭa Pravēśamu*). This condition was probably intended to preserve the peaceful atmosphere in the *Agrahāra* village so that the academic and religious activities in them would not be disturbed.

Revenue Department and the Religious Institutions: Another department of the central government, in the case of the Hindu kingdoms, which appears to have had some connection with the religious institutions was the revenue department. This department in the Vijayanagara empire was known as *Athavana* and it had, under its jurisdiction, the entire administration of the revenue of that empire.[41] It has been noted already how the *Pārupatyagāra* or *Maniagāra,* the *Sthalakaranamu,* the *Rāchakaranamu* and the *Ūrakaranamu* (*Grāmakaranamu*), the officials belonging to this department, were associated with the management of the Hindu religious institutions. As the central office of the revenue department maintained registers containing all the details about the revenue matters of the state, a section of it probably looked after the accounts pertaining to the lands of the religious institutions. This section must have maintained registers in which the extent of the land given to the religious institutions and the amount of the tax due from them to the state and the remission if any granted in their favour, were recorded. If any grants of land or proceeds of the taxes or tolls were made by the king, the provincial governor and the other government officials, a copy of the order must have been sent to the department. And also a copy of that order must have been sent to the revenue officials posted in the locality concerned (that is the place where the religious institution was situated). For instance, when Sadasiva Raya granted the remission of several taxes and tolls from several provinces of the empire for the maintenance of certain services at Tirupati, an order (*Rāyasam*) was issued to every ruling officer of the said provinces, *Nādus,* and the Temple trustees for guidance.[42] Similarly Venkatadri, the governor of Kandanavaolu Rajya of the Vijayanagara empire, when he, with the permission of his king Sadasiva Raya, exempted the *Mahājanas* of several *Agrahāras* from the payment of certain dues, issued an order to the *Doras (Amaranāyakas) Pārupatyagāras, Rāyasamvāru, Avasaramvāru* and *Rāchakarnālu,* connected with the administration of the *Sīma* (district) prohibiting them from collecting these dues.

Even when the Temple trustees made a grant of land belonging to the Temple, either to an outsider or to its own servants for executing its works, the government's revenue officials like the *Sthalakaranamu* and *Grāmakaranamu,* posted in the loally where the Temple was situated, appear to have been informed of the same. In some cases, the grant appears to have been made in their presence and with their signatures on it, as an attestation. An inscription of 1516 A.D. from Devagudi (Cuddapah dt.) which records the grant of some land by the trustees of Talakantidevi Temple of that place to certain people for having constructed the Temple compound wall, contains, at the end of it, the signature (*vrālu*) of the *Sthalakaranam* Lingaraja Basavayya.[43] The presence of this local revenue official at the time of the grant and his attestation to it, indicates his participation in the management of that Temple. It was intended, probably, to enable him to take a note of the transfer of the ownership of the land and enter it in the government revenue registers. Thus, the revenue department's permission for the transaction is implied. A similar procedure seems to have been adopted in the Muslim state. Whenever a grant of land or the proceeds of taxes or tolls was made to a religious institution, either by the royal donors or the private individuals, the revenue officials of the government posted in that locally where the institution was situated, were informed about the same. For example, the Qutbshahi *Farmān* of 1585 A.D. which was issued to confirm the grant of the village Madhol to the Chisti Saint, Hussain Shah Wali, was addressed to *Karkūnan* and *Dēsāiyān,* the revenue officials of the Arki-Paragana in which that village was situated. Those revenue officials were instructed not to disturb the amount of revenue from that village.[44] Similarly, another Qutbshahi *Farmān,* dated 1607 A.D. which records the renewal of the grant of allowance of Rs. 200 for the maintenance of the Mosque of Hussain Shah Wali situated in the Golkonda fort, was also addressed to the *Kārkūnan* and *Dēsāiyān* for information.[45]

Government enquiry about the management of the Religious Institutions and the redressal of grievances: The proper functioning of the religious institutions during the period was also ensured, to some extent, by the personal enquires about their working, the redressal of grievances, and the settlement of disputes, if any, by the kings and their subordinate officials from time to time. It is to be remembered that this was in addition to the keeping of the government representatives at the places of the religious institutions and sending the agents of the royal donors periodically to those places.

The keen personal interest and concern evinced by some of the Vijayanagara rulers for the welfare of the religious institutions in their empire is indicated in the *Rayavachakamu.* It states that Veera Narasimha, the predecessor of Krishnadeva Raya of Vijayanagara empire, used to summon the concerned officials every day to the court and enquire about the working of the religious institutions and their difficulties etc.[46]

The kings, their ministers, and other subordinate officials also visited the shrines and especially the popular among them, situated in their dominions, on various occasions. They, sometimes, visited them in connection with their military campaigns and other official tours. Though these royal tours and campaigns were undertaken for the explicit purpose of territorial conquests or to bring back the recalcitrant subordinate under control, the rulers availed these opportunities to visit the shrines on their way. On such occasion, they received representations from the authorities of the religious institutions for additional patronage. They also entertained complains about their mismanagement or misappropriation of their revenue or any other dispute that affected their normal functioning. They either personally looked into those grievances and tried to redress them on the spot or authorized somebody for the purpose. Many epigraphs and local-records attest to this type of activities of the rulers, besides their munificent gifts to the religious foundations. According to the *Kaifiyat* of Ramesvaram (Cuddapah dt.), Krishnadeva Raya visited that place (Ramesvaram) on his way to the siege of Kondavidu. On that occasion, the *Sthanikas* of Mukti

Ramesvara Temple made a representation to him and requested him to grant more revenue for the Temple, stating that the existing provision was not sufficient for the proper conduct of the Temple services. And the monarch is said to have granted one more village immediately.[47]

Even the government officials like ministers and provincial governors appear to have made it a point to enquire into the working of the religious institutions located in the neighborhood of their campaigns or tours, and to ascertain their satisfactory and proper functioning. According to an interesting epigraph of 1477 A.D. from Attirala (Cuddapah dt.), one Avasaram Annamarasayya, an important official under Saluva Narasimha Raya, visited the village Araturevula on the day of *Gōkulashṭami,* while camping at Siddhavatam, and enquired into the affairs of the Temples of that place. Finding that the worship in those Temples had been stopped due to the mismanagement of their revenue, including that coming from the excise duty (*tālla-eeṅdula-Suṅkamu*) the above said official rectified it and arranged for the proper conduct of worship in those Temples.[48]

The government of the day did not hesitate even to punish the Temple officials, when it found that they indulged in the misappropriation of Temple property. According to an inscription from Tirumalai-Tirupati, Saluva Narasimha, the Vijayanagara emperor, when he visited the place, ordered, as a punishment, the confiscation of the house and house-site of Nambi-Sirappayya, the Temple priest, who had misappropriated the jewellery of God Venkatesvara.[49]

Sometimes, the government had to settle the disputes among the Temple servants which affected the worship and services in certain Temples. An inscription belonging to the last quarter of 16th century A.D. from Ontimitta (Cuddapah dt.) refers to a dispute between the artisans and priests of the Raghunayaka Temple of that place over certain privileges connected with the car-festival and its settlement by a Vijayanagra subordinate Mattla Ananta Rajaiha.[50] Another epigraph from Sambaturu (Cuddapah dt.) of 1551 A.D. also refers to the settlement of a dispute between the trustees of the local Chennaraya Temple and the Ayyagars regarding sharing of certain house-sites and lands, by Narasingayya Deva Maharaja, the Vijayanagara governor of Gandikota *Sīma*[51].

Sometimes the government appears to have delegated these judicial powers to its local officers. An epigraph from Tirupati village (Godavari dt.) states that during the reign of Kapileswara Gajapati, when the *Mahājanas* of that place were unjustly enjoying the land of the local Temple, Raghudeve Narendra, the Viceroy of Rajamahendravaram province, interfered in the matter and authorized the treasury officer and the chief priest of the Temple to enquire into the matter and restore the land to the Temple.[52]

GOVERNMENT PROTECTION TO THE RELIGIOUS INSTITUTIONS AND THEIR PROPERTIES

Protection was offered by the government to the properties of religious institutions. Due to the liberal patronage extended by the rulers and their pious subjects, these religious institutions came to possess lot of properties, both movable and immovable, and became immensely wealthy. This wealth especially of the Hindu Temples attracted, sometimes, the greedy attention of thieves, robbers and even foreign invaders. It may be remembered that the wealth of the religious institutions was one of the factors which attracted the early Muslim invasion upon the country south of Vindhyas.

The routine arrangements made locally either by the religious institutions themselves or by their donors, who appointed watchmen and made provision for their maintenance, ensured the protection of their properties from thieves and robbers, in normal times.[52]

In addition to this, the government also extended protection to the village and other properties of the religious institutions through its own police, system, which was as well meant for guarding its own villages. The references, in the epigraphs, to the payment by the religious institutions of the military cess or the police tax in the form of *Durgadannāyi-vartanan, Kāvali-kānike* and *Talārikatnam* to different officials of the government, which would be discussed in the following pages, provide an ample testimony of the responsibility, the government of the day took for protecting their properties.

Sometimes, even the above arrangements made for that purpose proved to be inadequate and the government had to make special arrangements for the same. According to a local record, an adventurer called Yakarla Yarrama Nayudu troubled the Brahmans of the Rollamadugu *Agrahāra* very much by committing thefts in that village, during the reign of Krishnadeva Raya of Vijayanagara, and obliged them to abandon that *Agrahāra* and migrate to another village known as Rayavara. Later on, the Raya who came to know the plight of the people of that village and its neighbourhood, is said to have appointed the same Nayudu, who committed the thefts, as the *Kāvalgar* of that locality to protect the people and the pilgrims passing from that locality from the bandits.[54] According to an epigraph from Goturu village (Cuddapah dt.), during the reign of Sadasiva Raya the Temple-village of Puspagiri which was also an *Agrahāra,* was plundered by robbers.[55] This epigraph records the grant of *Neṭṭurupaṭṭu* (an endowment made to the person who died fighting for the sake of others) by the Brahmans of Pushpagiri to one Perugu Basivi Nayudu who had lost his life while fighting those robbers. This Nayudu appears to have been deputed by the government to protect that *Agrahāra.*

The Hindu state felt it an obligation to provide the necessary protection not only to the religious institutions and their properties but also to the pilgrims visiting them. Especially the Hindu Temples used to attract, as they do now, throughout the year, a large number of devotees. Particularly, during the days of their annual festivals, thousands of pilgrims used to flock from far and wide to some of the popular shrines like those of Tirupati, Srisailam, Ahobilam and Simhachalam. We know from the Portuguese accounts of the 16th century that, a large number of pilgrims from the whole of East Coast used to come to Tirupati to attend its annual festival.[56] Journeys along the public roads, followed by the pilgrims proved, sometimes, risky and insecure. These pilgrim routes, especially in the forest areas, were the haunts of bandits and wild animals who caused havoc to the pilgrims. The bandits not only robbed the pilgrims of their belongings but sometimes in their greed for money even killed them. On the whole, the pilgrims had to suffer considerable hardships while journeying to the shrines. The atrocities of the robbers along the pilgrims routes, sometimes, affected the normal flow of pilgrims to the shrines and indirectly affected their income and functioning. In order to protect the pilgrims from robbers and wild animals, the Hindu government during this period used to post special officers with contingents of soldiers to guard the roads and passes leading to the pilgrim centres. The Dasaripalle *Kaifiyat* states that, while Achyutadeva Raya was ruling at Vijayanagara, robbers killed traders and pilgrims and robbed them of their valuables at the Jyoti pass in the Nallamalai hill ranges (Kurnool dt.) on the highway leading to the shrine of Ahobilam. As a result, the flow of pilgrims and traders from the places like Baddevolu, Khambam Porumamilla to Ahobilam, during the days of the Temple annual festival, was affected. Achyutadeva Raya, who was appraised of the situation, according to the same source, appointed one Siddappanayudu to curb the activities of the robbers and to make the passage of the pilgrims in that route safe.[57]

But in times of political disturbances or civil war and especially when the central government was not strong enough to ward off the foreign invasions or curb the anti-religious activities of its subordinates the position of the religious institutions became still vulnerable. This, in turn, increased the responsibility of the government to protect them all the more. The fateful battle of Rakshasi Tangadi, which weakened the position of the Vijayanagara empire, may also be said to have disastrously affected the fortunes of the Hindu religious institutions in the Telugu districts of that empire. We find a number references, in the local records and inscriptions, to the plunder and destruction of the Hindu Temples by the invaders. Even the local Hindu chiefs, upon whom the hold of the central government was weakened in the post-Tallikota period, did not hesitate to plunder these institutions. The Hande chiefs of Anantapur, one of the Vijayanagara subordinates in alliance with the Qutbshahi army robbed the Temple of Ahobilam of its wealth and disrupted the worship in it. Sri Ranga I, the

Vijayanagara monarch, according to an inscription of 1584 A.D. from Ahobilam, had to send an army under Kondaraju Venkataraju and Tirumalaraju to recover the Temple and renew worship in it.[58] Similarly, the wealth the Tirupati Temple during the period of Achyutadeva Raya, tempted the Portuguese of the west-coast of India to plan a plundering raid on it. But that was averted by the timely arrangements made for its protection by the Vijayanagara government.[59]

GOVERNMENTS'S FISCAL POLICY TOWARDS THE RELIGIOUS INSTITUTIONS

No doubt the government extended patronage in the shape of grant of lands, cash, proceeds of revenue etc. to the religious institutions, and as noted before, the patronage of the government was the mainstay of their finances. But it should be remembered, at the same time, the government did not exempt these institutions from its fiscal regulation. The latter, like the ordinary citizens, had to share the state's financial burden. There is ample evidence to show that the properties of the religious institutions and those of their functionaries, though recognized, in principle as taxes-free endowments (*Sarvamānya*),[60] were liable to pay various taxes which contributed considerably to the state exchequer. Even the devotees visiting these shrines had to pay certain taxes. The epigraphic evidence to the conversion of the endowments granted in the previous period, into tax-free endowments and the granting of various remissions and commissions to them by the rulers, also make it clear that they did not always necessarily enjoy tax exemptions.

From the inscriptions we gather that various taxes were collected by the governments of the Hindu kingdoms from the Hindu religious institutions in their dominions.

Taxes on the lands owned by the Religious Institutions: As land revenue was one of the basic sources of its income, the Hindu state collected various taxes on the lands of the religious institutions.

During the Kakatiya period a tax called *Parapaṅgamu* appears to have been levied on the lands owned by the religious institution.

An inscription of 1303 A.D. from Tadikonda Village (Guntur dt.) refers to this tax as Kakatiya government's due from the Temple of Kamesvara of that place, on its dry and wet lands.[61] This tax means one fourth share of rent on the lands granted to gods and Brahmans.[62]

The Vijayanagara and Gajapati governments appear to have levied a tax known as *Śrōtriyas* on all the cultivable land and owned by the Temples, the *Maṭhas* and the *Agrahāras*. An inscription of 1448 A.D. from the village Parachuru (Guntur dt.) refers to the tax *Śrōtrīya-katnalu* due to the Gajapati government on the *Mānya* lands belonging to the Brahmans of *Agrahāras* and the Saiva and Vaishnava Temples of that places.[63] It records their remission by a certain Inkolani Tirumala Reddi. Similarly an inscription of 1563 A.D. from Siruvolla village (Rayalaseema) also refers to this tax *Srōtrīyas* as due from the Temple villages (*Dēvata-grāmas*) and *Agrahāras* on their endowment lands (*Kuṭra vrittulu*) till then collected by the Vijayanagara government, and their exemption by Ahobalayya, a provincial governor under Sadasiva Raya.[64] This tax *Śrōtrīya* means a low-quit-rent.[65] Normally, the lands owned by the religious establishments got a preferential treatment in this regard compared to the lands owned by the peasants in the *Bhandāravāda* villages, that is, the villages owned by the government. Though it is very difficult to give the exact rates of taxation in these two cases, it can be stated that the religious institutions paid land-tax at a lower rate than that paid by the ordinary peasent. This tax collected from the religious institutions in the Tamil districts of the Vijayanagara empire was known as *Jōdi*.[66]

Kaṭnam, Kānike and *Veṭṭi-vēmulu* are some of the other taxes collected by the Hindu governments on the lands belonging to the religious institutions. These taxes, beside that of *Śrōtrīya* are mentioned in an epigraph of 1544. A.D. from Kotapadu village (Kurnool dt.) as dues payable to the palace (government) by the *Mahājanas* of Kotapadu and Kesanipalle *Agrahāras*.[67] N. Venkataramanayya defines *Katnam* and *Kānike* as taxes that originated from the practice of making periodical presents to the superiors.[68] And *Veṭṭi-vēmulu* means a tax paid in lieu of *Veṭṭi* (unpaid labour).[69]

A few more taxes collected by the Hindu governments from the religious institutions, either on their lands or on the produce, are mentioned in the epigraphs of the period. An epigraph of 1314 A.D. from the village Penumuli (Guntur dt.) refers to the taxes *Gaḍḍuga* (a kind of tax or fee), *Māḍa* (a tax paid in cash) *Kānike* (a present to the government official), *Puṭṭi-pahindi* (a tax paid in cash on each *Puṭṭi* of land), *Puṭṭikolupu* (the measured heap of grain to be presented to the Temple on the produce of a *puṭṭi* of land), and *Upakriti* (an offering consecrated by long use and paid to the king or officials of state) which were due from the lands belonging to the Temples and *Mahajanas* in 22 villages to the government.[70] An inscription of 1558 A.D. from Mangalagiri village (Guntur dt.) mentions, besides some of the above mentioned taxes. *Siddhāyamu* (a faxed assessment on land in accordance with revenue records or a tax) and *Radelu* (meaning not known) paid by the people of all castes living in that Temple village, to the government.[71] Another inscription of 1581-82 A.D. from Bukkapatnam village (Anantapur dt.), mentions *Nagari-birāda* (the same as *Nagari-kaṭnam,* a tax or present paid to the government), *Birudulu* (a kind of tax in coin) and *Āsavechchālu* (meaning not known) as dues on the lands owned at Bukkasagaramu and Anantapuram by the Temple of Chaudeswari of Krottacheruvu-Bukkasagaram to the government and their remission by Megoti Timmanayudu, an agent of the Vijayanagara king.[72]

That the government collected the water-cess from the religious institutions for the use of its tank for irrigating their lands, is known from an inscription of 1587 A.D. from a village (Nellore dt.).[73] It states that a certain Damera Timmanayudu remitted that water-cess (*Neella-pullari*) due on the lands of the Temple of Ganga of the place.

Taxes on live-stock of the Religious Institutions: the government levied taxes even on the properties in live-stock (*Jeevādhanamu*) belonging to the religious institutions. Especially the Hindu Temples of the period, maintained a large number of cattle which included cows, bullocks, buffaloes, goats and sheep for their use. The government collected the grazing tax called *Pullari* from these institutions for permitting the grazing of their cattle in the government waste lands. An inscription 1314 A.D. from the village Penumuli (Guntur dt.) refers to this tax as *Paśuvula-pullari.*[74] It states that Errayalenka, the gate-keeper of Kakatiya Prataparudra II remitted this grazing tax due to the government from the Temples and the *Mahājanas* in the 22 villages. An inscription of 1336 A.D. from the village Tangeda (Guntur dt.) refers to the *Pullari* as a due to the government from the herdsmen of the Temple of Ghantala Ramanathadeva of that place and its remission by the orders of Tangeda Madala Nayudu who was ruling that region.[75] This tax is referred to as *Śūlavari* (Tamil word) in an epigraph of 1427 A.D. from Tiruttani village.[76] It quotes an order of the Vijayanagara king that no taxes other than this tax (*Śūlavari*), payable to the treasury at Chandragiri, should be collected from the Temples of that province including the Temple of Tiruttani village.

Taxes on pilgrims and other Religious taxes: The Hindu governments of the period used to collect certain taxes from the devotees who came in thousands to the Hindu shrines on festival days. At Tirupati, according to an inscription of 1534 A.D. from that place, *Pērāyam* was levied by the Vijayanagara government from the devotees during the days of *Purուttāsi-Tirunāl* or *Brahmōtsavam.*[77] If further states that Krishnadeva Raya granted the proceeds of that tax for the services of Sri Venkatesvara Temple of that place. An epigraph of 1405 A.D. from the village Tamballapalli (Chittoor dt.) refers to the tax *Kānike* (of 25 *Honnu*) derived from the devotees during the *Śivarātri* festival as a due to the government.[78] It is not known whether this tax, levied by the Vijayanagara government on the devotees, was similar in nature to the Pilgrim-tax collected by the Mohammedan governments. It is known that in the 12th century A.D., the Pilgrim-tax was collected at Bahuloda (Gujarat) by the municipality on behalf of the Hindu government.[79]

There are references, in some of the inscriptions of the period of Devaraya II, to a tax called *Vibhūti-kānike* as a royal due from the devotees visiting the Hindu Temples.[80] These inscriptions coming from both the Telugu and the Tamil districts reveal that this tax collected from all the Saiva and Vaisnava temples of Chandragiri-*rājya* by the Vijayanagara government till 1427 A.D., was remitted by the royal order in the year. This tax appears to have been a voluntary fee paid by the devotees while receiving the sacred ashes, and collected by the Temples on behalf of the government.

The government of the period appears to have collected fines or penalties for offences or crimes in the villages belonging to the religious institutions. A Telugu epigraph of 1556 A.D. from the village Bhupatisamudramu (Bellary dt. Karnataka) refers to this tax (*Tappuchēsinavarivalla-vachchina-aparādham-pannu*) as due of the government from the *Agrahāra* of Bhupatirayasamudramu alias Sarvajnakriyasaktipuram.[81] It records the remission of this fine alongwith several other taxes by the Vijayanagara provincial governor *Mahammandalesvara* Ramaraju Tirumalayyadeva.

That the Hindu government of the period levied religious taxes, on the people in the villages belonging to the religious institutions, is known from a few inscriptions. For example, an epigraph of 1549 A.D. from the village Jillella (Cuddapah dt.), refers to the religious tax known as *Mahārāja-prayōjanālu* levied by the government on the people in the village of Jillella owned by the Temple of Ahobilam Narasimha.[82] This tax seems to have been levied by the Vijayanagara government on the villages (held both by the government and the religious institutions) in certain location. The amount was utilized for the maintenance of deities whose protection was sought for the welfare of the villagers.[83]

Police-taxes or Military Cess: The Hindu state collected various taxes from the religious institutions for performing police functions in the villages belonging to these institutions. These taxes were paid for providing protection to their villages and properties from thieves and robbers.

An important tax belonging to this category, paid by the Hindu religious institutions, was *Durgavartana* or *Durgadannāyivartana.* It was paid to the commandant of a fort in return for the protection offered by him to the villages in the neighbourhood of his fort. According to the *Kaifiyat* of Chennur (Cuddapah dt.) an amount of sixty *Varāhas* was fixed as *Durgavartana*, to be paid by some eight villages belonging to the Temples and *Maṭha* of Puspagiri to Gandikotadurgam per annum, by an official of Achyutadeva Raya in the year 1541 A.D.[84] An inscription of 1530 A.D. from Mopuru village (Cuddapah dt.) also refers to *Durgadannāyivartana* amounting to 235 *Varāhas* per annum, payable by villages belonging to the Temple of Bhairesvara of that village to the Gandikota fort.[85] But a record of 1565 A.D. from the same village (Mopuru)[86] refers to both Durgavartana and *Dannāyivartana* separately as if they were two different taxes payable to the Gandikota fort by the *Dēvatagrāmas* (Temple villages) and *Agrahāras* in the Gandikota *Sīma*. But they appear to be the two different names of the same tax but used here in juxtaposition. In any case, the collection of this military-cess from the Temples implies the responsibility of the government to protect the wealth of the Hindu religious institutions from thieves, robbers and even foreign invaders. As this tax is prominently mentioned in the epigraphs of the Rayalaseema districts which formed a part of the Vijayanagara empire throughout the period under study, it is not unreasonable to infer that it was collected for the religious institutions only by the Vijayanagara government. And the counterparts of this tax, in the Tamil and the Canarese areas of the Vijayanagara empire were *Dannāyakara-magamai* and *Dannāyakara-swāmya* respectively.[87]

A damaged inscription of 1534 A.D. from Rayachoti village (Cuddapah dt.) refers to the tax *Grāmakāvali* as a due to the government from Mandem and other villages belonging to the Temple of God Visvesvara of Rachavidu, and the grant of the proceeds of that tax to the same Temple.[88] Similarly an epigraph of 1547 A.D. from the village Kattaragandla (Cuddapah dt.) refers to the *Kāvali-kānike* due to the government from the villages belonging to the Temples and *Agrahāras* in Gandikota *Sīma* and their remission (along with those of the *Amaragrāmas* and *Bhandāravādagrāmas*) by Nandyala Timmaraja under Sadasiva Raya.[89] These two terms *Grāma-kāvali* and *Kāvali-kānike* are used to denote the same tax to be paid to the *Kāvalgār* for protecting the villages belonging to the religious institutions. *Kāvalgār* was a police official under the Vijayanagara government and was in-charge of policing in the villages of a *Sthala* (equivalent of modern Taluq). He appears to have been a subordinate of *Durgadannāyaka* (provincial military commandant). The above mentioned police taxes appear to have been collected even on the lands belonging to functionaries of the religious institutions. A damaged inscription of Vijayanagara period from Paluguralllapalli village (Cuddapah dt.) refers to this tax as due on the lands granted to the doness for the musical services in the Temples of Somesvara and Chennakesvara of that place and its remission for Temple services.[90] The difference between *Kāvali-kānike* paid by the Temple servants on their *Inām* lands and *Durgavartana* paid by the Temples on their villages, to the government is proved by a reference to these two taxes side by side in an inscription of 1545 A.D. from the Village Mopuru (Cuddapah dt.) as dues to the government.[91]

Finally, an inscription of 1443 A.D. from a village in Prakasam district refers to another tax of this category known as *Talāri-kantam* which was due to the government from the Temple of God Narasimha of that place.[92] It records the remission of this tax by *Dalavāyi* Devaraya Vadayulu, an officer under Pratapadeva Raya of Vijayanagara. It was levied to be paid as remuneration to the *Talāri,* who like the police-*patel* or *Kōtwāl* of modern times, performed the police functions in the villages and towns. He protected them from brigands and thieves. He was one of the *Ayagārs* of the village during the Vijayanagara period and received some remuneration and *Inām* lands for his services.[93] During the days of the Temple festivals when a number of devotees used to flock to these institutions, the services of this official, to keep watch and ward, appear to have been of utmost importance.

Taxes on Professions in the villages of the Religious Institutions: The government levied various taxes on professions and properties of the private individuals in the *Devadāna, Maṭhapura* and *Brahmadēya* villages, as in the case of the ordinary villages. An inscription of 1546 A.D. from a village of Cuddapah districts refers to *Maṅgala-pannu* (a tax on barbers) and *Dommara-pannu* (a tax on acrobats) collected by the government from the villages belonging to the Temple of Tiruvengalanatha of Mutukuru.[94] An epigraph of 1555 A.D. from Markapuram village (Kurnool dt.) refers to *Iḷḷari* (house-tax which amounts to the property tax), *Gānugari* (tax on oil-mills), *Maggari* (tax on looms), *Mudrayam* (a duty levied to stamp the heaps of grain brought for sale in the market) and *Aṅdiśāṅtiśuṅkam* (perhaps a tax on professions of various castes) paid by the 18 villages belonging to the Temple of Chennakesava of Markapuram.[95]

The government got some income from the tax on the profession of prostitution which prevailed at the places of the religious institutions and especially in the annual Temple-fairs. There is a reference, in an inscription of 1556 A.D. from Markapur village (Kurnool dt.) to the collection by the Vijayanagara government of *Laṅja-suṅkam* i.e., a levy on prostitutes, at Markapuram during the days of the annual festivals of the Temple of Chennakesava of that place.[96] It records the grant of the proceeds of that tax for the Temple services by Madaraja Narapadeva, a government official. Similarly, an inscription of 1557 A.D. from the village Chedalavada (Nellore dt.) also refers to the tax *Ranku-talārikamu* levied on prostitutes by the government during the days of the annual festival of the Temple of God Raghunayaka of the village.[97] It records the remission of that tax during certain days of that festival (from the day of flag-hoisting to *Phālguna Bahula* 30) by Mandapati Appalaraju, a Vijayanagara government official.

From this, it can be assumed that the prevalence of prostitution even in the annual fairs held at the sacred shrines of this period is an established fact. References to the levy of tax on that profession and its remission on certain occasions by the Vijayanagara government officials clearly show that this profession, like any other profession in that empire, was recognized, regulated and taxed by the government. This evidence supports the statement of Abdur Razak that the pay of 12,000 *fanams* per day paid to the 12,000 police men of the city of Vijayanagara was derived from the proceeds of the brothels.[98] And the term *Lañja-talārikamu* applied to this tax on prostitutes as mentioned above also suggests that, probably, it was a due to the *Talāri,* the official in-charge of police functions, either in a village or a town.

Tolls on merchandise: The government, during this period, used to get a considerable income by levying tolls on various articles of merchandise sold at the shrines on normal days as well as on festival days and even on the roads leading to these shrines. An inscription of 1443 A.D. from Singarayakonda village (Prakasam dt.) refers to the tolls levied by the government on various categories of merchandise, including slaves and live-stock such as horses, bullocks, cows, buffaloes etc., carried for sale on the road leading to the Temple of Narasimha of the same village and to their remission by an official of Devaraya II during the seven days of the festival of the God.[99] Another epigraph of 1515 A.D. from Srisailam (Kurnool dt.) also refers to the tolls levied on the loads of pack-horses, bullocks, asses and head-loads, and collected from the merchants coming to Srisailam *Jātara* by the government and to their remission by Krishnadeva Raya who visited that place along with his queens.[100]

Sometimes, even the merchandise meant for the Temple use and even when it was carried by the Temple transport system (bulls and carts), was not exempted from the government tolls. An epigraph of 1547, A.D. from Porumamilla (Cuddapah dt.) records the collection of tolls, by the government, on articles of merchandise carried by the Temple bulls from Udayagiri and Pakanati *Sīmas to the* Sakali *Sīma* and meant for the services of God Ahobilesvara of the same place.[101]

That the Government collected tolls on articles of food meant for the Temple functionaries is indicated in an epigraph of 1465 A.D. from the village Chodavaram (Vizag dt.). It states that the toll or duty on salt (*Uppu-gaḍyam*) due to the government from the members of the board of trustees (*Sthānamvāru*), dancers (*Sāni-naṭṭuvulu*) belonging to the Temple of God Vallabharaja of Dattada, were remitted by a government official.[102]

Oppressive Taxation and exemptions by the government: It is to be noted that the method of collection of these taxes and tolls from the religious institutions was, sometimes, oppressive. The tax-collectors, sometimes, became rapacious and extracted, without the knowledge of the government, certain taxes which had been exempted. During periods of political anarchy and civil war, the oppression of the revenue officials became all the more increased. This resulted, in some cases, in the desertion of the people of the villages belonging to the religious institutions and necessitated the government intervention.

An inscription of 1309 A.D. from Nandaluru village (Cuddapah dt.) states that the *Mahājanas* of Nelandaluru *Agrahāra* complained to Kakatiya Pratapa Rudra II about the unjust collection of taxes (*Suṅkamu, Sādamu* and *Avanāya*) from that *Agrahāra* village and its four hamlets by the previous rulers (*Kritamu Ēlinavāru*).[103] It records their remission by that Kakatiya ruler. Similar cases of oppression in the collection of taxes and tolls from religious institutions are known from the inscriptions of the Vijayanagara period. According to an epigraph of 1553 A.D., the *Dēvadāna* and *Brahmadēya* lands which had been tax-free since the time of Chikkadevarāya were assessed in kind and cash owing to certain political disturbances.[104] It records that Bhandarada Timma, a Vijayanagara official rendered them once again tax-free. Another inscription of 1538 AD states that several taxes had been unjestly imposed by the previous rulers on tax-free lands held by the Temple of Perusomula village (Kurnool dt.)[105] It further states that they were remitted by Hanumayyadeva, a Vijayanagara official. N. Venkataramànayya quotes from a contemporary Telugu work as follows: "The Turukas of Golkonda eat cows; but Bacamarasa consumes all the Brahmanas of Kondavidu; which of them better, Turuka or Bacamarasa?".[106] This illustrates how some of the Vijayanagara government officials extracted money from the functionaries of these religious institutions and earned notoriety for themselves.

That the worship in Temples was affected due to the oppressive nature of taxation, is indicated by an inscription of the Vijayanagara period from Nandyala (Kurnool dt.).[107] It states that Virajiyya, the Temple priest of Nandyala, unable to pay *Kānike* and *Kaṭnam*, ran away from his place and he consented to resume his office only after the remission of those taxes by a government official. Similarly, an interesting epigraph of 1547 A.D. from Kommuru village (Guntur dt.) refers to the desertion of the villages belonging to the Agastesvara Temple of that place, due to the unjust collection of certain taxes from the Brahmans and dancing women in those places.[108] It also states that those unjust taxes were remitted by a government official with a view to repopulating those villages.

It is to be remembered, at the same time, that the government used to grant, sometimes, exemptions and remissions of these taxes and tolls. At times, it realized that these levies collected at some of the shrines were detrimental to the Temples and the pilgrims thronging them, and took the wise step of remitting them, at least on festival days. Almost all the epigraphs mentioning these taxes as the dues of the government also refer to the remission of some of them either by the rulers or their representatives on various occasions and for various reasons. These exemptions and remissions were granted, sometimes, on a large scale, to a number of Temples and some other times they benefited only one or two individual Temples.

Rates of Taxes: However, the amount of some of these taxes is mentioned only in a few inscriptions. For instance, an epigraph of 1530 A.D. from Mopuru village (Cuddapah dt.) mentions 60 *Varāhas* as the amount paid per annum as *Durgavartana* by some eight villages belonging to the Temples and *Matha* of Puspagiri to Gandikotadurgamu.[109] Similarly, an inscription of 1555 A.D. from Markapur village (Kurnool dit.) gives the total amount of various tolls *Illari, Pullari,.Gānugari, Maggai, Mudrāyam* and *Andiśānti-śuṅkam* due to the government from the 18 villages belonging to the Temple of Chennaraya of that place, as 150 *Varāhas.*[110] But on the basis of the information like this, it is very difficult to give the rates at which these levies were made. And it is also not possible to know the exact mode of this collection with the help of the evidence available.

6

Relations with the Society

The religious institutions during the period under study were all-comprehensive and multipurpose organizations. Through their many sided activities, they exerted considerable influence on all aspects of the contemporary society. In this chapter, an attempt will be made to assess the impact of their intellectual, political, social-welfare, economic and cultural activities on the society.

The religious institutions, both Hindu and Muslim, contributed to the enrichment of the religious life of the contemporary society. The activities conducted by the religious institutions were responsible for bringing religion within the reach of the common man, making it a living force.

The Hindu religious institutions—the Temple, the *Maṭha* and the *Agrahāra*—profoundly influenced the spiritual life of the contemporary Telugu society. The main purpose of constructing Temples, consecrating the *Archa*-idols in them, and conducting various rituals for them was meant to invite the attention of all the people to congregate and to rouse or substantiate their relationship with God. The rituals and worship, which the priests performed in the Temples on behalf of the society, were believed to promote happiness, welfare and success of the members of the society. The influence emanating from the rituals was also considered to have benefited the devotees.

The daily worship and service of the images of the deities and the grand celebration of their annual festivals created a lot of religious fervour among the people who gathered to witness them. The Temple festivals which consisted mainly of processions and spectacular enactment of mythological episodes had a special significance for the entire community. The bringing of the sacred images or their prototypes (*Utsava Vigrahas*) from the Temples and taking them out in procession in the streets of the village or the town, enabled all the people, including those like untouchables who were, generally, denied entry into the Temple, and the sick and disabled who were unable to go to the Temple to have a Darshan of God.

The recital of sacred hymns, the invoking of Lord's name with His various epithets (*Nāma Saṅkīrtana*) and the exposition of the *Iṭihāsas* and the *Puranas* by eminent religious teachers in the Temple precincts kept up the religious fervour of the people, by adding to their religious knowledge. The music, dance and drama which were performed in the Temples every day and on special occasions, acted as great media of popular religious instruction. These and other arts such as the *Yaksagānas, Harikathas, Kūchipūdi Bhāgavatham* and the like which depicted the religious themes served to created spiritual awakening and religious enthusiasm among the masses.

The spiritual activities pursued by the occupants of the Hindu *Maṭhas* also helped the spiritual enlightenment of the Hindu society. An epigraph of 1298 A.D. from Cuddapah, describes Aghora Sivacharya (probably, the pontiff of the Puspagiri *Maṭha*) with the epithets: *Yama-niyama-prānāyāma-pratyāhāra-dhyāna, Maunānuṣhtāna, Japasamādhisheela Gunasampannulu.*[1] Almost the same qualifications are ascribed to another Aghora Sivacharya, probably the occupant of the same office as that of above mentioned teacher, in an inscription of 1403 A.D. from Somireddipalli village. (Cuddapah dt.).[2] Sri Vidya Sankara, the pontiff of the Advaita *Maṭha* of Sringeri and the spiritual teacher of Vidyaranya, is also described with similar epithets in an undated epigraph from the village Akkampalli (Cuddapah dt.).[3] From these references, it appears that the pontiffs and other occupants of the Hindu *Maṭhas* always engaged themselves in contemplation, meditation, spiritual discussions etc. Their other pursuits appear to have been intense study of the ancient scriptures, their interpretation, and writing commentaries on them in order to popularize their respective religious systems.

The members of the Hindu *Maṭhas* strove not only for attaining the highest spiritual experience for themselves, but also worked for the spiritual wel-being of the society. One important means by which the Hindu *Maṭhas* established their sway over the religious life of Hindu society was the propagation of their respective tenets through their members, and especially their pontiffs. Of course, and for which their occupants dedicated themselves. Various methods were adopted by the members of the various *Maṭhas* to propagate and popularize their religious persuasions among the people. One important method was undertaking of religious tours and conducting discourses. Sri Sankaracharya, the founder of the Advaita *Maṭhas,* while prescribing certain rules and regulations for the pontiffs of the *Maṭhas,* in his *Maṭāmnāyasētu* lays down that:

> the usual tendency of social movement is towards absence of righteousness; inspite of the laws, people are naturally selfish and disturb the social harmony, therefore the responsibility of the acharyas occupying the pontifical seats of the monasteries is very great; they should be always on the alert; should spare no pains to remove the forces of the evil; they should never stay in one place; but should always be moving about within their own appropriate territorial jurisdiction.[4]

This gives us some idea about the high ideals set before the pontiffs of these *Maṭhas* The heavy responsibility of removing the forces of evil, maintaining the righteousness and social harmony was entrusted to them. And they were expected to be always on the move for that purpose.

The preceptors of Hindu *Maṭhas* of the period were, normally, great adepts in preaching and made it the mission of their lives.

Accompanied by their disciples, they toured the country extensively and held religious discourses for the propagation of their respective sects. The religious discourses helped, to a great extent, the dissemination of religious, ethical and moral values to the people in every nook and corner of the country. The *Jiyars* of Ahobila *Maṭha*, during this period, played a very important role in the propagation and spread of Vaishnavism in Andhra desa. Adivan Sathakopa *Jiyar*, the founder of that *Maṭha* carried on vigorous propaganda and established Vishnava faith in the country.[5] Narayana *Jiyar*, the second pontiff of the same *Maṭha* visited Tirupati and stayed there for sometime as part of his religious tours and discourses.[6] *Srimath Vaishnava Siddhānta Pratisthapanachārya*, one of the titles held by Vyasatirtha,[7] the head of the Madhwa *Maṭha* of Krishnadeva Raya's period, clearly indicates the prominent role played by that teacher in the propagation of Vaishnavism in the land. Those religious tours, during which they expounded their philosophy to their followers, enabled them to establish mass contacts.

Another means of religious propaganda carried on by the preceptors of the *Maṭhas* were the religious disputations or debates. These disputations, held between the religious teachers of rival schools, evoked a lot of popular enthusiasm. Normally, the royal court or the precincts of the Temples, provided the venue for such debates. In the course of these debates, each teacher tried to establish the superiority of his own school over that of others. The defeat of one *Āchārya* was, usually, followed by the total conversion of his disciples and followers into the fold of the victorious opponent. The contemporary literature throws ample light on the zealous activities of these religious teachers of various *Maṭhas* and *Samayas* to get as many converts as possible to their faiths from among the kings, their subordinates and subjects.

Through their association with the management of the Temples also, the Hindu *Maṭhas* played a prominent role in moulding the religious life of the society. As noted already, the pontiffs of the *Maṭhas*, as the *Sthānāchāryas*, *Sthānikas* and Supervisors of the Temples, had a voice in the direction of their affairs.

The religious activities pursued in the *Agrahāras* had a beneficial influence on the society. Especially, the sacrifices performed by the occupants of the *Agrahāras* were meant to contribute to the spiritual well-being and material prosperity of the society. The Vedic religion was kept alive in the country mainly because of this sacrificial activity. And in fact, this type of religious activity was confined, during this period, only to the *Agrahāras*.

Similarly, the Mosque, the *Khānqāh*, the *Dargāh* and the *Āshūrkhāna* of Islam, of the period in Andhra Desa, exerted profouned influence on the spiritual life of the contemporary Muslim society. It is a general belief among the Muslims that, the prayers performed in a Mosque purify the heart, control the passions and enable the devotees to always remember God. The occupants, especially, of the *Khānqāhs* lived a life of asceticism and austerity. Their spiritual practices and the instruction given by them in various branches of spiritualism, benefited not only the occupants of those institutions but also the lay followers. The saints were generally believed to have influence with God, and the ability to perform miracles like possessing extraordinary powers of blessing, healing and protective effect. Anything touched by them and handed over to the people was considered efficacious. People used to approach them seeking solution for their problems both spiritual and material. Similar miracles were attributed to the *Dargāhs* and *Āshūrkhānas*. By and large, the spiritual activities of these institutions and their occupants contributed to the welfare of the society. By stressing the higher values of the spirit and by giving the people a ready-made philosophy, they enabled them to face the hard realities of life.

IMPACT OF THE INTELLECTUAL ACTIVITIES

The Religious Institutions of the period were great centres of intellectual activity and considerably enriched the intellectual life of the contemporary society. When there were no regular educational institutions run by the state for imparting education to its subjects, it was the religious institutions that fulfilled this need, to some extent, through their educational activities. This service of promoting learning was rendered by them through their patronage to educational institutions and scholars as part of their establishment.

The Temples: Some of the *Ghaṭikāsthānas* or the schools attached to the Temples, which functioned as the important centres for learning the Vedas and the *Sastras* during the pre-Kakatiya period in the Telugu country,[8] appear to have continued to do so during the period under study also. An inscription of 1404 A.D. from the village Sarpavaram (East Godavari dt.) refers to the school (*Ghaḍiyāramu*) established by a certain Goli Soma Reddi, in the Temple of God Bhavanarayana of Sarpavaramu.[9] It also records the grant of some land for the maintenance of two Brahmans, Aubhala Voju and Singa Voju, probably the teachers connected with that institution. But due to the absence of any further details, it is not possible to know either of its size or of the subjects taught in it. An inscription of 1291 A.D. from Simhachalam (Vizag dt.) gives the interesting information that a Temple donor made an endowment in the Temple of God Narasimha, providing for the teaching of *Kāṇdava Śākha* and *Taittiriya Śākha* by two *Ghaḍiśāsi Brāhmanas,* and the *Purāṇas,* Grammar, Poetry, Dramatreatise, (*Purāṇa vyākaraṇa kāvya nātakabidanālupathiṃpinche*) by three *Viḍivat Brāhmanas.*[10] Another inscription from Simhachalam Temple, dated 1383 A.D., refers to the appointment of a certain Vodya Peddibhatlu for teaching the Vedas (*Vēdādhyayanamu*) to the Brahmans residing in that place, and the provision made for their maintenance from the Temple treasury.[11] So, it is clear that some of the Temples made arrangement for the teaching of not only religious subjects but also secular subjects like Grammar, Drama, Poetry etc., and they maintained different teachers for teaching different subjects. They made provision for the maintenance of the teachers by granting them lands etc. The students were also normally provided with various facilities like food and shelter, free of cost. Of course, these teaching arrangements made in the Temples were generally meant for the Brahman pupils.

Other important sciences cultivated by the Hindu Temples of the period are Astronomy and Astrology. Those two sciences were closely related. A Kannada inscription from Alampur (Mahbubnagar dt.) of the year 1521 A.D. records the grant of an endowment by Gaura Dannayaka Narayanayya (a Vijayanagara official) for the astronomical services in the Temple of Bala Brahmesvara of the place.[12] Astronomers were needed by the Temples to fix the timings for conducting various religious services performed daily and periodically. The *Muhūrtam* or the auspicious time, for the conduct of various religious services in the Temple of Tirupati, in the 16th century, A.D. was fixed by an Astrologer of that Temple known by the name Iyuni Appa.[13]

The religious discourses and debates by eminent religious teachers and scholars which were usually arranged in the precincts of the Temples also helped the spread of knowledge especially of religious character. A copper plate inscription of 1514 A.D. from Pedadandluru village records that in a disputation held in the Temple of Virupaksha of that place, Chauduri Tirumala Somayajulu defeated Avanuri Ananta Sastri; and the victor was granted three villages as gift by Chikkavodayalu.[14] This type of debates, no doubt, helped the scholars to satisfy their ego by establishing their superiority over others. At the same time, they also helped the common people, atleast the educated among them, to acquire religious knowledge.

Besides these, many of the Temples had arrangements in them for the reading of religious scriptures and the recitation of the sacred names of the deity either every day or on certain days of a week. An inscription from Tirupati refers to the grant made by Devaraya II to 24 Brahmans engaged for the *Vēdapārāyanam* in the Sri Venkatesvara Temple of that place, in the year 1433 A.D.[15] Another epigraph of 1545 A.D. from the same place states that Potlapati Timmaraya, a Vijayanagara subordinate arranged for the recitation of *Tiruveṇkatamahatmyam* every day in the presence of the deities, Sri Venkatesvara, Govinda Raja, Achyuta Perumal and Varadaraja Perumal of that place.[16] Similarly an inscription of 1350 A.D. from Simhachalam records the provision made for the reading of *Purusasūktamu* at the time of *Abhishēka* to Lord Narasimha, by one Kesava Bhagavata.[17] Another record of 1396 A.D. from

Simhachalm refers to the recitation of *Viṣnu Stōtram,* by Varadabhatlu at the time of offering the sacred light (*Dhūpāvasaram*) to the God Narasimha of the place.[18] And another epigraph of 1417 A.D. from the same place (Simhachalam) records the provision made for reading the *Purāṇam* and *Narasimha Kavachamu* in the presence of the God Narasimha.[19] No dobut, the reading of the Vedas, the *Purāṇas* and *Sthalamahatmyams* and the recitation of the sacred names of the deity in the Temples on certain occasions was meant for inspiring religious devotion and fervour among the devotees and for popularizing the religion to which that particular shrine belonged. But at the same time, it also helped, to some extent, the spread of theological knowledge among the common masses visiting them.

Finally, the various sculptures and paintings in the Temples and the performance of dance and drama, which were generally based on religious themes from the *Purāṇas,* Epics, etc., greatly helped the dissemination of knowledge both religious and secular among the devotees and especially the illiterate pilgrims frequenting the shrines. In view of the teaching arrangements made in some of the Hindu Temples of this period, it is quite reasonable to infer that they also maintained their libraries attached to them where various manuscripts were preserved. The *Āgamas* insist that the Temple of a first magnitude must have a library attached to it. The *Saṅkīrtana Bhandāram* attached to the Temple of Sri Venkatesvara of Tirupati where the copper plates of thousands of *Saṇkīrtanas* (devotional songs) composed by the musician poets of the famous Tallapaka family were preserved, can be regarded, in a way, as a library.

The Hindu Maṭhas: The Hindu *Maṭhas* of the period were great centres of learning. The promotion of traditional learning besides that of religion, appears to have been one of the primary functions of these institutions.

The members of the *Maṭhas,* especially their pontiffs, besides being religious preceptors, were highly learned and cultured persons, proficient in many branches of learning. They had a number of works, both religious and secular, to their credit. Visvesvara Sivacharya, the founder-pontiff of the Pasupata Golaki *Maṭhas* in

Andhra Desa, was a highly learned Vedic Scholar; and he was the president of the *Vidyā-Maṅtapa* (the hall of instruction) of Kakatiya kings Ganapati's place.[20] The pontiffs of the *Maṭha* of *Tengalai* Srivaishnavas, situated at Ahobilam, were great scholars. Narayana *Jiyyar,* the second head of this *Maṭha,* was the author of *Pūrva Paksha Mīmāmsa, Siddhāṇta Mīmamsa* and *Śrītatva Siddhajnāna.*[21] *Ubhaya Vēdāntāchārya,* the title held by Parankusa *Jiyyar,* the sixth pontiff of the same *Maṭha,* indicates his proficiency in the *Upanishads* and the Tamil *Prabaṇdham.* Likewise, Sri Van Sathakopa *Jiyyar,* the seventh head of the same *Maṭha,* is the author of a Sanskrit Drama *Vāsantika Parinayam.*[22] Many of the heads of the Madhwa *Maṭhas* of the period were also great men of learning. Vyasatirtha, the founder-pontiff of the Vyasa (Madhwa) *Maṭhas* at Tirupati and Vijayanagara wrote a number of works on religion, logic etc. which include *Tarka-tāndava, Nyāyāmrita, Sudhā Maṇdāra Maṇjarī, Mādhwa Tātparya-Chaṇdrika* and commentaries on several *Upanishads.*[23] The titles, *Padavākya Pramānagna* and *Sakala Vidhvajjana-manah-Padmavana-Saupāṣtika.*[24] assumed by this pontiff highlight his scholarship.

Being themselves great scholars and writers, the members of the Hindu *Maṭhas* drew around them a number of scholars and poets and advanced the cause of literature by extending patronage to them. Some of the major *Maṭhas* like Sringeri *Maṭha* appear to have maintained poets and scholars as part of their establishments on the model of the contemporary royal courts. A certain scholar, Vishnu, who wrote *Purushōttama Bhārati Charita* containing an account of the lives of four pontiffs of the Sringeri *Maṭha* during the period of Devaraya I of Vijayanagara is referred to as the *Maṭha Āsthāna Kavi,* (Poet-laurate) of that *Maṭha.*[25] Vamana Bhatta Bana Kavi, the poet who is credited with a number of works in Sanskrit and other languages and who was, honoured in the court of the Reddi kingdom of Kondavidu, described himself in his work, *Sabda-Chandrika* as a spiritual disciple of Vidyaranya of Sringeri *Maṭha.*[26] The *Maṭhādhipatis* encouraged poets and scholars, through their spiritual influence, to compose books on religious themes. Mukti Santabhikshavrittiraya, the head of the Bhikshavritti *Maṭha* of Srisailam in the first quarter of the 15th century A.D., encouraged Telugu poets, Gaurana[27] and Srinatha, to write *Navanātha Charita* and *Śivarātri Mahatmyamu* respectively. The latter dedicated his work to Mummaya Santayya, a disciple and the agent of the above mentioned Guru.[28] Madayagari Mallana, the author of *Rāja Sēkhara Charita* in Telugu, was a spiritual disciple of Aghora Sivacharya of the same Bhiksha *Matha.* In the colophon of his work mentioned above, he describes himself as *Śrīmadaghōra Śivāchārya Guru Karunāviśēśa labda-sārasvata.*[29] Nandi Timmana, the author of *Pārijātāpaharanamu,* describes himself in it as the disciple of Aghora Sivacharya (*Āghōra Śivaguru Śiśyuṇdu*).[30] And Sri Adivan Sathakopa *Jiyyar,* the founder of Ahobila *Maṭha,* was the Guru of Allasani Peddna, the poet-laureate of Krishnadeva Raya's court. Peddana describes his spiritual teacher as the asylum of all learning.[31]

The *Hindu Maṭha* served a useful purpose as a teaching and disciplinary institution. It was one of the most important agencies of defusing knowledge among people. Most of the *Maṭhas* appear to have had, in them, teaching arrangements meant to benefit not only their occupants but also the outside students who came for that purpose. The students were normally provided with free-boarding and lodging facilities by the *Maṭha.* In the Golaki *Maṭha* at Mandaram of the Kakatiya period, there were three teachers for teaching the Vedas and five teachers for teaching logic, literature and the *Agamas;* provision was made for the maintenance of students free of cost with lodging and boarding facilities.[32]

The curriculum of the subjects which were studied and in which instruction was given in the *Maṭhas* was both religious and secular, of course, with a stress on the former. The Advaita *Maṭhas* appear to have stressed the study of Brahmanic or Vedic literature. The *Maṭhas* belonging to the theistic sects such as Saivism and Vaisnavism, must have stressed the study of their respective theologies. The subjects in which instruction was given in the Golaki *Maṭha* including religious subjects like Rig, Yajur and Sama Vedas, *Āgamas,* and secular subjects like logic and literature.[33] The Lingayat *Maṭhas* concentrated on the study of the *Āgamas* and allied Veera Saiva literature.[34] Vedic hymns, *Upanishads,* Tamil *Prabhandhams, Dharma Sāstras* and *Purānas* were studied in the Srivaishnava and the Madhwa *Maṭhas.*[35] Some of the theistic *Maṭhas* like those of the Veera Saivas and *Tengalai* Srivaisnavas chose the vernacular languages as the medium of instruction.

Most of the *Maṭhas* of the period, which played such an important and crucial role in the promotion of the religious and secular learning in the country, appear to have maintained their own libraries. There is a reference in two inscriptions of the year 1432 A.D. from Sringeri (Karnataka) to the existence of a library attached to the Advaita *Maṭha* of that place.[36] They also make a mention of two librarians, Kavi Krishnabhatta and Kavi Sankara Bhatta of the same library. This indicates that this particular library was well-stocked and was systematically maintained. The librarian must have been in-charge of the various manuscripts composed by the successive pontiffs of that *Maṭha* and its various collections. For the proper maintenance of the library of Sringeri *Maṭha,* Bukka II of Vijayanagara made an endowment.[37]

In view of the numerous collection of manuscripts consisting of theological works, biographies of the pontiffs and the other hagiological works, which have been found in the various *Maṭhas,* it is quite reasonable to infer that the library of the *Maṭha* was a fairly well-recognised institutions, though they are very rarely referred to. The libraries of the *Maṭhas* (and Temples), thus, became the repositories of spiritual and secular knowledge and ensured the survival of at least a part of the legacy of our ancient literature.

The Agrahāras: Similarly, the *Agrahāras* of the period were important centres of intellectual activity. In fact, they occupy among the Hindu religious institutions, the foremost place, as the promoters of traditional learning. The promotion and the propagation of learning was one of the important and basic purposes for which they were created and granted to the Brahman scholars. The term *Vidvan-Mahājanas,* used to denote the elders or the principal inhabitants of the *Agrahāra* villages, amply indicates their learning and scholarship. The two of the six duties (*Satkarma*),[38] enjoined upon the *Agrahārikas* and referred to in many of the grants of the period, namely *Ādhyayana* and *Adhyāpana* also make it clear that one of their basic and primary functions was to study and to give instruction.

It appears that some of the *Agrahāras* had the provision for the maintenance of schools in them.[39] These schools must have provided elementary education to Brahman pupils of the *Agrahāras*. But it was the individual scholars, noted for their scholarship in various branches of learning, that played a significant role in the pursuit and the transmission of learning in the country. They appear to have taught the students in their homes which served as some kind of residential schools (*Gurukulas*).[40] The students desirous of acquiring specialization in various branches of learning were drawn to them from far and wide. They studied different subjects under different teachers either simulataneously or one after the other. Their various needs such as food, shelter, and clothing were catered to, free of cost, by the teachers themselves.[41] Thus, due to the fostering care of the royal donors, the teachers and the students in the *Agrahāras* were enabled to pursue intellectual activities undisturbed by the wants. Mallampalli Somasekhara Sarma describes these *Agrahāras* as one kind of Chartered Universities or *Vidyāpīthas*.[42]

The learning promoted in the *Agrahāras*, as noted earlier in connection with their history, was both religious and secular. For example, the 108 Brahmans who were brought from various places and given shares in the *Agrahāra* of Vilasa by Vennaya Sarma, the principal donee of that *Agrahāra*, are described in the Vilasa grant of (1330 A.D.) Prolaya Nayaka as "well versed in Vedas and *Sastras*".[43] Among them there were mathematicians, grammarians, philologists, logicians, philosophers, jurists, astrologers, poets, exegetists and experts in *Āgamas* and various sacrificial lore.[44] Other secular subjects, the study of which appears to have been popular, were music, medicine (*Āyurvēda*) and the like.[45] The Kommu-Chikkala inscription of Anapota Reddi describes a certain Pinnamarya, presumably the recipient of an *Agrahāra*, as *Śakunabrahma* (one who was an expert in the Science of Omens).[46]

The Muslim Religious Institutions: The Muslim religious institutions of the period in the Telugu country, like those of

Hindusim, were great centres of intellectual activity and promoters of learning. They played a significant role in diffusing knowledge, especially, among the followers of Islam.

Most of the Mosques of the period appear to have had schools (*Maktāb* or *Madarasa*) attached to them for the maintenance of which endowments were made. *Taḍhkiratul Muluk* records that Ibrahim Qutbshah built Mosques in each town and village of his kingdom. He appointed *Mullā*-teachers in all these Mosques and made it compulsory for all Muslim children to attend those Mosque-schools.[47] The Jami-*Masjid* built (north-east of Charminar, Hyderabad) by Muhammad Quli Qutbshah in the year 1597 A.D., had a school in it. According to *Mahānamah,* this school served the needs of both the Hindu and the Musalmans; and the government paid the salaries of the teachers teaching in it.[49] The facilities for the stay and for the food of the teachers as well as the pupils seems to have been provided in these Mosque-schools. Sherwani, while describing the Syedabad Mosque (Hyderabad), built in 1605 A.D., expresses the similar opinion. He states:

> "We also know that every Mosque of any pretensions had a school attached to it, and the rooms all round the Mosque might well have served as a kind of boarding school where both teachers and pupils lived together."[50]

In these schools, the students were probably imparted elementary education. Theology, being the most important of all the branches of knowledge of the Muslims, must have received special attention in them.

Similarly, the *Khānqāhs* of the Sufi saints of Deccan during the period of the Bahmanis and those of the Andhra Desa under the Qutbshahis, were great centres of learning. Their pontiffs and their disciples were great scholars and writers in Arabic, Persian, Urdu and even in the local languages. Syed Muhammad Hussain Gesu Daraz who established his *Khānqāh* at Gulburga during the region of Feroz Shah Bahmany, was a great scholar. He is said to have compiled more than a hundred works in several languages and on the topics of Sufism, religion and ethics. He was conversant with Sanskrit language also.[51]

The birth and growth of the Urdu language or Dakhni, a mixture of Persian and Indian languages, in Northern India as well as the South was mainly due to the efforts of the Sufi saints of the period. Their attempts to spread their tenets in an easy medium of communication with the local people, appear to have contributed to the growth of this language. Nizami, writing about the contribution of the Deccan Sufis, observes:

> "The eagerness of the Sufis to establish a direct contact with the common man and share the joys and sorrows of his life, led to the growth of a new medium of communication called 'proto-Urdu'...."[52]

That the study of the local languages like Telugu and Sanskrit, was cultivated in the *Khānqāhs* in Andhra Desa, is known from the work *Śriṅgāra-mañjari.* The authorship of this work in Telugu as well as in Sanskrit is ascribed to Akbar Shah, the son of Syed Shah Raju II, the pontiff of a Sufi *Khānqāh* at Hyderabad during the period of Abul Hasan Tanesha.[53] This is a clear proof of the fact that the ascetics of the *Khānqāhs* endavoured to learn the language of the local people in order to converse with them on the mysteries of Sufi philosophy.

The *Khānqāhs* of the period were important centres for the diffusion of education and many of them appear to have had schools and colleges attached to them, where instruction (in religious and secular subjects) was given. The above mentioned Gesu Daraz of Gulburga had organized a *Madarasa* (College) attached to his *Khānqāh.* In that institution students coming from various parts of Deccan were given instruction in various branches of Islamic learning.[54] Some of the subjects, on which the Pir (Gesu Daraz) and his chief disciples gave lectures in that *Madarasa* included *Tafsīr, Hadīth, Sulūk, Kalam, Fiqh,* and commentaries on various works on Sūfism written by the *Pīr* himself.[55]

One important branch of knowledge cultivated successfully in the Muslim institutions of the period and put to public and royal use was the science of horoscope. One of the main reasons for the liberal patronage extended by the people and monarchs in the Vijayanagar empire to the *Dargah* of Babayya of Penugonda was on account of the successful forecast made by the occupants of that institutions. The grant of a large number of villages and lands by the Vijayanagara monarchs like Vira Narasimha, Sadasiva Raya and Venkata II, was meant for encouraging the study of horoscopy (*hōra*) in that institution.[56]

IMPACT OF THE POLITICAL ACTIVITIES

The religious institutions exerted a profound influence over the contemporary political life. The members of these institutions did not bury themselves exclusively in religious activity and did not remain indifferent to the political changes that were taking place around them. On the other hand, they did every thing, including engaging themselves in politics, diplomacy and intrigue to influence the contemporary political life in many ways. Their influence, in most cases, was benevolent and changed many a time the very course of the history of the Telugu country. They served the state in many capacities as guides, philosophers and friends.

It may be remembered that, especially, the Hindu religious institutions and the religious teachers connected with them played a crucial role in rousing political consciousness in the country during the period of Tughluq rule. They wee instrumental in the creation of new Hindu kingdoms which liberated the country from the Muslim yoke. This is amply indicated by the acts of the founders of these kingdoms. They described themselves as those who acquired their kingdoms with the grace of either some god or some religious teacher. Some of them also chose to rule their kingdoms on behalf of God considering themselves merely as his representatives on the throne.

According to Anitalli Grant of Kaluvacheru[57] and the Gurija grant.[58] Kapaya Nayaka acquired his kingdom and ruled it by the grace and commands of Visvesvara. This Visvesvara was presumably the God Visvesvara of Kasi, from whom Kapaya must have taken his inspirtation. Prolaya Vema Reddi, the founder of the Reddi kingdom, is described in an inscription of 1346 A.D. as one who acquired the grandeur of the kingdom by the grace of his spiritual Guru Goderaya Gangaya Deva.[59] This religious teacher appears to have inspired his royal disciple in his political enterprise of establishing an independent kingdom. The crucial role played by Vidyaranya in the foundation of the city and the empire of Vijayanagara is too well-known. Harihara and Bukka, its founders, are said to have achieved their objective with the advice and blessings of this ecclesiastical statesman. As a matter of fact, the *Kaifiyat* of Tadipatri (Anantapur dt.) states that Vidyaranya, after the foundation of the empire, sat on its throne for a couple of years and then crowned Harihara and Bukka.[60] Several other *Kaifiyats* from Rayalaseema region also give a similar information. Harihara, the first ruler of the empire, ruled as the Vice-regent or the agent of Virupaksha, a deity in the local Temple, and adopted Sri Virupaksha as the sign manual of the empire. This act was intended, probably, to get the divine sanction for the political act. The reconversion of these two brothers, before they were crowned as kings, must have been the work of the religious teachers of the Advaita *Maṭha.* It is one of the most glorious epochs in the history of the Hindu religious institutions, when they exhibited such a liberal and catholic spirit in readmitting them into the fold of Hinduism, which had, normally, no scope for such act. The rulers of these kingdoms endeavoured to revive the activities of the religious institutions which suffered a setback under the Muslim rule and extended liberal patronage to them.

These acts on the part of the rulers were, probably out of gratitude for the help they received from the religious institutions. By doing so, they might have also sought to enlist the support of all the Hindus and especially the Brahmans for their political enterprise. They tried to take full advantage of the hold of the religious institutions on the society to consolidate their political power. On the other hand, the members of the religious institutions also might have felt that their safety and survival lay in the political independence of the Hindu kingdoms. On the whole, there was a happy interaction of political and religious institutions for their mutual benefit. And this can be seen throughout the period under study.

The members of the Hindu religious institutions continued their association with the royal court, and involvement in the contemporary politics throughout this period. As the spiritual guides and philosophers, they shaped the course of conduct of their royal disciples and contributed greatly to the political stability of the Hindu kingdoms. The supreme spirit of tolerance which characterized the religious policy of Vijayanagara, in the initial stages, was mainly due to the influence of the teachers of the Advaita *Maṭha* of Sringeri. They were able to infuse a liberal spirit into the policies of these monarchs. Similarly, the pontiffs of the Vaishnava and Madhwa *Maṭhas* of Tirupati and Ahobilam played a benevolent role in the Vijayanagara court politics during the period of its Second and Third dynasties. Sripadatirtha and Vyasatirtha, the successive pontiffs of the Madhwa *Maṭha,* acted as spiritual preceptors of Saluva Narasimha and Krishnadeva Raya respectively.[61]

It is quite interesting to note that many of the pontiffs of the *Maṭhas* of this period behaved like temporal princes and assumed temporal titles *Srimatrājādhirāja.*[62] *Vodayalu,*[63] *Rāya.*[64] etc. Their offices were called *Āsthānams* and their spiritual seats (*Peeṭhams*) were designated as *Simhāsaṇams* (thrones).[65] Bigger *Maṭhas* like Sringeri *Maṭha,* with a number of branches all over India, called their area of spiritual jurisdiction *Sāmrājyamu.*[66] Of course, the assuming of temporal titles and maintaining royal ensignia by these *Mathāḍipatis* was intended to show their supreme position in their own filed i.e., the spiritual field. At the same time, it also indicates the enviable place of prestige held by them in the royal courts and the society.

Some of these monks even went to the extent of constructing forts and maintaining army. Bhikshavritti Santa Lingayya of Bhiksha *Maṭha* of Srisailam, the *Dharmakarta* of the Temple of Mallikarjuna of the place and a contemporary of Krishnadeva Raya, constructed a fort in the neighbourhood of Srisailam and stationed a garrison in it for the protection of the villages belonging to the Temple and his own *Maṭha.*[67]

Some of the pontiffs even took up arms and participated in wars in support of their patron kings. *Navanātha Charita* refers to a victory won over the Gajapati by Mukti Santa Bhikshavritti Raya, the Veera Saiva pontiff of the Bhiksha *Maṭha* at Srisailam.[68] According to the same source, he seized the *Sāptaṅgās* (royal insignia) of the Gajapati. R. Subrahmanyam maintains that this pontiff might have fought that war as an ally of Mallikarjuna Raya of Vijayanagara.[60] Whatever might be the truth in this claim, one thing i.e. the participation of the pontiff in the war, is obvious. This is also confirmed by a statement in the *Velugōtivāri Vamśāvali* which credits the Velama prince Madaya Linga with a victory, on behalf of Kapilesvara Gajapati, over this Mukti Santabhiksha Vritti.[70]

Even in the selection of the successors to the throne, the help of the religious institutions was sought by the rules of this period. *Mādalapañji,* the Oriyan work, gives the interesting information that Bhanudeva IV, the childless last ruler of the Ganga dynasty of Orissa, picked up his heir in the form of a boy (the future Kapilesvara Gajapati) near a Temple according to the instructions given in his dream by Lord Jagannatha.[71] Kapilesvara Gajapti, the founder of Suryavamsi Gajapati dynasty, is believed to have selected his successor Purushottama Gajapati following the wishes of the same God.[72] Jagannatha was the guardian deity of the Gajapati kingdom, and its rules like their predecessors, the Gangas, considered themselves to be his mere servants holding the kingdom in trust.[73] This overlord subordinate relationship between these rulers and God Purusottama-Jagannatha is indicated in an epigraph of Kapilesvara from Srisailam dated 1460 A.D.[74] In it, Kapilesvara Gajapati is described with the titles *Puruṣōṭṭama puṭra* and *Rāhuta.*

Sometimes, the precincts of some of the important shrines, during this period, served as the places of coronation ceremony of the rulers. According to *Achyutābhyūdayam,* Achyuta Raya celebrated his coronation ceremony at Tirupati before he was crowned formally at Vijayanagara.[75] The next Vijayanagara monarch Sadasiva Raya was also crowned at Tirupati before his second coronation at Vijayanagara.[76] On that occasion, he is said to have received from the Treasury of the Venkatesvara Temple of that place a great deal of money, intended to be used against the usurper.[77] The main purpose behind these coronations of the monarchical candidates in the presence of gods of the important shrines was, probably, to give religious sanctity to the succession. It was also, probably, intended to register the claim of that candidate, to which God himself was to be a witness, before his formal crowning ceremony, which was uncertain. Any way, God with His shrines were involved in politics and was made a party to the political transactions. And according to the above information, the Temple management also took sides in the war of succession and gifted money from the Temple treasury to be used by one candidate against the other.

The Muslim religious institutions played a similar role in the political life of the contemporary Muslim society. For example, the Mosque, besides being basically a centre of religious and spiritual activity, was also associated with many important acts in the Muslim kingdoms. It was the place where the coronation ceremony of some of the rulers was performed. The coronation of Alauddin Hsan Bahman Shah, the founder of the Bahmany Sultanate, was performed in the Mosque of Qutbuddin Mubarak Shah Khilji, situated at Daulatabad.[78] All important proclamations were made in the Mosque. The very fact that the *Khuṭba,* in the name of the ruler, was read from the pulpit of the principal Mosque indicates its importance in the political life of the Muslim society. Even in the 17th century, Aurangazeb, when he conquered Bider as Mughal Viceroy, hastened to the principal Mosque of that place to have the *Khuṭba* recited in the name of the emperor Shah Jahan. It was done as a proclamation of the latter's sovereignty in the newly conquered territory. The performance of coronation and the declaration of sovereignty was, no doubt, intended to get the religious sanction to the political act. At the same time, it also enabled the rulers to enlist the moral support of the religious leaders connected with those institutions and their followers among the common masses.

Similarly, the functionaries of the *Khānqāhs* of the period took an active part in the contemporary politics and exerted a profound influence in the political life of the society. The early tradition of the Sūfi saints, who were the occupants of these religious establishments, especially in Northern India, was against their participation in the politics of the state. They kept away from the royal court with the fear that it would infringe on their independence. In fact, they considered it beneath their dignity to visit them. But the saints of the latter period, especially in Decean and Telugu country, deviated from this tradition and accepted the patronage of the state for their institutions. They extended their cooperation and goodwill to the rulers. This good-will appears to have gone a long way in helping the early Bahmani Sultans to consolidate their political power in the newly established kingdom. They became spiritual preceptors of the Sultans and performed their coronations. The coronation of Alauddin, the founder of the Bahmani kingdom, was performed by Shaikh Sirajuddin Junaidi, the Sultan's preceptor.[79] The sultans gave grate value to the allegiance of these saints to their political power and enlisted their moral support for their enterprises.

Similarly, the saints of the *Khānqāhs* of the Qutbshahi period in Andhra Desa, also, took an active part in the political life of the country. Hussain Shah Wali, a descendant of Gesu Daraz of Gulburga, became a son-in-law of Ibrahim Qutbshah and occupied the position of the superintendent of public works and the commander of 10,000 army in that state.[80] But it is interesting to note that Shah Raju I, the brother of Hussain Shah Wali was one of the key persons involved in an unsuccessful conspiracy engineered with the object of deposing Muhammad Quli Qutbshah from the throne.[81] The episode connected with the accession of Abul Hasan Taneshah, the last ruler of the Golkonda kingdom, also illustrates the influence of the religious institutions on the political life of the country. This ruler, before his marriage to the daughter of Abdulla Qutbshah and before his accession to the throne, was an ascetic and a regular member of the *Khānqāh* of Shah Raju II, situated at Hyderabad.[82] The spiritual influence and power of the pontiff of that *Khānqāh* went a long way in the acquisition of the Qutbshahi throne to his disciple, Abul Hasan. The influence and the hold of this pontiff on the common masses and nobility must have definitely helped that ruler to consolidate his position in the early period of his rule.

But it should also be noted at the same time, that the pontiff of these *Khānqāhs* came out with bold criticism of the rulers, whenever they found that the behaviour of the rulers was against the precepts of religion and established morals. There were many instances when the saints defied the authority of the rulers in such circumstances. Shaikh Zainuddin Dawud, an eminent *Khalifa* in the *Khānqāh* of Burhanuddin Gharib of Gulburga, was very much critical of the Sultan Muhammad I's addiction to wine and his indifference to moral and ethical principles of Islam. He refused to owe his allegiance to that Sultan by absenting himself at the time of the latter's coronation. He also sided with two rebels against the Sultan. And it was the Sultan who had to finally come down and reconcile himself tactfully with the saint.[83] this incident clearly shows that the rulers could not afford to antagonize the religious leaders.

Religious Institutions as an integrating factor. The influence and the activities of the religious institutions of the period transcended the barriers of language, race and state. For example, the Hindu *Maṭhas* of Andhra Desa, most of which were branches of central *Maṭhas* situated outside, were great inter-state organizations. The activities of their members were not constrained by the considerations of state or languages. The Golaki *Maṭha* established by the Pasupata Saiva teacher Visvesvara Sivacharya at Mandaram village (Guntur dt.) and its various sub-branches established in all the three modern regions of Andhra Pradesh, were the branches of the parent Golaki *Maṭha* situated in Central India (Dahala country), originally founded by Sadbhava Sambhu.[84] Golaki *Maṭhas* of Andhra Desa were not exclusively meant for the people of Andhra Desa alone. On the other hand, a number of people from outside Andhra Desa were employed in it. Visvesvara Siva brought from Gauda (Bengal) and Chola (Tamilnadu) countries, a number of people to act as accountants, managers, village guards and scholars in his *Maṭha* at Mandaram. Its musicians were from Kashmir.[85] Moreover, the founder-pontiff of these *Maṭhas* in Andhra

Desa i.e. Visvesvara Siva, himself was from Radha in Gauda country (Bengal). Another thing that proves the inter-state influence of these *Maṭhas* is that the above Visvesvara Sivacharya, who is described as the *Rāja-guru* (*Deekṣha Guru*) of Kakatiya Ganapati Deva, had Malva, Kalachuri and Chola kings as his disciples[86] indicating his wide influence that transcended the barriers of the states.

Similarly, the Madhwa *Maṭhas* established by Narahari-thirtha at Simhachalam, and Vyasatirtha at Tirupati were the branches of the parent Madhwa *Maṭha* situated at Udipi in the Kannada country, and they must have been manned by a number of mendicants from that country. And like this, examples can be multiplied. In the same manner, some of these institutions commanded respect from people belonging to all languages, races and even religions. An inscription of 1550 A.D. from the village Chitrachedu (Anantapur dt.) gives very interesting information about the inter-state influence of the pontiff of the Bhikshvritti *Maṭha* of Srisailam.[87] It describes the *Narapati* (Vijayanagara), the *Aśvapati* (Deccan Sultans) and the *Gajapati* (Orissa) kings as the 'three spiritual sons' of Santa Bhikshavritti Ayyavaru, the pontiff of the above *Maṭha*. It is not known from any other sources whether these monarchs and especially the Deccan Sultans and the Orissa rulers were ever influenced spiritually by this pontiff, or came into contact with him personally. But it is quite probable that some of the people and especially the Veerasaivas, residing in all these kingdoms must have definitely looked to this pontiff of Veerasiva *Maṭha* at Srisailam for spiritual guidance.

Likewise, the Hindu Temples of the period were great unifying factors and contributed considerably to the national unity. Some of the major Hindu Temples situated at places like Tirupati, Srisailam and Simhachalam were religious centres of all India fame. They used to draw, as they do even now, especially during the times of their annual festivals, pilgrims from the entire country south of Vindhyas. In an inscription of 1497 A.D. from Ramapuram village (Anantapur dt.), Srisailam has been referred to as the *Dakshina Vāranāsi* (Varanasi of South),[88] indicating its importance as a Saiva centre of all India basis. As a matter of fact, it is included among the 12 great Saiva *Kshētras* of India.[89] Thus the Hindu Temples were the meeting places for the people of different nationalities, races and linguistic groups and facilitated exchange of views and helped the spread of common culture.

The Temples also helped the spread of spiritual conceptions quickly in the country. The major Hindu Temples attracted not only the ordinary devotees but also the great teachers of various religions. These religious luminaries frequented these places for the diffusion of their teachings among the devotees who visited these shrines from far and wide. This greatly helped the quick propagation of their concepts in the country.

It is the same with the Muslim religious institutions. Especially the *Khānqāhs* and the *Dargāhs* of the Muslim saints helped, national integration through their all pervading influence. They enabled the people of various social situations, religions and races to come together. They attracted into their fold not only the Muslims but sometimes even the Hindus. The *Khānqāh* of Syed Muhammad Gesu Daraz of Gulburga appears to have been visited by the Hindu *Yōgis* with whom its *Pīr* had discussions on religion.[90] He is quoted to have stated at one place, "The human seed is just the same, prophets, saints abdalautads are from one seed, so are Kafirs, hypocrites, thieves etc."[91] This shows the broad and liberal outlook of some these saints who understood the oneness of mankind in those days of religious and racial bigotism. Similarly, the Babayya *Dargāh* of Penugonda had its followers among the Muslims and the Hindus and enjoyed the patronage of both.[92] Nizami, in his introduction to his article 'Sūfi movement in deccan', writing about the integrating influence of the Sūffi saints, observes:

> 'Considered in its broad cultural perspective, it was through the medium of mysticism that the Muslim culture group adjusted itself with the local milieu and all those social and linguistic barriers which had separated the South from the North began to yield to the pressure of new all-India trends. The reciprocity of relationship between the Khānqāhs of the

North and the South and the Pan-Indian organizational pattern and perspective of some of the spiritual orders helped in bringing the north closer to the South and initiated a new phase of rapprochement between regions, creeds and culture."[93]

IMPACT OF THE SOCIAL WELFARE ACTIVITIES

The religious institutions of the period were great social welfare and charitable organizations. Many a time, they also acted as agents for executing the charities of the rich and pious members of the society. Charity, which is of a comprehensive nature, was expressed in different ways depending upon the capacity and the convenience of the donors. The usual from of charity was to give villages, lands, grain, money and other items of property for maintaining religious and educational institutions and for providing shelter, food and water to the needy persons free of cost. Of course, these charities could be conducted by the individual donors themselves independent of the public institutions. But it appears that the religious-minded and the charity-through the religious institutions, in whom they found great and recognized agents to carry on their charitable deeds. This was most probably on account of the sanctity attached to these institutions and also due to their being the places to which people of various communities and localities came regularly and on festival days. They might have felt that their charities, if conducted through these religious institutions, might cater to the needs of various classes of people so that more religious merit might accrue to them. Thus, the religious institutions provided an outlet to the charitable urge of people and enabled them to extend their charity to the needy members of the society. We find that most of the charities, during the period, were conducted through religious institutions.

It can be stated in this connection that the religious institutions of the period of whatever religion contributed, in one way to the economic socialism of the society. By exploiting the religious sentiments and charitable instinct of the rich and the wealthy members of the society, they induced them to contribute generously from their income to the general welfare of the society. Thus, they counteracted the general trend on the part of a few individuals towards the accumulation and concentration of wealth in their hands. They lessoned the gulf between the rich and the poor and leveled indirectly the economic imbalances in the society.

Temple Charities: One of the important charities conducted through the Hindu Temples, irrespective of their religious affiliations, is to provide food and shelter to the needy. This service was conducted through the establishment of feeding-shelters known variously as *Satram*, *Bhōga Saṭramu*, *Anna-Saṭram*, *Ambali-Saṭram*, *Rāmānūjakutam*, etc. The feeding-houses, where free lodging and boarding facilities were provided to the general travellors and pilgrims, though specifically endowed by donors, were attached to the Temples and managed by them. Prolaya Vema Reddi, the founder of the Kondavidu kingdom, is said to have established *Satras* at a number of pilgrim centres where food of various types was offered to the needy. This is also indicated by his title *Aganya punya-ksēṭra-saṭra Datta bahuvidhāhāra* referred to in an inscription of 1345 A.D. from Amaravati.[94] Some of these Temple *Satras* were exclusively meant for the people belonging to certain communities and sects. The Zakkampudi inscription mentions the existence of two separate *Saṭrams* at Bezawada, one meant for the Jangamas and the other for the Brahmans. They were endowed, for their upkeep, by the Gajapati prince Hamvira son of Kapilesvara.[95] An inscription of 1521 A.D. from Alampur (Mahbubnagar dt.) records that, in the feeding-house attached to the Temple of God Bala Brahmesvara of the place, provision was made for feeding twelve Brahmans every day.[96] There are references in some of the inscriptions from Tirupati to a *Satram*, which was exclusively meant for the Brahmans.[97] This *Saṭram* was instituted by Krishnadeva raya and endowed by his queens. Even the *Rāmānujakūtams*, which were a special feature of the Srivaishnava temples of the period, appear to have catered, exclusively, to the needs of the people of srivaishnava sect.[98]

Some feeding houses attached to the Temples were meant for the general travellers and the pilgrims. An inscription of 1520 A.D. from the village Chadipirela (Cuddapah dt.) clearly states that a certain Chennaya made a land grant to a *Dharma Sattaruvu* (choultry) presumably attached to the local Temple, for feeding Brahmans and Satanis among the pilgrims going to Tirupati.[99] Another inscription of 1536 A.D. from Malkonda village (Nellore dt.) states that the *Saṭram* attached to the Temple of Narasimha Swami of Somarajupalli was endowed by a Vijayanagara official for feeding 24 travellers daily.[100] Some times, this charity was conducted at the Temples to meet the demand on special occasions like the annual festivals. An epigraph of 1561 A.D. from Miduturu village (Kurnool dt.) records that Dalavayi Bundinayaka; a Vijayanagara official granted some land to a *Satra* at Srisailam for the feeding of the pilgrims (*Śivarātri-paruṣa-saṭra*) visiting the place during *Śivarātri* festival.[101]

Most of the Temple feeding houses were, normally, meant to serve the pilgrims and the general travelers irrespective of caste and creed. In two *Satrams*, instituted at Tirupati in the later part the 16th century A.D. by a certain Matla Kumara Anantaraja, the people of all classes were provided food of very good quality.[102] During those days, when the modern quick transport and conveyance facilities and the hotel facilities were absent and when the pilgrims and the general travelers could not carry all their necessary items with them for fear of the robbers, etc., free lodging and boarding facilities for them at various places was an absolute necessity. And this need was fulfilled, to a great extent, by the feeding houses attached to the Temples. And in fact, the precincts of the Temples themselves provided shelter to the travelers. William Methold, an employee of English east India Company, stationed at Masulipatam from A.D. 1618 to 1622 writing about the religious life of the people in the neighbourhood of his factory writes: "They (Temples) stand always open, and prove in some places the best receptacles for Travellers..."[103]

These feeding choultries were maintained by the Temples usually with the proceeds of the villages, lands, taxes etc. granted, by the pious donors, as permanent endowments, especially for that purpose. An inscription of Sadasive Raya's period from Nandavaram village (Kurnool dt.) records the gift of four villages for the maintenance of a *Sastra* by Suluru Balayya, presumably a government official.[104] Aravidu Kondaraja, a Vijayanagara subordinate, granted in 1550 A.D. ten villages yielding an annual income of 5,713 *Rēkhai-pon* (gold coins) for feeding the Srivaishnava pilgrims in Tirupati.[105] In this feeding house attached to the Nammalvar shrine at Tirupati, In the year 1547 A.D. about 2000 Srvaishnavas irrespective of caste were fed daily in a sumptuous manner.[106] Sometimes, the Temple donors arranged for the issue of their share in the *Prasādam* to the *Sātras* attached to the Temples. This was done probably to supplement the income from the permanent endowments, like villages, lands etc. and to meet the additional requirement during the period of Temple festivals. Sometimes the donors paid cash into the Temple treasury with the stipulation that its interest should be utilized for the maintenance of feeding houses attached to that Temple. An inscription of this period from Tirupati records that a certain Hariyappar paid 3000 *Panam* into the treasury of Temple of Venkatesvara of Tirupati, a portion of which was to be utilized for the feeding 12 Brahmans daily in a *Saṭram* at that place.[107]

These feeding houses, though attached to the Temples and were under the general supervision of the Temple authorities, had their own organization consisting of the functionaries like managers,[108] men for supplying various items, cooks, etc. The *Ramanujakūtam* established by Saluva Narasimha Raya and attached to Tirupati Venkatesvara Temple was under the management of Kandadai Ramanujayyangar, a Srivaishnava teacher of the place and the spiritual teacher of the above monarch.[109] Another *Saṭram* instituted by the same monarch at Tirupati was placed under the control (*Ādhipaṭyam*) of a certain Hastigiri Ayyan, who was granted, for his remuneration, a share in the sacred food by the authorities of the Venkatesvara Temple.[110]

An interesting charity conducted through the agency of the Hindu Temple comes to our notice in an epigraph of 1545 A.D.

from Tirupati.[111] It states that Vitthalaraja, a Vijayanagara subordinate, by granting three villages of God Venkatesvara arranged for the free distribution of clothes to the devotees who congregated for *Puruttāsi-tirunāl* (annul *Brahmōtsvam*) at Tirumalai and for the free supply of butter milk to the thirsty pilgrims at the entrance of the Temple. A similar arrangement (i.e., the supply of butter-milk in large quantities to the pilgrims coming to attend the *Puruttāsi Brahmōtsavam* at Tirumalai-Tirupati) made by a certain Namisettiyar, is referred to in an epigraph of Sadasiva Raya's period from that place.[112] The quality of the food offered in the Temple feeding-houses is indicated in an epigraph of Veera Narasimha Raya's period (Tuluva dynasty) from the village Pullapalle (Cuddaph dt.).[113] It refers to the items used in the preparation of food in the *Brāhmana-stra* attached to the Temple of Istakamesvara Bhairave of the place. They included, rice, green-gram, ghee, two varieties of curries, butter-milk, betel leaves and areca-nuts,

Water pandals: The maintenance of water-*pandals* or water-sheds, where drinking water was provided free of cost to the thirsty people, was another charity conducted through the agency of the Hindu Temple. That this charity, like that of providing food and shelter, was an absolute necessity during the period is proved by a number of references in the contemporary inscriptions to the establishment of water-sheds. To perpetuate this charity, the donors entrusted their management to the temples by making a permanent land of monetary endowment to the Temples by making a permanent land or monetary endowment for the purpose. An inscription of 1520 A.D. from Tirupati records that Srinivasan, the son of an accountant of the Venkatesvara Temple of the place, paid 700 *Panam* to the Temple treasury for the maintenance of a water-pandal near Sri Govindaraja Temple. And the Temple trustees bound themselves to run that service through the yield from the land in which the above money was to be invested.[114] An inscription of 1318 A.D. from Palakol village (Godavari dt) gives the information that the donor made arrangement, in the water-shed, (*Sali-pandiri*) instituted by him, for the supply of water (*Udaka-dānamu*) by a

Brahman this arrangement for the supply of water by a Brahmin was probably to enable the people all costes including the Brahmins to be benefitted by that service. Some of the donors who instituted water-shed service through the Temple also made provision for the planting and raising of trees, probably, intended to give shade to the people who came for water. A certain Vemula Ragavayya, according to an inscription from Kondapadu village (Guntur dt.) granted a piece of land to the Temple and another piece to Tammala Veeraiah in that village as *Chalivēṅdra-Mānya* for constructing some wells, suppling water to the water-shed (*Chalipaṅdali*) and raising 100 trees, in the year 1576 A.D.[116]

Sometimes, the charity of providing drinking water, instituted in the Temples, was extended to benefit cattle also. An inscription of 1516 A.D. form Tadipatri (Cuddapah dt.) refers to such service (*Dharma-gādi*) instituted by a certain Timmanayudu in the Temple of God Chennakesava of the place and the land grant for the men who supplied water for it.[117] Another important charity conducted through the Temple and which benefited and is benefiting even now, a number of pilgrims visiting the shrines, is the act of building a flight of steps either for the ascent to or the descent from the sacred hills where famous shrines were situated. As noted already in the preceding chapters, many rulers of Andhra Desa in the 14th century A.D. claimed, in their grants, credit for this type of charity.[118] And even the instituting of *Ghaḍiyarō-pachāra* (Time-keeping service) in the temples indirectly served the society. An inscription 1505 A.D. states that a certain Bhandaru Setti instituted the *Ghaḍiyarōpachāramu* in the Temples of Gopinatha-devara for announcing the time to the Temple priests for performing the worship.[119] This service, though primarily meant for announcing time to the Temple priests and other functionaries to perform various rituals according to their timings, also enabled the people of that particular locality or village where the temple was situated, to know the timings to conduct their daily routine according those timings. In a way, it served the purpose of a community clock.

Maṭha Charities: the Hindu *Maṭha* of the period, like the Hindu Temple was a great charitable institution and conducted many philanthropic activities. It provided lodging and boarding facilities to the poor travellers and the pilgrims visiting the shrines. As most of these *Maṭhas* functioned as auxiliaries to the important Hindu shrines, they also used to maintain *Satras*. The Golaki Matha at Mandaram of the Kakatiya period had the provision for feeding, at all times all (poor) people from the Brahmana down to the Chandalas who came and asked for food, presumably in the *Saṭra* attached to it.[120] An inscription of the 14th century A.D. from Tirupati records the arrangement made by a certain Singaya-Danayaka for feeding 32 Srivaishanvas in the Sitakaragandan *Maṭham* of that place.[121] Similarly the feeding house (*Maṭha-satramu*) attached to the monastery of the Suddhasaivas built near the Temple of Tripurantakesvara at Tripurantakam village (Kurnool dt.) is referred to in an epigraph from that place belonging to the Kakatya period. This *Maṭha-satram* was to cater to the needs of the guests and visitors (*Aṭidhi-abhyāgtulu*).[122]

The Hindu *Maṭhas* of the period appear to have extended medical facilities to the contemporary society. It is interesting to note that the Golaki *Maṭha* at Mandaram[122] maintained a maternity hospital, a general hospital and one doctor. All these services were understandably, meant for the use of the general public, besides that of the *Maṭha*. It is quite reasonable to infer that the *Maṭhas* promoted the study of sciences like *Āyurvēda* and Yōga for the benefit of their mendicants as well as for the general public. They might have prepared drugs for treating various diseases and extended those facilities to the people of the locality and especially belonging to their sect.

Agrahāras as Charities: The *Agrahāras* of the period in Andhra Desa, like other religious institutions, were important charitable institutions. The Brahamans in the *Agrahāra* were not only to accept the gifts but also to perform the act of gifting. As a matter of fact, the performance of a gift (*Dāna*) is one of the six duties (*Satkarma*) enjoined upon the *Agrahāra* Brahman.[124] They gave instruction to the needy students by providing various facilities, like food, shelter etc. to them free of cost.[125] Besides, they were also expected to give food to the visitors of their places. According to *Rāyavāchakam*

Veera Narasimha, the Vijayanagara emperor used to ascertain every day in the court from the official concerned, whether the *Agrahāra* Brahmans were performing this duty (*Aṭidhi-santarpana*).[126]

Charities of Muslim religious institutions: The Muslim religious institutions – the Mosque, the *Khānqāh* and the *Dargāh*, of the period, like those of Hinduism, were great social-welfare agencies and conducted charities of various kinds. As a matter of fact, *Zakat*, one of the five fundamental principles of Islam profounded by prophet Mohammad, enjoins on the Muslims to express their gratefulness to god by helping the created (Mankind) out of what they were given by God. Naturally the religious institutions of Islam appear to have laid considerable stress on charity and benevolence towards the follow beings. This went a long way in giving relief to the poor and needy members of the society.

The various charities conducted by the Mosques during this period in Andhra Desa are referred to in the inscriptions and foreign accounts. Many of them appear to have maintained Caravan-*Sarais* or inns, the counterparts of the Hindu *Saṭras*, which acted as the choultries and feeding houses for the travellers and mendicants. Tavernier, the French traveler, who visited Hyderabad in A.D. 1638-39, states that the Mosques of Qutbshahi period were also used as waiting-halls or inns for travelers.[127] The Mosque at Aliabad (Hyderabad) built by a certain Malik Almas in the year 1615 A.D. had a *Sarai* with 83 rooms, attached to it, presumably meant for the travellers.[128] Boarding and lodging facilities were, probably, provided to the travelers in those inns by the Mosques, either free of cost or on nominal charges. The French traveler, Thevenot, who visited Hyderabad in 1667 A.D., writing about the *Nīmet-ullah* Caravan-*Sarai*, attached to a Mosque, at Hyderabad, where he and his party lodged themselves, states that he hired two little chambers in that *Sarai* at 2 Rupees a month.[129]

Public feeding, through Alm-houses attached to the Mosque, seems to have been one of the important charities conducted during this period. Maḷik Aminul Mulk Khan, *Vazier* and *Mīrjumla* of Muhammad Qutbshah, who supervised the construction of

Jamay *Masjid* (near Charminar, Hayderabad) is said to have made two monetary endowments. One of them of 80,000 Rupees per annum was meant for the feeding of the holy persons in the above Mosque.[130] In the Mecca Masjid (situated north of Charminar, Hyderabad A.D. 1617-1669) during the Qutbshahi period, 36 mounds of food was cooked and distributed to the poor everyday.[131] The feeding of the poor in the Mosque, sumptuously, on certain sacred days annually, is another feature of the charity. An inscription of 1657 A.D., from the Salih Begams Mosque (Hyderabad city), records the provision made by Salih Begam Sayyida, the donor, for the annul feasting in that Mosque.[132] Similarly, a Persian epigraph of 1674 A.D. from Hyderabad city records the provision for feeding of the poor in the month of *Muharram* in the alm-house attached to the Mosque of Miyan Mishk of that place.[133] It also refers to the *Abdarkhāna*, attached to that Mosque where cold-drinks were distributed during the same month.

Some of the Mosques of the Qutbshahi-period had *Hammāms* (bath rooms) attached to them and meant for the public use. The Jmi *Masjid*, in Golkonda Fort of the period of Sultan Quli, had a *Hammām* where *lungis* or printed towels of the finest variety were presented to those who came for a bath in it. It also provided the bath-room, water and a free hair-cut by the barbers who were paid by the state.[134] Similar arrangements were made for the people who came to Jamay *Masjid*, built in 1597 near Charminar for prayers.[135] The Persian epigraph of 1674, mentioned above, from Hyderabad refers to the provision of 15 *Huns* made for the remuneration of the shampooers and for the maintenance of the bath and the bath sheets in the Mosque.[136]

One of the cardinal principles aimed at and implemented by the occupants of the *Khānqāhs* of the period, besides the spiritual and intellectual activity, was to give comfort to the fellow human beings and to help the needy and poor. Many of these saints disdained the possession of private property and distributed among the needy and poor whatever gifts come to them. When Sultan Muhammad bin Tughluq sent a gifts of 3,000 *Tānkas* to

Burhanuddin Gharib of Daulatabad, that saint is said to have added twenty *Tānkas* from his *Khānqāh* and distributed the entire amount among the poor and needy immediately. They *Khānqāhs* also appear to have catered to the needs of the poor travelers and mendicants by providing lodging and boarding facilities free of cost.

IMPACT OF THE ECONOMIC ACTIVITIES

The religious institutions of the period in the Telugu country were also great centres of economic activity. Their influence on the economic life of the contemporary society is to be measured in terms of services, employment, production of goods, investment and profits which enhanced considerably the wealth and welfare of the society.

Employers: Next to the state, the religious institutions were the largest employers in the country. The various endowments made to these religious institutions by the donors were, no doubt primarily meant for the maintenance and upkeep of their various, religious and charitable services. But these services ultimately benefited the people of various sections of the society. They provided the means of livelihood for a large number of persons, both male and female and both directly and indirectly. As noted earlier, they employed administrators, priests, accountants, musicians, dancers, artisans, cooks and various other menial servants who attended to their various services. All these persons were provided with full-time employment. But besides those who were directly benefited, there were a large number of other people whose services were requisitioned for the time being for various services and who were indirectly benefited by these institutions.

These institutions, as noted earlier, were great land-lords and owned extensive agricultural and pasture lands, groves and gardens of flowers and vegetables. They provided livelihood for a large number of farmers, agricultural laboures and gardeners who worked on them. Sometimes, these institutions played an important role in the reclamation of waste land and extension of cultivation. How the religious institutions, sometimes, helped the rehabilitation and reclamation of the villages is known from the *Kaifiyat* of Nivart-Sangam.[137] It stated that the two Jangama brothers, Santa-bhiksha-vritti and Vira-bhiksha-vritti who were the agents of the bhiksha-vritti *Maṭha* of Srisailam, founded a village by clearing the jungle on the site of a ruined village in the year 1498 A.D. It further states that the income of that new village, Atmakur, was used for the religious services in the Temple of Mllikarjuna of Srisailam, Some of the religious institutions embarked upon agricultural improvement by undertaking the construction of irrigational tanks and canals in the villages belonging to them. The inscriptions from Tirupati are replete with references to this type of activities undertaken by the *Sthānattār* of the Srivenkatesvara Temple in its villages. Similarly, it is interesting to note that, Hussain Shah Wali, the Sūfi saint of golkonda was instrumental in building the present Hussain Sagar tank, in Hyderabad city.[138] No doubt, the supervised its work, in his capacity as the superintendents of public works in that Qutbshahi state and as a son-in-law of the Sultan Ibrahim Qutbshah. It indicates the philanthropic interests and concern shown by that saint for the economic welfare of the contemporary society. The impetus given by the religious institutions to the intense cultivation in the villages and lands granted to them ensured, no doubt, the increased revenue to them. But, at the same time, it indirectly benefited the cultivators and the agricultural laboures. Besides contributing considerably to the economic prosperity of those villages, it exerted great influence on the general economic life of the society. This contribution, in view of the large number of the villages held by the various religious institutions in the country during this period, is quite significant. And it can be stated that these institutions in one way supplemented the work of the state in raising the general standard of living in the country.

In the same way, the work of construction and conservation of the buildings, their decoration with carvings and sculptures, and the making of images required, especially in the Hindu Temples undertaken by these institutions or by the devotees on their behalf, created a lot of employment in the country. This hectic building activity needed the services of contractors, engineers, supervisors, architects, sculptors, painters, masons and labourers. For example, the construction of the Mecca-*Masjid* at Hyderabad, started by Sultan Muhammad Qutbshah in the year 1617 A.D. and which continued under the next two Sultans, provided employment to 8,000 masons and laboures, for a number of years during its construction.[139] And in view of the prolific buidling activity connected with these religious institutions in the country during the period which is proved by the abundant references to them in the inscriptions, it is quite reasonable to state that they gave employment to thousands of people.

Finally, the religious institutions of the period, were great consumers and consumed a large number of articles of various types, such as foodgrains, dairy-products, spices, incense, garlands, cloth, jewellery vessels, fire-wood etc. Of course, many of these especially the foodgrains, dairy products, etc. must have been collected by them as the owner's share from the tenants who cultivated their lands. But they had to purchase the remaining things. Naturally, they provided the means of livelihood for a number of people who were engaged in the production and the supply of these items. The people who were benefited by them were the traders, the artisans of various professions like the gold-smiths, black-smiths, carpenters, potters, basket-makers, weavers, tailors, oil-mongers, garland-makers, wood-cutters, cow-herds, etc. Moreover, the various articles consumed in these institutions ultimately benefited the society. They were consumed, besides their functionaries, by the devotees and other poor and needy members of the society. The charities of the distribution of food, drinking water, medical facilities, monetary and other gifts conducted by these institutions and which benefited the society, have already been referred to.

Some of the religious institutions of the period appear to have acted as banks and helped the needy people by lending money. An epigraph of 1567 A.D. from the village Porumamilla (Cuddapah dt.) refers to the execution of a sale-deed in favour of the god Gopalakrishna towards the clearance of the loan of an amount of 20 *Ghaṭṭi-Varāhas*, taken by a certain Puranam Chennabhattlu from the treasury of the temple.[140] Similarly, the acceptance of monetary endowments, from the donors, by the temples with the stipulation that the interest on gift amount alone would be spent for conducting the services instituted in their name, almost amounted to the conducting of banking business by them. An epigraph of 1542 A.D. from the village Chidipirala (Cuddaph dt.) records the gift 50 *Māḍas* for the maintenance of a perpetual lamp in the Temple of Agastesvara of the place by certain Polreddi and Basavireddi, stipulating that the amount might be utilized by the *Sthānikas* of that temple who received it either for purchasing some land or taking some land on lease. It further states that the produce of that land alone should be spent for the lamp, without disturbing the principal amount and if any one of the *Sthānikas* happened to disobey that arrangement he should surrender his share of gift money along with the land.[141]

We come across a number of references to this type of endowments in the case of the Sri Venkatesvara Temple of Tirupati for example, an epigraph of 1514 A.D. from that place[142] states that a certain donor Yagna Narayanabhatta deposited 10,000. *Narpanam* in the treasury of the Venkatesvara Temple of that plece as *Poliyaṭṭu* (capital) for the purpose of an offering to the deity (8 *Tiruppōnakam* each day) as his service. And the Temple trustees gave an undertaking to perform that service with the income derived from the investment of the principal amount in improving irrigational facilities in Temple villages.

Trade and Commerce: The consumption of various commodities for the performance of the services in the religious institutions and the requirement of the pilgrims gave a lot of impetus to the growth of trade and commerce in the locality where they were situated. Many of the villages and towns where the important shrines were situated, were also important centres of trade which served the needs of not only the shrines and their pilgrims but also those of the people of the neighbouring villages. The references, in a number of epigraphs of the period as mentioned earlier, to the levying of tolls and other duties on the various articles of merchandise sold at the Hindu shrines on normal days as well as on festival days and even on the rods leading to them, and to their exemption either wholly or partially by the government,[143] amply testify to the brisk trade activity carried at those places. An epigraph of 1559 A.D. from the village Chadalvada (Prakasum dt) refers to the various taxes collected by the Vijayanagara government on the sale and purchase of various articles of foodgrains by the merchants in the Temple village of Chadalavada on ordinary days and festival days, indicating the trade activity at the place.[144]

The fairs-*Jātara* of the Hindu Temples and *Urs* of the Muslim *Dargāhs*-held on the occasion of their annual festivals, which usually drew thousands of pilgrims, gave similar boost to trade and commerce. Besides the pilgrims, a large umber of traders also used to attend these annual fairs where all types of articles of daily use as well as those of curiosity were for sale. The Russian traveler Nikitin who visited Deccan in about 1470 A.D. gives evidence to the annual fair held in connection with the Mahasivaratri festival at Srisailam, the famous Saiva pilgrim center (Kurnool dt.) of the period. He observes:

> "I . . . agreed with some Indians to go to the Parvat . . . where stands their chief būtkhanah (Siva Temple) . . . whe Market by the būtkhanah lasts for five days . . . They go to Parvate to worship their but; that is their Jerusalem or Mccea in the Moslem tongue . . .[145]

The brisk trading activity on the occasion of the annual fair of the Srisailam Temple is also indicated by an epigraph from that place dated 1516 A.D. it refers to merchants coming to Srisailam *Jātara* carrying their articles of merchandise on horses, bullocks, assess and head-loads and the remission of tolls on them by Krishnadevaraya.[146]

Trade and commerce flourised along the pilgrim routes, i.e., the roads leading to the important pilgrim centres. The villages and towns situated on those routes also sometimes became important centres of trade. As noted before, there are several epigraphs referring to the trade and the duties levied on merchandise by the government of the day. An inscription of 1443 A.D. From Singarikonda village (Prakasam dt.) refers to the levy of tolls, by the government of Vijayanagara, on a variety of merchandise such as slaves and livestock including horses, bullocks, cows and buffallos and on all kind of grains, oils, women's clothes and other beautiful articles carried for sale on the road leading to the Temple of God Narasimha of the same place during the days of festival of that God.[147] Sometimes, new villages were built on the pilgrim routes for the convenience of the pilgrims and mendicants visiting the important shrines. The Rudravaram *Kaifiyat* (Kurnool dt.) states that Kakatiya Prataparudra II got the jungle cleared and the village Rudravaram built on the road leading to shrine of Narasimha of Ahobilam for the convenience of pilgrims and mendicants going to that shrine.[148] It further states that he did so at the request of the ascetics of the place when he visited it on his way from Ahobilam. These references amply indicate the important role played by the religious institutions in the country's internal trade in particular and its economic life in general.

IMPACT OF THE CULTURAL ACTIVITIES

The religious institutions of the period in Andhra Desa were important cultural centres around which the cultural life of the contemporary society revolved.

Patronage of Art: One of the most important services rendered by the religious institutions is their patronage to arts. It has often been remarked that art in India is the hand-maid of religion. This is to a great extent true of the religious institutions in the Telugu country. Arts like architecture, sculpture, painting, music, dance and drama, were promoted and successfully harnessed for religious purposes by these institutions. They helped the cultivation of these arts by providing livelihood to the artists and craftsmen who were well versed in them. Next to the state patronage, that is, the patronage, it was that of the religious institutions which contributed greatly to the development and preservation of these traditional arts in the country. Most of them are able to survive even to this day, partly, because of the patronage extended to them by the institutions.

The extant monuments belonging to the institutions of both Hinduism and Islam and especially the Temples and Mosques, can be described as the galleries or the store-houses of the arts of this period. They bear out the great level to which the art of the period reached under the patronage of the religious institutions. Many of the Temples of the Kakatiya and Vijayanagara period contain, besides the architecture, many sculptures, carvings and paintings of beautiful workmanship illustrating various episodes from the religious texts. The art of the Kakatiya period can be seen in the Temples of Warangal Fort, Hanumakonda, Palempet, Pillalamarri, Panagal etc. *Krīḍābhirāmam* refers to the existence of the mural paintings contained on the walls of the Temple of Palnad heroes in the Fort of Warangal during the period of Prataparudra II. These paintings illustrated the themes from the history of Palnad heroes like, Brahmanaydu.[149] Nadindla Gopamantri, the governor of Kondavidu Fort during the reign of Krishnadeva Raya, states in his work *Krishnārjuna Samvādamu* that he got the Temple of God Raghavesvara of Kondavidu covered with paintings (*Chiṭra Varnamulu Gāvinchi*).[150] The best example of Vijayanagara sculptures and paintings in the Telugu country are those contained in the temples of Lepadshi, Jataprolu, Tadpatri and Srisailam. The Temples, especially at Somapalle (Chittoor dt.) (C.1578 A.D.) and at Lepakshi (Anantapur dt.) (C. 1541 A.D.) Contain beautiful paintings of this period. They depict the themes from the *Mahābhārata*, the *Rāmāyana* and the *Purānas.*[151]

Similarly, the Mosques of the Qutbshahi period, situated at Hyderabad, contain, besides the architecture and carvings, inscriptions written beautifully in many styles of calligraphy such as *Nastāliq*, *Naskh*, *Kūfic*, *Tughra* and *Thulth.*[152] The promotion of the art of calligraphy is an important contribution of the Muslim religious institutions to the field of art.

The other arts, besides those mentioned above, patronized by the religious institutions of the period are dance, music and drama. Music and dance usually formed a part of the rituals in the Hindu Temples. Even the Temples of moderate size and resources appear to have maintained their own dancers, musicians and singers, both male and female, to entertain the deity at the time of the daily rituals and during the special ceremonies and festivals. The major Temples appear to have maintained several *Melas* or bands of these artists in their service. The *Nātyamaṅtapa* or *Raṇgamaṇtapa*, where these arts were performed, had been an essential part of the Temple building-complex of the period. The Temple music was both vocal and instrumental. An epigraph of 1350 A.D. from Simhachalam, gives the following compositions of the band of dancers and musicians of that Temple: 8 dancers (*Paṭrulu*), 2 drummers (*Maḍḍela-kāṅdru*), 1 vocalist (*Gāyni*), one women each to play respectively the instruments called *Tūkīnamu* (flagolet), *Śaṅkhu* (conch), *Āvarjamu* (brazen kettle-drum), *Bhēri* (kettle drum), *Mihvuri* (a kind of drum), *Brahma-mihvuri* (a kind of big drum) and *Sumaṅta-kahali* (a kind of trumpet), and a pair of women to play on the *Kamsyatālamu* (bronze cymbals).[153] As noted earlier in connection with the Temple servants, some of the Temples maintained teachers to train their artists in their arts and sometimes the royal donors used to depute trained dancers from their courts to render service in some of the famous Temples.[154]

Some Temples' used to patronise drams (*Nāṭaka*) which were staged in the Temples' precincts on the occasion of the periodical festivals. Some of the Temple dancers, probably, were also actors. On the occasion of the *Vasaṅtarāyamahotsava* of God Prasanna Gopaladeve at Rajasala (Rajukonda, the capital of Velama kingdom), *Ratnapāṅclika,* a Sanskrit drama by Singabhupala II (ruler of the same kingdom) is stated to have been enacted.[155] Similarly, Pasupati Naganatha, the court poet of the Rcearal Velama kingdom, wrote a drama *Madana Vilāsabhāna* meant for staging on the occasion of the spring festival of God Kalyana Narayana. Sometimes, the troupes of actors, actresses and musicians appear to have been invited to enact these dramas. It is stated in *Krīḍābhirāmam* that this drama itself was enacted on the occasion of the festival of God Bhairava of Mopuru (Cuddapah dt.) by a dramatic troupe (*Naṭṭuvulu*) belonging to *Dōrasamudra* (Dwarasamudra, Karnataka).

Cultural Centres: The religious institutions of the period were important centres for the cultural activities of the people of the locality where they were situated. They were almost like the town-halls or community-halls of the modern period. This can be clearly seen in the case of the Hindu Temples. Marriages, investiture of the sacred thread and other similar ceremonies were usually performed in the Temple precincts. As noted earlier, it was the place where religious debates and discourses were held by religious teachers and scholars. It was the place where all entertainment programmes, such as *Harikathas*, *Burrakathas*, *Yakṣagānas* and puppet shows for the people of the village or locality were conducted. The *Vipravinodinis* (professional jugglers who entertained the Brahmans) and *Dommaras* (acrobats also exhibited their skill, usually, in the Temple precincts. *Krīḍābhirāmam* refers to some of these entertainments performed in the Temples of the Fort of Warangal during the period of Kakatiya Prataparudra II. It states:

> The new comers (Manchena and Tittabha Chetti), them saw and heard some dancing and music in a Palnad Temple. The girl who danced and sang displayed such a vigour and talent in her perfomance that the onlookers were extremely enthused and inspired to imitate some of those blood curdling events."[156]

The same work also refers to the singing of the story of Kamesvari's love by the *Jakkula* maid, and the performance of frightful acts of religious frenzy by the *Mailāra* heroes, etc. in the precincts of some of the Temples of that place.[157] *Paṅditārābhya Charitra* describes the various entertainments provided to the pilgrims keeping holy vigil on the night of the *Mahaśivarātri* day at Srisailam (Kurnool dt.) during this period.[158]

These entertainment programmes, like drama, dance, music and singing, which formed a part of the Temple life and which usually depicted the religious themes, played an important part in the cultural life of the people of the period. Besides having great educational and religious value, they provided sufficient entertainment to both the literate and illiterate masses of the locality as well as to the devotees visiting them. Similarly, the annual festivals of the Hindu Temples, especially the important of them which used to draw very great concourse of people from the neighbourhood, were marked by the performance of various types of cultural activities. They provided great entertainment to the people of all walks of life. William Methwold, an employee of the English East India company, stationed at Masulipatam, from A.D. 1618 to 1622, gives an interesting eyewitness account of the annual festivals of the Hindu Temples of the neighbourhood of that place. He observes:

> Only once a year, on their (Temples') anniversary day, they keep their festivals, and to some of them repair many thousands of people (as I myself have seen); some for devotion, and they fast 24 hours, wash their bodes, and burn lamps within or as neere the pagode as they can get; some to see their friends, children, or kindred, which will not fail to meet them in such a general liberty; others for profit (as peddlers to great fair), the whoores to dance, puppet-players and tumblers with their exquisite tricks, one whereof I will mention, with the admiration of such as saw it, or understanding shall read it. A tumbler, fetching his run, did the double sommersel (sommerset) without touching the ground with any part of his body, until he fell again on his feet, keeping his body in the aire until he turned twice round, a strange activity, and with me and others which saw it, shall not loose the wonder it carried with it. Others bring charmed snakes and Vipers in baskets. Which they let loose, and with their hands put in againe, piping unto them, and receiving their attention; very many beggars there are, and they practice several ways to move compassion, for such as have not natural defects as blindness, lameness & c. Some lie upon thornes with their Naked bodies, other lie buried in the ground all but their Heads, some all but their hands, and diverse other such trickes they put up on the poor peoples charity, whose reward is for the most part a handful of rice or a small piece

> of money that may be the half part of a farthing. About midnight the saint (Deity) is drawne forth in procession, handsomely carted and well clothed, with much clamour of drummers, trumpets hoboyes (oboes); and such like, that country musicke, and very artificial (skilful) fireworks, wherein they have a singular dexterity, followed without order or distinction of place, sex, or person; and having circled their limits, they drawn him back again . . . [159]

Meeting Places: The meetings of the village elders to decide on various matters concerning the village appear to have been usually held in the precincts of the local Temple. The village court (*Sabha* or *Dharmasāna*) usually met in the *Mantapa* or verandah of the local Temple, and settled the civil and criminal disputes of the village. *Krīḍībhirāmam* refers to the settlement of a dispute between a foreign paramour and the mother of a courtesan by *Dharmasāna* (the elders court), which met in the porch of the Temple of Bhairava in the city of Warangal, during the period of Kakatiya Parataparudra II.[160] The reason for holding this court in the precincts of the Temple was, probably, due to the belief that the people, who were usually religious minded and god-fearing, would not utter lies in the presence of the deity and would abide themselves by the decision taken in it.

The Temple precincts also usually served as a venue for the meetings of the communal organizations which assembled these to settle various matters concerning the affairs of their religious creed or trade or any other profession. Especially, the guilds belonging to the traders of various regions used to hold their meetings in the precincts of the celebrated Temples, situated at a central place, so that it would be convenient for all the members to attend them. For example, an epigraph of 1292 A.D. from Tripurantakam (Kurnool dt.) states that the merchants hailing from various countries (*Nānādēsa Pekkaṅdru*) for settling the affairs relating to either their religious creed or community (*Samayakāryānikai*) met in the presence of God Tirpurantaka Mahadeva of that place.[161] It also records their grant to that God, of duties on several articles of merchandise sold in certain villages. Similarly, an inscription of

1549 A.D. from Srisilam (Kurnool dt) states that the *Pekkańdru* (guild of traders) belonging to fifty-six countries met in the *Mukhamantapa* (Portico) of the Temple of God Mallikarjuna of the place, during the days of *Śivāratri* festival for transaction of their trade matters *(Samaya-kārya-nimittamu).*[162] On that occasion they made an endowment to the god. The holding of these meetings in Temple precincts was, probably, intended to give a religious sanction to the decisions taken at such meetings, it also enabled them to have a vision of their patron god to whom they, very often, made endowments out of their profits of customs duties on the articles sold by them. And the smaller organizations of these communities, probably, held their meetings in the local Temples of their places.

7

Conclusion

Religious Institutions, as elsewhere in India, played a major role in shaping the history of the Telugu country. The present study has endeavoured to reconstruct the history of different religious institutions that flourished in Andhra Desa and influenced the society during the three hundred years from A.D. 1300 to 1600.

This period covered by the study is quite distinctive in the history of Andhra Desa. While the beginning of the 14th century A.D. where the study starts, marks the beginning of the decline of Hindu political power under Kakatiyas and Gangas and the commencement of the Muslim rule, the end of the 16th century A.D. where the study comes to a close, saw the eventual consolidation of the Muslim political power under the Qutbshahis. This period of three centuries witnessed momentous political and religious changes with whom the fortunes of the religious institutions were inextricably linked.

The Hindu Temples which were the most important of the Hindu religious institutions, were in a flourishing condition in the Telugu country at the begging of the 14th century A.D. Among the Hindu Temples again, the Temples belonging to the Saiva sects were the most predominant at this point and the next place of importance belonged to those of Vaishnavism and Sakti cult.

The early Muslim invasions and the establishment of the Tughluq rule severely affected the fortunes of the Temples. During that period, many of them were destroyed and desecrated and some were converted into Mosques by the new rulers.

The fortunes of the Temples were revived following the re-establishment of the Hindu rule. The rulers of Musunuri, Velama, Reddi and the Sangama dynasties extended liberal patronage to these institutions. Though, they did not attain their position of the pre-Muslim period with regards to their prosperity, organization and activities, the relative strength and popularity of the Temples belonging to the various sects of Hinduism during the period of the above dynasties, remained the same as that of the Kakatiya period. But regional variations have been noticed in the fortunes of the Temples during this period which mainly depended on the corresponding political changes. The Temples of Telangana region during the period of Musunuri and Velama dynasties were less prosperous and less active than those of the Rayalaseema and the Coastal Andhra regions.

The regional variations in the fortunes of the Temples have been more clearly noticed from the middle of the 15th century onwards. In the Telangana region which after this date was under continuous Muslim rule, the Bahmanis at first and the Qutbshahis afterwards, the Temples gradually declined. The inadequate state support and the unequal competition with the Muslim religious institutions were the main reasons for their decline. Among the Temples of the Rayalaseema and the Coastal Andhra regions, the former were better in position than the latter during this period. The stable political conditions and the liberal royal patronage enabled the Temples of the Rayalaseema region to become very prosperous and active.

The sect-wise fluctuations among the Hindu Temples corresponded mainly to the dynastic and religious changes of the contemporary period. Under the Saluva and the Tuluva dynasties of Vijayanagara empire whose rulers showed special favour to the Srivaishnavas and Madhwas, the Vaishnava Temples became quite influential and rich.

The Hindu Temples received another great setback in their progress with the fall of the Gajapatis by 1538 A.D. and the decline of Vijayanagara after 1565 A.D. The consequent expansion of the Qutbshahi rule proved disastrous to the interests of the Temples especially in the Coastal Andhra and the Rayalaseema regions. Towards the end of the 16th century which marks complete decline of the Hindu rule and the consolidation of Muslim rule, the Temples in Andhra Desa were in a state of decline.

The *Maṭha* was an important Hindu religious institution in Andhra Desa at the beginning of the 14th century A.D. While the Saiva *Maṭhas* were in a predominant position throughout the Telugu country at this juncture, those of Vaishnavism were limited in number and were situated only at places like Tirupati and Simhachalam. During the period of Tughluq rule they became inactive. In the post-Tughluq period they became, once again, active. Many of them situated at places like Srisailam, Tirupati, Simhachalam, Pushpagiri and Alampur continued to function during the remaining period under study. But no evidence has been found for the existence of the *Maṭhas,* except for those of Alampur, in the Telangana region during the above-mentioned period. In the Rayalaseema and the Coastal Andhra regions, a few new *Maṭhas* belonging to the Srivaishnava and Madhwa sub-sects were established at places like Ahobilam, Simhachalam and Tirupati. The Vaishnava *Maṭhas* became quite active and prosperous due to the influential position enjoyed by their respective sects in the contemporary royal courts. The period covered by the last quarter of the 15th century A.D. and the first three quarters of the 16th century, witnessed the climax in the influence of these *Maṭhas.* The decline of the institution of the Hindu Temple consequent upon the decline of the Hindu political power, naturally led to the decline of the Hindu *Maṭha* towards the end of the 16th century A.D.

The *Agrahāras* in Andhra Desa also passed through a number of fluctuations in their fortunes which, to a great extent, depended on the contemporary political changes. They were in a flourishing condition at the beginning of the 14th century A.D. when the Telugu Country was under the Hindu rule. Their activities suffered a serious setback during the Muslim invasions and the Tughluq rule. This has been amply indicated in the contemporary epigraphs which also indicate the revival of the former under the new Hindu kingdoms, established after the Tughluq rule. Especially in the Coastyal Andhra and the Rayalaseema regions, which were under the Reddi and the Vijayanagara rule, the *Agrahāras* were in a flourishing condition. The gradual expansion of the Muslim rule, under the Bahmanis and the Qutbshahis in succession, led to the decline of the *Agrahāras*. After the battle of the Rakshasi Tangadi many *Agrahāras* were destroyed and a number of them were confiscated by the Muslim state.

The Mosques, the most important of the Muslim institutions, were very few in Andhra Desa at the beginning of the period under study. The establishment of the Tughluq rule in 1323 A.D. gave some impetus to the growth of this institution. A few new Mosques were built at some of the places like Rajahmundry and Bodhan in the conquered country. The growth in the Mosque building activity was in consonance with the growth of the Muslim political power. The establishment of the Bahmani rule in the Telangana after the middle of the 15th century A.D. and its expansion afterwards into the Coastal Andhra gave a new spurt to the building of the Mosques. A number of them were built under the patronage of the Bahmanis. Under the Vijayanagara patronage also, a few of them were built in the Rayalaseema and the Coastal Andhra. The period of the Qutbshahi rule has been an important stage in the history of the during this period a number of Mosques, some of them very grand, were built with state patronage at Golkonda and Hyderabad. They became very rich and influential. An important feature noted in the history of the institution of the Mosque in Andhra Desa is that some of them were converted from the Hindu Temples or built with the material that came from the ruins of the latter. This practice has been found throughout the period under study. The Mosques in Andhra Desa were in a flourishing condition towards the end of the 16th century A.D.

Evidence has been found for the existence of only a few *Khānqāhs* in Andhra Desa at the beginning of the 14th century A.D.

Their history during the Tughluq and the Bahmani period is almost blank. During the Qutbshahi period also, the existence of only a few of them has been attested. The existence of only a limited number of them during the Qutbshahi period was mainly due to the general decline of this institutions in the Muslim world by that period. Moreover, this institution in Andhra Desa was superseded by this time by the *Dargāh,* another Muslim institution.

The history of the *Dargah,* another important Muslim institutions in Andhra Desa, has been traced from the pre-Muslim period. The growth in the influence of this institutions was in accordance with the growth of the Muslim political power. The important *Dargāhs* which figured in the study are those of Baba Sharfuddin (Ob. 1287 A.D.) situated in the Barkas locality of old Hyderabad, of Baba Fakruddin (Ob. 1294 A.D.) at Penugonda (Anantapur dt.) and of Kadi Ziauddin Multani Warangali (Ob. 1590 A.D.) situated at Urs village near Warangal. They were patronized by the rulers and the ruled. Especially their *Urs* festivals used to be attended by a good number of people belonging to all religions, races and languages. Towards the end of the 16th century A.D., which marks the climax of the Muslim political power, the *Dargahs* in Andhra Desa were in an influential position.

The *Āshūrkhāna,* an institution belonging exclusively to the Shia sect of Islam, was of late origin. There are only few *Āshūrkhānas,* situated in and around the city of Hyderabad, which belong to the period under study. They belong to the reigns of Ibrahim Qutbshah and his successor Muhammad Quli Qutbshah. The establishment of the *Āshūrkhānas* and the celebration of *Muharram* festival became an important feature of the Muslim religious life of the period. The Qutbshahi rulers, being stanch Shias, encouraged this institution with a view to popularize the Shia sect in the Telugu country.

The Hindu Temple, for managing its affairs, had an organization consisting of a number of functionaries. The number of categories of the Temple staff and the designation of some of them closely resembled those of the contemporary Hindu state. The first category, the Managerial staff, included mainly the Temple Superintendent, the Temple Treasurer, and the Accountants who were also included in the Temple trust-boards.

The second category of the functionaries, known variously as *Archaka, Pūjāri* and *Naṃbi,* performed the daily worship and other religious rituals. In many Temples, they were also associated with the management.

The third category, known variously as *Ūdigālavāru, Nibaṇdha Kāṇdru, Koluvulavāru,* and *Kaṇdācharamvāru,* comprised the numerous non-priestly staff attending to the miscellaneous functions.

It has been found that people belonging to certain communities were specially employed for certain services in the Temples. Almost all the functionaries were appointed on hereditary and full-time basis and received remuneration both in cash and in kind. Some of the categories of the Temple servants were organized as corporate bodies.

The Hindu *Maṭha,* organized on the basis of monarchical principle, had a pontiff known by designation as *Maṭhādipati* or *Jiyyar.* The pontiffs were normally Brahmans. But in the case of Veera Saiva *Maṭhas,* non-brahmans acted as pontiffs. The *Maṭhādhipati* engaged *Kāryakartas* and *Mudrakartas* who were also *Maṭha's* regular members to assist him in managing the affairs of the *Maṭha*. Besides them, there were a few servants to attend to the menial services.

The *Agrahāras* were autonomous and self-governing villages.

The organization of the Mosque was simple and its functionaries were a few. At the time of the establishment of a Mosque itself, its trustee, known as *Mutawali* was appointed on hereditary basis. The other important functionaries of a Mosque were *Imām* or the leader of the congregational prayers and a few menial servants.

The *Khānqāh,* like the Hindu *Maṭha* was organized on the basis of monarchical principle. Its pontiff, generally known as *Shaikh* or *Pir*, was at the apex of its organization. He presided over its congregations and gave instruction to his disciples. The spiritual disciples of the *Shaikh* were-known as *Murīd.* His chief disciple known as *Kalipha* became his successor. But usually the succession to the pontificate was hereditary.

The head of the *Dargāh's* organizations was *Mutawalli,* who was generally a descendant of the deceased saint to whom the *Dargāh* belonged. The post of *Mutawali* was hereditary. He was the owner of the properties of the *Dargāh* and decided all matters concerning it. *Sajjāda* was the manager of the *Dargāh.* He was appointed by the *Mutawalli* and was given a fixed salary.

The chief functionary of the *Ashrākhana* was its trustee known as *Mutawalli.* He was appointed at the time of the crection of the *Āshurkhāna.* His post was hereditary. The next important functionary of this institutions was its caretaker known as *Mujāver* who also held his post hereditorily and got a fixed salary.

The religious institutions, being basically service-oriented in nature, were concerned in managing their finances only to the extent of meeting their requirements.

The income of the religious institutions was mobilized from various sources which have been classified under two main categories–long-term or fixed assets and short-term or current assets. The first category comprised both movable and immovable properties and included villages, lands, gardens, buildings, cattle, jewellery etc. The second category consisted of the proceeds of taxes, tolls and other monetary endowments. The donors of the religious institutions belonged to a wide cross-section of the society. They were mainly the kings, their subordinate officials, feudal nobles, corporate bodies, communal organizations and private individuals, in order of importance.

Every religious institutions possessed landed property, the quantum of which was dependent on its size and popularity. In a majority of the cases, they leased their cultivable lands including groves and gardens to the tenants who gave the former a portion of the produce, as the owner's share. They derived considerable income from their cattle which mainly consisted of cows, bulls, buffaloes, sheep and goats.

The income of the religious institutions from their short-term assets included the proceeds of the taxes and tolls granted to them by the government. It has been noticed regarding the mode of collection of the proceeds of taxes and tolls, that sometimes the donors themselves took the responsibility of collecting and depositing them with the religious institutions and sometimes the latter was asked to take that responsibility.

It has been found that important items of expenditure of the religious institutions included mainly the remuneration of their functionaries, purchasing various articles for food and other religious services, charities and other social services, construction and conservation of their buildings and taxes. The ratio of the amount spent on these items depended upon the nature of the institutions and its size.

The income of the religious institutions was, normally, sufficient for their expenditure. The rich among them, which had more income than expenditure, invested their suplus money, sometimes, in acquiring new properties and thereby got some more income. But some of them ran into financial difficulties in times of unfavourable conditions and were compelled to resort to borrowing by mortgaging their properties. Sometimes they sold their properties to overcome the financial difficulties. These financial difficulties affected their functioning also.

The preparation of the budget and keeping of the accounts as noticed in the case of some major Hindu Temples, and particularly the closing of the old accounts and the opening of the new accounts on the first day of the dark fortnight in the month of *Kārtīka* (i.e. *Deepāva!i*) shows how efficiently their finances were managed.

The chief patron of the religious institutions was the state. The governments of the period, whether Hindu or Muslim, earmarked a considerable part of their income and landed property for the maintenance of the religious institutions in their dominions.

In order to ensure the proper functioning of the religious institutions, the government exercised supervision and control over the management of the affairs of the latter situated in their dominions. Many of the governments had a separate department headed by a minister in-charge of the religious endowments. The Revenue departments also had some connection with the management of the religious institutions. Lspecially in the case of the Hindu states, the provincial and dist-ict revenue officials were entrusted, many a time, with the responsibility of executing the grants and supervising the management especially of the Temples. In some cases, a departure was made from this practice and the governments appointed separate officials who acted as the executive officers and exercised control and supervision over the work of the trust-boards and prevented mismanagement. Even the government's lower level revenue officials also had some say in the administration of the religious institutions. Sometimes, the agent of the royal donors also participated in their administration. The proper functioning of these institutions was also ensured, to some extent, by the periodical visits by the kings and their subordinate officials. They personally enquired into their affairs, redressed the grievance, if any, and took action against the erring staff.

The government extended protection to the religious institutions, their properties and pilgrims from thieves, robbers and even foreign invaders.

The government, especially in the Hindu states, extended its fiscal regulations to the Hindu religious institutions, as in the case of the ordinary citizens in its own villages. The religious institutions paid various kinds of taxes and tolls to the government and contributed considerably to the state exchequer. Their properties, though supposed to have been tax-free endowments, were liable to be taxed in practice.

The religious institutions through their religious and spiritual activities, not only contributed to the evolution and propagation of their respective religious systems but also helped the maintenance of righteousness and harmony in the society.

The religious institutions were great centres of intellectual and educational activities and thereby considerably enriched the intellectual life of the contemporary society. The Temple, the Mosque, the *Maṭha* and the *Khānqāh* acted as the most important agencies of diffusing knowledge among the needy people. They maintained schools and colleges where religious as well as secular subjects were taught not only to their occupants but also to the outside students who came for that purpose. Similarly, the provision made in the Temples for the religious discourses and the reading of the religious texts helped the spread of religious knowledge among the people. Many of these institutions maintained a good collection of manuscripts, composed by their members and others.

The religious institutions were great centres of charity and provided shelter, food, drinking water, clothes and medical facilities to the needy pilgrims, students, general travellers and even to animals. When there were neither lodging and boarding houses nor hospitals in the modern sense of them terms, these services rendered by the religious institutions were of great social significance.

By encouraging philanthropic attitude in rich classes, these institutions counteracted the general tendency towards the amassing of wealth by a few rich individuals. Thus, they indirectly contributed to the economic socialism in the contemporary society. Similar activities of some of the religious and social organizations of the present day are, probably, the continuation of the traditions established by these religious institutions.

The religious institutions exercised a profound influence over the political life of the contemporary society. This influence, in most cases, was benevolent and changed, many a time, the very course of the history of the country. The members of these institutions and especially those of the *Maṭhas* and the *Khānqāhs*, did not shun the world and the people and bury themselves in spiritual and intellectual pursuits. On the other hand, they engaged themselves in politics, diplomacy and intrigue to influence the contemporary political life. As guides, philosophers and friends, they came to the rescue of the monarchs whenever the latter were in trouble. They were instrumental in the creation of new states and in deciding succession to the throne. The members of some of these institutions assumed royal titles and behaved like temporal princes. Sometimes, the influence and activities of these institutions transcended the barriers of the political state, language and race and contributed to the national unity.

An important function fulfilled by these religious institutions was to build a rapport and understanding between the kings and their subjects. In times, when there was no means of communication between the monarchs and the masses and mass communication in particular, these religious institutions functioned as mass media.

The religious institutions were also great centres of economic activity. Next to the state, they were the greatest employers and gave employment to a large number of people as administrators, priests, accountants, artists, artisans, cooks and menial servants, who attended to their various services. As land-lords, they employed a large number of cultivators and agricultural labourers. They played an important role in the extension of agriculture and reclamation of waste lands and helped in increasing the economic wealth of the society. Similarly, the work of construction, repair and decoration etc. undertaken by these institutions also created a lot of employment. As consumers of various merchandise, they provided livelihood for a number of people who were employed in producing and supplying those items.

Next to the state, these institutions created great job-potential. Especially the Temple was unique in the sense that it gave employment to a large number of women skilled in various arts. They also acted as banks in a limited sense by advancing loans to the needy.

The seeds of the Industrial Exhibitions and Fairs were laid in the activities like *Tirunāl, Jātara* and *Urs* held under the aegis of these institutions.

The religious institutions were great cultural centres around which the cultural life of the contemporary society revolved. They promoted various arts, architecture, sculpture, painting, calligraphy, music, dance and drama and harnessed them successfully for religious purposes. The artists and craftsmen were patronized and trained by the religious institutions. Besides these classical arts, the folk arts like *Yakśa-gānam, Burrakatha, Harikata,* puppet shows and jugglery were also promoted by them. The patronage extended by the religious institutions to these arts and cultural activities contributed greatly to their development and preservation. The precincts of the religious institutions were the meeting places for village assemblies and communal and professional organizations. The modern intellectual gatherings and art exhibitions have their parallels in similar activities of these institutions. They played the role of a modern town-hall, cinema theatre, art-galleries, etc. by providing entertainment in the form of musical concerts, dance, drama, puppet shows and the like.

Finally, it can be said that these religious institutions were the custodians of Indian culture and carries of Indian heritage.

References and Notes

Chapter-1

1. *Bharati,* Vol. 16, 1926, pp. 239-49.
2. *All the Kings' Mana: Papers on Medieval South Indian History,* Madras, 1984, pp. 68-89.
3. *Sada-e-Jaffaria* (Special *Muharram* issue,), Oct. 1978.
4. *Ibid.*
5. The general public, especially the people in the backward regions, who are far away from the influence of important religious and cultural centres, worshiped innumerable minor deities. Srinatha, the great Telugu poet of the Reddi period, while giving a description of the backward conditions prevailing in the Planati *Sīma* (in modern Guntur dt.) says in a *Catu* verse that the people of that region worshipped a number of minor Gods (*"Chinna Chinna rallu chillara devullu... pallennati sima palletoollu"*) (V. Prabhakara Sastri (ed.), *Chatupadya Manimanjari,* p. 126).
6. *Telangana Sasanamulu,* Vol. II, (Kakatiya Inscriptions) of 1096 A.D.
7. B., Butterworth and Venugopal Chetty, *Nellore District Inscriptions,* (Podili), p. 2 of 11th century, A.D.
8. K. Iswara Dutt, *Inscriptional Glossary of Andhra Pradesh,* p. 315 of 1170 A.D.
9. *South Indian Inscriptions,* Vol. No. 700, of 1262 A.D.
10. *SII.,* VI, No. 904, of 1291 A.D.

11. *SII, VI,* no. 81, of 1292 A.D.
12. *SII.*, X, no. 585, of 1445 A.D.
13. *Ibid.*, IV, no. 702, of 1518 A.D.
14. *Ibid.*, X, no. 743, of 1530 A.D.
15. *NI.*, (Darsi) p. 65, of 1538 A.D.
16. *Ibid.*, (Gudur), p. 19, of 1697 A.D.
17. *Inscriptions of Andhra Pradesh,* Cuddapah District II, no. 12 of 1370 A.D.
18. *Ibid.*, no. 44.
19. *Tirumala-Tirupati Devasthanam Epigraphical Series, passim.*
20. For *Paramahamsa* and *Parivrajakaaharya,* the titles of Ramanuja Jiyyar of *Tengalai* Srivaishnava *Maṭha* at Tirumalai, see *TDER* p. 92.
21. *Ins., Gloos.*, p. 6.
22. *SII.*, V. nos. 8 & 15.
23. *Telangana Sasanamulu* II, p. 169
24. In this study, the *Agrahāra* is treated as one of the religious institutions because of its predominant religious character though it differs from the other institutions in certain aspects which will be discussed in the second chapter.
25. Ziauddin Desai, *Mosques of India,* p. 7.
26. S. Baba Mala, 'The Sufi Convent and its Social Significance in the Medieval Period of Islam', *Islamic Culture,* V, 1997. Jan. p. 35.
27. *Ibid.*, p. 32.
28. H. K. Sherwani, *History of the Qutbshahi Dynasty,* p. 313.
29. Quoted from Stella Kramarisch, *The Hindu Temple,* p. 139.
30. *Ibid.*, fn. P. 139.
31. "*Tana pencina santanamu = dana santanambum = gritiyum = (da) na nallillunu Vanamunum jeruvunu gudiyunum jana-vinutamul = aina sapta santanambulu*" (The children brought

up by oneself, one's own children, (literary) work, ones' *Agrahāra,* garden, tank and Temple these are famous among men as one's seven children)., 'Gangadhara's Inscription from Karimnagar', *Tel., Ins.*, II, p. 169.

32. *Shorter Encyclopedia of Islam,* p. 336.
33. M. Somasekhara Sarma, *A Forgotten Chapter of Andhra History,* App. I.
34. *Ibid.,* App. II.
35. *Journal of Andhra Historical Research Society,* Vol. IV, p. 147, ff.
36. *Inscriptions of Andhra Pradesh,* Warangal District, no. 111.
37. *TTDE,* V, no. 89.
38. H. M. Elliot and John Dowson (Trans.) *History of India as told by its own Historians,* pp. 67-93 and pp. 557-65.
39. M. Elliot, (trans and ed.). *The History of India* (as told by its own Historians), The Mohammadan period.
40. J. Briggs (Trans), *History of the Rise of the Mahomedan power in India,* 3. Vols., Calcutta, 1908-1910.
41. J. S. King, *The History of the Bahmani Dynasty,* (founded on Burhan-i-Ma'asir), London, 1900.
42. J. Briggs, (Trans) *History of the Rise of the Mahomedan Power in India,* Vol. III, Calcutta, 1901, pp. 339-484.
43. Girdharilal Ahqar, *Tarikh-i-Zafarah,* Gorakpur, 1927.
44. Anonymous Historian, *Tuzuk-e-Qutbshahi* (Salarjung Library, Persian Manuscript Catalogue no. 412, pp. 475-78).
45. Abdul Jabbar Khan Malkapuri, *Mahbub-i-dhil-manam Tadhkira Auliya-i-Dakkan,* 2 Vols.

CHAPTER-2

1. This must have been the *Rūkha,* one of the three types of coins prevalent under the Kakatiyas, the other two being *Niṣhkamu* and *Chinnamu.*

2. *Siddēśvara Charitramu,* pp. 154-55
3. *Ibid.,* Intro. Pp. xxvii-xxviii.
4. Inscription of 1313 A.D. from Srisailam, *SII,* XVI, no. 504.
5. *Futher Sources,* I, p. 39.
6. *ED.,* III, p. 8
7. *ED.,* III, p. 559.
8. Ziauddin Barni states: "He (Malik Kafur) took from Ladder deo (Prataparudra II) all the treasure which he had accumulated in the course of many years – a hundred elephants, seven thousand horses, and large quantities of jewels and valuables. He also took from him a writing, engaging to send annual treasures and elephants..." (*ED.,* III, p. 203). This account is supported by Amir Khusru. He states that Malik Kafur left Arangal (Warangal) in 1310 A.D., after subduing its ruler, with all his booty; and 'a thousand camels groaned under the weight of the treasures..." (*Kazāinul Futūh"* p. 79). Similarly, Khusru Khan, Mubarak Shah Khilji's general, who subdued Prataparudra II in 1318 A.D. "received from the Rai five districts,... an annual tribute of more than a hundred strong elephants, as large as demons, 12.000 horse, and gold and jewels and gems beyond compute..." (*ED.,* III, pp. 560-61).
9. *Forgotten Chapter,* Appendix. I.
10. The Vaishnava Temple at Rajahmundry, which was converted into a Mosque during the invasion of the country by Muhammad-Bin-Tughluq in A.D. 1324, appears to have been looted, on that occasion, by the Muslim invaders who even killed the priests (see *Madras Dist. Gazetters – Godavari* supplement) – 1935, p. 395). The Hindu Temple of Bodhan was converted into a Mosque by Muhammad-Bin-Tughluq when that town was occupied by him. (see *AR of the Archaeological Department of H. H. the Nizam's Dominions,* 1914-15, pp. 3-4.
11. *A.R.,* 1912, no. 44.

12. *A.R.,* 1958, B. no. 12.

13. *IAP Wg.*, no. 104.

14. *Archaeological Bulletin,* no. 11 (A. P. Govt. Arch. Series no. 15, p. 57).

15. Quoted from S. Pratapa Reddi. *Āndhrula Sānghika Charitra,* p. 90.

16. N. Ramesan, (ed.), *Copper Plate Inscription of A.P. State Museum II,* p. 1.

17. *SII.*, XVI, nos. 1-35.

18. Vittalamba, wife of Harihara II, caused the construction of steps to the river Krishna from Srisailam mountain (L. R. 18, p. 404); Prolyaya Vema Reddi built a flight of steps leading to the river Krishna near Srisailam according to his Puvvada grant (C. P. Inscriptions of A. P. Govt. Museum, I, p. 173); According to Jatara-revu inscription, Mada I of Velama kingdom built a flight of steps down to the northern bank of the river Krishna near Srisailam for the pilgrims (Epigraphia Andhrika I, no. 8).

19. *Reddi Kingdoms,* p. 22 ff.

20. *A.R.*, 1962-63, B, no. 224.

21. *Briggs,* II, p. 305.

22. *IAP. Wg.*, no. 111.

23. Syed Ali Tabataba, *Burhan-i-Mathir,* p. 58.

24. *AR of Archaeological Dept. Hyderabad State for* 1915-16, p. 4.

25. *Briggs* III. (anon,) p. 355.

26. *Tarīkh-i-Qutbshāhī* (Ms.), f. 70.

27. *Briggs* III, p. 497.

28. R, Subrahmanyam, 'Vijayanagar Architecture', in *Medieval Deccan* II, p. 317 ff.

29. *TDER.*, p. 130.

30. Burton Stein, *All the Kings' Mana: Papers on Medieval South Indian History,* Madras, 1984, p. 70.

31. *SII.*, V, no. 1312.
32. *Ibid.*, VI, no. 1184.
33. *Mac, Mss,* 100, pp. 21-22.
34. *SII.*, XVI, no. 296.
35. *Mac, Mss.*, 20 (SA), pp. 8-37
36. *Ibid.*, 4 (SA), p. 19.
37. *Ibid.*, VI, p. 54.
38. *Briggs* III, p. 460.
39. *Briggs* III p. 444. It appears that the Temple near Adoni is no other than that of Ahobilam, and this incident of 1579 A.D. is the same as that of the sack of Ahobilam by Ibrahim Qutb Shah in the same year referred to before.
40. *Relations,* pp. 57-88.
41. *Ibid.*, p. 71.
42. *Ibid.*, p. 72.
43. T.K.T. Veeraraghava Charya, *History of Tirupati,* (1978), pp. 11 & 40.
44. The *Sanyasis* of Ancient India, belonging to the last stage of the four-fold *Āśhrama* system, described in *Upanishads,* and the ascetics belonging to the theistic Hindu sects of the early centuries of Christian era, were not cenobites. They did not lead a corporate life and did not belong to a particular monastic order with a fixed abode. They led a highly individualistic life and their life was of eremitic character. Of course, the Buddhists and Jains were the first to establish monastic orders in cenobitic from.
45. H. Charaborthy, *Asceticism in Ancient India,* pp. 178-79.
46. *Ibid.*, pp. 181-82.
47. *Ibid.*, p. 182.
48. *Studies in the Third Dynasty,* p. 324.
49. *EI,* XXXIII, p. 161.
50. *SII.*, III, no. 18.

51. *IAP.*, Wg., no. 15.
52. *AR.*, 1967, B. no. 3.
53. *Mac, Mss,* 104, p. 68.
54. Yazdani, (ed.), *The Early History of the Deccan,* I, p. 710.
55. *AR.*, 1959, B. no. 94.
56. *JAHRS.*, IV, p. 147, ff.
57. *Mac. Mss.*, 396, pp. 1. 13.
58. C. Elliot, *Hindustan and Buddhism,* p. 233.
59. *TDER.*, pp. 94-95
60. *Simhachalam Temple,* p. 151.
61. *TDER.*, p. 88.
62. *Ibid.*
63. Two inscriptions, one of 1352 A.D. from Srikurmam (*SII. V,* no. 1313) and another of 1358 A.D. from Simhachalam (*SII,* VI, no. 892), refer to the Narasimhabharati, the chief pontiff of those *Mathas,* issuing certain instructions to his disciples regarding the assets of the two *Maṭhas*.
64. *TDER.*, p. 93. These *Maṭhas* appear to have been additions to the already existing Jiyyangar *Maṭham* of the place.
65. V. Rangacharya, 'Historical Evolution of Srivaishnavism in South India', in *The Cultural Heritage of India,* IV, p. 182.
66. *TDER.*, p. 215.
67. *Ibid.*, p. 91-95
68. *Ibid.*, p. 92.
69. *Mac Mss.*, 139, p. 6.
70. *TDER.*, p. 278 According to an epigraph of Sadasiva Raya's period from Tirumalai-Tirupati (No. 65, *TTDI.*, V) Vedanta Sathakopa *Jiyar* was authorized to receive the donors share of Nandyala Naraparaja of the offered *Prasadam* and arecanuts and betel-leaves throughout the succession of his

disciples. This was apparently meant for the use in the local *Vadagalai Matham* (Sathakopan *Maṭham*) which was the branch of Ahobila *Maṭha.*

71. *TDER.*, p. 1146
72. *Ibid.*, p. 91-95.
73. *TTDE.*, III, no. 175.
74. *Bharati,* Sept. 1957, p. 69-73.
75. *Studies in the Third Dynasty,* p. 419.
76. N. Ramesan, (ed.,) *Copper Plate Inscriptions of A.P. Govt. Museum,* II, p. 42.
77. *SII.*, VI. No. 248.
78. *SII.*, XIV, no. 130., N. Ramesan (ed.), *op. cit.*, p. 13.
79. *Reddi Sanchika,* Annexure, pp. 15-16
80. An inscription of 1545 A.D. from Koruvampalle village (Cuddapah dt.) describes the donee of an *Agrahāra* as *Śatkarma–niratulu* (*Cudd. Ins.*, p. 149).
81. *SII.*, VI, no. 248.
82. Quoted from S. Pratapareddi, *Āndhrula Śanghika Charitra,* p. 125.
83. *Siddēśvara Charitramu,* pp. 154-55.
84. *Forgotten Chapter,* Appendix I.
85. Vilasa grant states; "King Prolaya restored to the Brahmans their *Agrahāras* which were granted to them by the former kings but forcibly taken away from them by those wrong-doers (*Turuśkas*). He revived the religious sacrifices with their uninterrupted smoke emanating from oblations…" (*Forgotten Chapter,* Appendix I).
86. N. Ramesan, (ed.) *C. P. Inscriptions of A. P. Govt. Museum,* Vol. I, p. 173.
87. *Reddi Kingdoms,* p. 261.
88. *SII.*, VI, no. 243.

89. Srinatha, *Kaśikhāndamu,* p. 11.

90. *Mac. Mss.* no. 101, p. 105.

91. *Mac. Mss.,* 4 (S. A.), p. 19.

92. *NI.,* II, p. 667.

93. *AR.,* 1967, D. no. 3.

94. *Kr., Rm.,* p. 50.

95. A. Watson, *The War of the Goldsmiths' Daughter,* Chapter III. P. 49.

96. The inscription of Ghiathuddin Tughluq from Rajahmundry', in *EIM,* 1923-24, p. 13.

97. *EIM.,* 1919-20, p. 16.

98. Syed Ali Tabataba, *Burhān-i-Māthir,* p. 58.

99. *AR.,* 1964, D. nos. 1 & 2.

100. *AR., of Archaeological Dept. of Hyderabad State for 1915-16,* p. 4.

101. *AR.,* 1924, B. no. 246.

102. G. Mackenzie, *Manual of Krishna dt.* (1883 A.D.), p. 87.

103. *VR.,* I (Chittoor) no. 158, p. 490.

104. *Briggs* II, p. 431.

105. Anonymous Historian, *Tarīkh-i-Qutbshahī,* (MS), p. 70.

106. *Landmarks,* pp. 110-112

107. Quoted from, M. A. Abdul Muid Khan, *Arabian poets of Golkonda,* p. 27.

108. Z.A. Desai, 'Architecture—Bahmani Succession State' in *Medieval Deccan* II, pp. 296-97.

109. *Landmarks,* p. 15.

110. *AR.,* 1963-64, D. no. 17.

111. Z.A. Desai, *op cit.,*

112. *Landmarks,* pp. 27-28.

113. *Ibid.*

114. *EIM.*, 1925-26, p. ff.
115. *Madras Dist., Gazetter,* Godavari (supplement) 1935, p. 395.
116. *AR., of the Archaeological Dept., of H.H. the NIzam's Dominions,* 1914-15, pp. 3-4.
117. *AR., of the Archaeological Dept., Hyderabad State for* 1915-16, G. Yazdani.
118. Anonymous Historian, *Tārīkh-i-Qutbshāhī* (MS) p. 70.
119. K.A. Nizami, *Some Aspects of Religion and Politics in India during the Thirteenth Century,* p. 59.
120. S. Baba Mala, 'The Sūfi Convent and its social significance in the Medieval period of Islam in *IC.*, V, 1977, Jan, p. 35.
121. K.A. Nizami, 'Sufi Movement in Deccan', in *Medieval Deccan,* II, p. 178.
122. *Malkapuri,* I, pp. 163-173 and 193-195.
123. *AR.*, 1967, D. no. 2.
124. For the date of his death, See *AR.*, 1967, D. no. 1.
125. The corresponding period in Western Deccan marks the zenith of the growth of the *Khānqāhs* especially belonging to the Chisti Sūfis. Their decline started towards the end of the 15th century A.D., which coincides with the decline of the Bahmani Sultanate.
126. *Quṭbshāhi dynasty,* p. 254, fn. No. 204.
127. *Landmarks,* p. 74.
128. *Ibid.*
129. *Quṭbshāhi dynasty,* p. 601.
130. *Malkapūri,* pp. 245-48.
131. *Ibid.*
132. *Malkapuri,* I. p. 164.
133. *Ibid.*, p. 246.
134. *Ibid.*, p. 248.
135. *AR.*, 1967, D. no. 2.

136. *Ibid.*, 1911-62, pp. 89-90.

137. T. Srinivas, 'Rājukonda and its Remains' *The Journal of the Hyderabad Archaeological Society,* 1916. July.

138. *Ibid.*

139. *Ālāmpur Sanchika,* 1970, p. 18.

140. A.A. Bilgrami, *Historical Sketches of H.H. the Nizam's Dominions,* pp. 571-75

141. Hazarat Ali was the cousin and son-in-law of the Prophet.

142. Ghulam Hussain Khan, *Gulzar-i-Asfiyah,* p. 551; A.A. Bilgrami, *Masir-e-Deccan,* p. 4.

143. *A.A. Bilgrami, Masir-e-Deccan,* p. 10.

144. Rahat Azmi, 'Hyderabad ke Muqadas Tabarrukat' (Urdu article) in *Sadā-e-Jāffarīya,* 1978, Oct. pp. 37-56.

145. Muhammad Ali Khan, *Tazkara-e-Zakīriah,* p. 166.

146. Hadi Ali Baqari, 'Hyderabad ke Qadim Ashurkhane' (Urdu article) in *Sada-e-Jāffarīya,* 1978, Oct., p. 63.

147. *Landmarks,* pp. 22-24

148. *Ibid.*

149. *Qutbshahi Dynasty* p. 366, fn. No. 91.

150. *Landmarks,* p. 99.

151. Mirzah Nizamuddin Ahmed, *Hadiqatos Salātin,* p. 58.

Chapter-3

1. *SII.*, XVI, no. 502.

2. *Ibid.*, X, no. 12.

3. *Ibid.*, X, no. 465 & *Ibid.*, XVI, no. 502.

4. *The Archaeological Bulletin* no. 11, (A. P. Govt. Archaeological Series-15); p. 57.

5. Srinatha, *Śivarātrimahatmyamu,* Pītika, p. iv.

6. The various kinds of officers belonging to the civil and military departments and royal household in the Kakatiya

kingdom appear to have been divided into 72 categories and the term '*Bāhatari Niyōgam*' was used to denote them. The Kayasta Gangaya Sahini held the office of the '*Bāhattara Niyōgādhipati*' in the year 1251 A.D. under Kakatiya Ganapti Deva (*SII.*, X, no. 332). Similarly an epigraph of 1290 A.D. describes Gandapendara Ambadeva Maharaja, a Kakatiya official as *Bāhattara Niyōgadhipati,* (*SII.*, X. no. 464). *Rāyavāchakam* refers to the existence of *Debbairendu Niyōgālavāru* (72 categories of employees) in the Vijayanagara government, which included the *Pālēgars, Amarānayakas,* religious teachers, musicians, etc. (*Rāyāvachakam, ASPP.*, III, pp. 13-14).

7. *TTDE.*, I, no. 187.
8. They were laymen in the sense they were not permanent and regular functionaries of the temple doing day-to-day service as the *Archakas* and accountants.
9. See T. K. T. Veeraraghava Charya, *History of Tirupati,* Vol. I (1977), p. 374; same author, *History of Tirupati* (1976), p. 11.
10. *Mac. Mss.*, 272, pp. 48-56.
11. *AR.*, 1941, B. no. 238.
12. *SII.*, XVI, no. 238.
13. *NI,* II., p. 608
14. *SII.*, XVI, no. 74.
15. *SII.*, IV, no. 280.
16. N. Venkataramanayya, in his '*Studies in the History of Third Dynasty of Vijayanagara*' (p. 331) also remarks that each Board of the *Sthānikas* of this period had a President known as *Sthānapati* or *Sthānacharya.*
17. *Cuddapah Inscriptions,* p. 348.
18. *Mac. Mss.*, 137, p. 69.
19. The administration of these Temples during this period appears to have been vested in a committee of Vaishnavas

(C. V. Ramachandra Rao, *Administration and Society in Medieval Andhra (A.D. 1038-1538) under the Later Eastern Gangas and the Sūryavamsi Gajaptis,* p. 346).

20. *SII.,* V. no. 1214.
21. *Ibid.,* VI, no. 1646.
22. *Ibid.,* V, no. 1214.
23. *Ibid.,* XIV, no. 20.
24. M. A. Waheed Khan, (ed.), *Stone Sculptures in the Ālampūr Museum,* Ins. No. 22.
25. *Ibid.,* Ins. Nps. 3, 4, 7, 8, 11, 12, 14, 15, 18, 20 & 22.
26. *Mac., Mss.,* 137. p. 69.
27. *SII.,* XVI, no. 238.
28. An inscription of 1482 A. D. from Tirupati refers, clearly, to the supervision of the *Sthānattar* over the construction and repair of the buildings belonging to the Venkatesvara Temple (*TTDE,* II, no. 79.)
29. *Ibid.*
30. 'Kaifiyat of Rāmēśvaram', *Mac., Mss.,* 133, p. 42.
31. *TDER.,* pp. 276-77.
32. *Ibid.*
33. A large number of epigraphs, especially from Tirupati, Simhachalam, and Srikurmam refer to the *Sribhāṅdaram* of the Temples of those places transacting money matters.
34. inscription of 1556 A.D., *SII.,* IV, no.280.
35. *SII.,* XVI, no. 98.
36. *Ibid.,*VI, no.1008.
37. *AR.,* 1924, B. no. 152
38. *AR.,* 1922, B. no. 169.
39. *TDER.,* p. 222. Some of the temples of the period appear to have maintained a separate granary for storing their food grains. An inscription of 1318 A.D. from Draksharamamu

(Godavari dt) refers to the *Viviḍha-ḍhānyalaymulu* (granaries for storing different types of grain), besides the *bhaṅdāgāramu* attached to the Temple of Bhimesvara of that place (*SII.* IV no. 1379). Simiarly, an epigraph of 1305 A.D.from Srikurmam (Srikaulam dt.) refers to the existence of a *Kōśtamu* (granary) besides the *Sribhaṅdāram* in the temple of that place (*SII.*, V. no. 1151).

40. *TDER.*, p.216
41. *TTDE.*, II, no. 79.
42. *Ibid.*, no. 35.
43. *NI.*, III, p.1363
44. *SII.*, VII, no. 569.
45. Inscription of 1281 A.D., *Simhāchalam Temple*, p. 96.
46. Inscription of 1309 A.D., *SII* V. no. 1214.
47. *SII.*, VI, no. 876.
48. *TTDE.*, II, nos. 114-120.
49. *Ibid.*, V, no. 82.
50. *Ibid.*, II, no. 132.
51. *Ibid.*, II, no. 135; See also T.V.K. Viraraghavacharya., *History of Tirupati Temple* (1977), I, p. 170.
52. *TTDE.*, I, pp. 175-76.
53. *Ibid.*, II, no. 132.
54. *Ibid.*, II, nos. 115, 116, 130.
55. *TDER.*, p. 278; SII, XVI, no. 932.
56. *SII.*, XVI, no. 932.
57. *Ibid.*, no. 260.
58. Of course, in the case of the Temples like those of Tirupati and Simhachalam, though the Srivaishnavas captured their management during the period of Ramanujacharya, the original *Archakas*, that is, *Naṁbis* belonging to the *Vāikhānasa Āgama* continued to conduct worship in them.

Srinivasa Bhattar, the officiating priest of Raghunatha Temple at Tirupati, in the middle of the 15th century A.D. was a great scholar and is said to have written a commentary on Kalidasa's *Sākuntala Nātaka* (*TDER.*, p. 67).

59. *NI.*, I, no. 333.
60. *Mac., Mss.*, 106, p. 68.
61. *Further Sources II,* p. 138.
62. *SII.*, X, no. 531.
63. *Ibid.*, no. 737.
64. *TTDE.*, III, no. 157.
65. 'Inscription of 15th or 16th century A.D. from Udayagiri' (Nellore dt.), *NI,* III, p. 1360.
66. 'Inscriptions from 'Śrīkūramam', *SII.,* V, nos. 1172, 1187, 1204 and 1214.
67. *Cudd., Ins.*, p. 179.
68. *SII.*, V, no. 1183.
69. *Ibid.*, IV, no. 702.
70. *Mac. Mss.*, 245, pp. 40-31
71. *TTDE.*, II, no. 135.
72. *VR.*, I, p. 691.
73. *SII.*, VI, no. 1091.
74. *Ibid.*, X, no. 742.
75. *Ibid.*, IV, no. 1379.
76. *Ibid.*, VI, no. 890.
77. *Ibid.*, VI, no. 941.
78. *Ibid.*, VI, no. 955.
79. *AR.*, 1916-17, pp. 143-144.
80. *TDER.*, VI, p. 205.
81. *SII.*, VI, no. 818.
82. *Ibid.*, no. 1099.

83. *Ibid.*, no. 84.
84. *NI.*, III, p. 1360.
85. *TDER.*, p. 259.
86. *SII.*, VI, no. 941; *Mac. Mss.* (S.A.) 23, pp. 67-69.
87. *Mac. Mss.*, 404, pp. 103-113.
88. (Simhāchalam) *SII.*, VI, (Śrīkūrmam) *SII.*, V.
89. C. V. Ramachandra Rao, *Administration and Society in Medieval Andhra (A.D. 1038-1538) under the Later Eastern Gangas and the Suryavamsi Gajapatis,* pp. 303-04.
90. *TDER.*, pp. 85-87
91. *Ibid.*, p. 85.
92. *SII.*, IV, no. 280.
93. *Ibid.*, VI, no. 938.
94. *Ibid.*, VI, no. 1240.
95. *Mac. Mss.*, 127, p. 30.
96. *Ibid.*, 270, p. 51.
97. *Mac. Mss.*, 260, pp. 3-4
98. *AR.*, 1938, B. no. 22.
99. *Mac. Mss.*, 245, p. 42.
100. *AR.*, 1953-54, B. no. 22.
101. *Mac. Mss*, 388, p. 3.
102. *SII.*, VI, no. 1035.
103. T. K. T. Viraraghavacharya, *op.cit.*, (1976) p. 25.
104. *Cudd. Ins.*, pp. 351-52.
105. *TDER.*, V, nos. 89.
106. *Ibid.*, no. 125.
107. *TDER.*, p. 278-79.
108. *NII.*, p. 23.
109. *Cudd. Ins.*, p. 493.
110. *Ibid.*, p. 677-78.

111. *SII.*, VI, no. 84.

112. *SII.*, VI, no. 950 & 954.

113. C. V. Ramachandra Rao, *op. cit.*, pp. 251-259.

114. *SII.*, VI, no. 81.

115. *TDER.*, p. 94.

116. Nilakanta Sastri, *Development of Religion in South India*, p. 116.

117. 'Gadikota *Kaifiyat*' (*Mac. Mss.* 124, p. 60); Gollapalli *Kaifiyat* (*p. 101-102, Mac. Mss. 105*) refers to Govinda Bharati, the pontiff of the Puspagiri *Maṭha* as the receipient of the Gollapalli village and several other villages in the Dravida country in the hands Sadasiva Raya in the year 1540 A.D. His name definitely indicates that he was of Advaita religion. And it can be also inferred that the *Maṭha* at Puspagiri was a branch of that of Sringeri.

118. 'Malkāpuram Inscription of Kākatīya Rudrama Devi's period', *JAHRS.*, IV., p. 147. ff.

119. P. Srinivasachari, & P. B. Desai, *Kannada Inscriptions of A.P.*, no. 112, (A.P. Govt. Arch. Series No. 3).

120. Quoted from N. R. Kulkarni, 'Advaita Philosophy and Karnataka' in *Karnātaka Darshan*, p. 276.

121. 'Malkapuram Inscription of Kākatīya Rudrama Devi period', *JAHRS.*, IV, p. 147 ff.

122. *TDER.*, p. 92.

123. *Ibid.*,

124. *Ibid.*, p. 276-77.

125. K. R. Venkataraman, *Brahma Vidya Simhāsanamu*. Translated by T. Ramalingeswara Rao, (1977), p. 190-91.

126. *Ibid.*

127. *TDER.*, p. 214.

128. *SII.*, XVI, no. 235.

129. *Ibid.*, no. 257.

130. *Ibid.*, no. 296.
131. *Mac. Mss.*, 104, pp. 70-71.
132. *SII.*, X, no. 388.
133. *Ni.*, (Podili), p. 39.
134. *AP. AR.*, A. 1939, no. 5.
135. *NI.*, (Kanigiri), p. 22.
136. *Studies in the Third Dynasty,* p. 160.
137. M. Soma Sekhara Sharma, 'Mana Prāchina Vidyā Samsthalu' *Bhārati,* Vol. 16, (1926), pp. 239-249.
138. *SII.*, X, no. 496.
139. *Ibid.*, XVI, no. 122.
140. M. Soma Sekhara Sarma, *op cit.*
141. *Studies in the Third Dynasty,* p. 160.
142. *Cudd. Ins.*, p. 595.
143. *Kākatīyas,* p. 185.
144. 'English Summaries of Farmans and Sanadas', *Firmāns and Sanads of the Deccan Sultāns,* no. 4, p. 13.
145. *AR.*, 1963-65, D. no. 4.
146. *Landmarks,* pp. 79-84.
147. K.A. Nizami, *Some Aspects of Religion and Politics in India during the Thirteenth century,* p. 206.
148. S. Baba Mala, 'The Sūfi Convent and its social significance in the Medieval period of Islam' in *IC.*, Vol. V., 51, 1977, Jan. pp. 44-45.
149. *Ibid.*, p. 44.
150. M. S. Siddiqui, 'Origin and Development of the Chisti order in the Deccan, 1300-1538 A.D.' *I.C.*, 1977, July. Pp. 216-17.
151. G. Yezdani, *Bidar–Its History and Monuments,* p. 109-110.
152. *Medieval Deccan,* II, p. 181.
153. M. S. Siddiqi, 'Syed Muhammad Al-Hussain Gesu Daraz (1321-1422)', *IC.*, July 1978, p. 179-180.

154. *Ibid.*

155. *G.* Yezdani, *op.cit.,* p. 185.

156. *Malkāpūri,* I, p. 248.

157. S. A. Asgar Bilgrami, *Landmarks of the Deccan,* p. 74.

158. M.S. Siddiqui, *op. cit.,* p. 180.

159. M.S. Siddiqui, *Sūfis of the Deccan (A.D. 1347-1538),* p. 345.

160. *Malkāpūri,* pp. 164-65.

161. Rahat Azmi, 'Hyderabad Ke Maqaddas Tabarrukat' (Urdu Article) *Sadā-i-Jāfāriya,* 1978, Oct., pp. 37-56.

162. *Landmakrs,* p. 99.

163. *A Guide to Hyderabad,* 1976, pp. 33-34.

CHAPTER-4

1. Inscription of 1315 A.D. from Srisailam, *SII.,* Vol. XVI, no. 504.

2. *TDER.,* p. 33.

3. Sundaram K. The Simhachalam Temple, Waltair, 1969, p. 141.

4. *SII.,* XVI, no. 299.

5. *Mac. Mss.,* 105, pp. 101-2 & *Ibid.,* 124, pp. 1-60 respectively.

6. *AR.,* 1911, p. 87.

7. *Landmarks,* p. 74.

8. *EIM.,* Vol. 1935-36, p. 27.

9. *SII.,* XVI, no. 86; *Ibid.,* no. 165.

10. The eight kinds of enjoyment include-habitation, bed, raiment, jewels, women, flowers, perfumes and arecanuts and betel-leaves.

11. N. Venkataramanayya states that the holders of the *Sarvamanya* grants were under no obligation of any kind and enjoyed the fruits of the land or village granted to them without paying any tax to the government (*Studies in the Third Dynasty,* p. 183).

12. See Chapter V, p. 251 and also my article "Taxation and the Hindu Temple in the Telugu Districts under Vijayanagara Empire" Pub. in the *Proceedings of the Indian History Congress,* 1978.
13. *EI.*, V, p. 9.
14. *IAP.*, Wg. No. 110.
15. *EI.*, V, p. 53.
16. *Landmarks,* pp. 79-84.
17. *SII.*, VI, no. 227.
18. *TDER.*, p. 32.
19. *Ibid.*
20. 'Chennur *Kaifiyat'*, *Mac. Mss.*, 140, p. 98.
21. *TTDE.*, II, no. 97.
22. 'Chāgalamarri *Kaifiyat'*, *Mac. Mss.*, 100, p. 86.
23. *TDER.*, p. 131.
24. *Simhāchalam Temple,* p. 146.
25. *Epigraphy Report for 1920,* p. 146.
26. *LR.*, 55, p. 424.
27. *SII.*, XVI, no. 174.
28. T.K.T. Veeraraghavacharya, *History of Tirupati* (1976), f.n. p. 21.
29. Burton Stein, *All the Kings' Mana: Papers on Medieval South Indian History,* Madras, 1984, pp. 68-89.
30. *Epigraphy Report* for 1920, p. 114 (no. 655/1910).
31. *Studies in the Third Dynasty,* p. 336.
32. M. Somasekhara Sarma, 'Mana Prāchina Vidyā Samsthalu', *Bhārati,* Vol. 16, 1926, Ugadi, p. 243.
33. *SII.*, XVI, no. 199.
34. *Mac. Mss.*, 267, pp. 49, 50.
35. *TTDE.*, II, no. 67.

36. *SII.*, XVI, no. 280.
37. *TDER.*, p. 9.
38. *SII.*, X, no. 471.
39. *Ibid.*, no. 548.
40. *Ibid.*, VI, no. 70.
41. *Ibid.*, VI, no. 760.
42. *Ibid.*, no. 743.
43. *TDER.*, p. 9.
44. *Ibid.*
45. See Chapter V, pp. 255 and 256.
46. *SII.*, XVI, no. 227.
47. *TTDE.*, V, no. 154.
48. *Ibid.*, no. 89.
49. *TDER.*, p. 35.
50. *VR.*, I, no. 213.
51. T.K.T. Viraraghacharya, *op.cit.*, p. 25.
52. *TDER.*, p. 35.
53. *Ibid.*, p. 273.
54. *Mac. Mss.*, V. ('Nizampatnam *Kaifiyat'),* p. 72.
55. *Ibid.*, 272, p. 56-57.
56. *NI.*, (Ongole) 132.
57. *Mac. Mss.*, 272, pp. 9, & 10.
58. *EI.*, VI, p. 22.
59. 'Kōdūru *Kaifiyat*', *Mac. Mss.*, 96, pp. 65-66.
60. *Landmarks*, pp. 79-84.
61. See chapter V, pp. 268-69, for details about the taxes paid by the religious to the government.
62. *Mac. Mss.*, 133, p. 50
63. *Ibid.*, p. 32.

64. *AR.*, B. 1938, no. 200.
65. *IAP.*, Wg, no. 86.
66. *Mac. Mss.*, 231, p. 12.
67. *Ibid.*, 269, p. 32.
68. *APPB.*, 1932-33, *AR.*, 1932-33, no. 351.
69. *AR.*, 1938-39, p. 90.
70. *Ibid.*, 1939, B. no. 431.
71. *Cudd. Ins.*, p. 49.
72. 'Duvvūru *Kaifiyat'*, *Mac. Mss.*, 115, p. 47.
73. *Mac.*, *Mss.*, 127, pp. 96-115.
74. *Studies in the Third Dynasty*, p. 229.
75. *Ibid.*, pp. 232-33.
76. *Mac. Mss.*, 104, pp. 70-71.
77. Barth, *Religions of India*, pp. 281-282
78. *NI.*, II, p. 952.
79. *TTDE.*, V, no. 154.
80. *VR.*, III, (Vizag), p. 1686.
81. *Ins. Gloss.* (Intro.), p. cx-cxiii
82. *VR.*, I, p. 486.
83. *NI*, I, p. 331.
84. Quoted from *Qutbshāhi Dynasty*, pp. 654-56.
85. *TTDE*, V, no. 89.
86. 1 *Rēkhaipon=10 panam;* 1 *Varaha=15 panam* or 1½ *Rēkhaipon.*
87. 'Epigraph from the Mosque of Miyān Mishk', *Landmakrs*, pp. 79-84.
88. *VR.*, I (Anantapur) no. 78.
89. *Mac. Mss.*, 269, pp. 149-50.
90. *AR.*, 1924, B. no. 179.

91. *Ibid.*, 1941, B. no. 328.
92. *SII.*, XVI, no. 330.
93. *Simhāchalam Temple*, p. 142.
94. *SII.*, VI, no. 1184.

CHAPTER-5

1. *Siddēśvara Charitramu*, pp. 154-55.
2. It is probably the first of the three types of coins-*Rūkha, Nishkamu,* and *Chinnamu* in vogue during the Kakatiya period.
3. *Siddēśvara Charitramu*, pp. 154-55.
4. *SII.*, XVI, no. 504.
5. *Reddi Kingdoms*, p. 259.
6. Quoted from Mahalingam, *Administration and Social Life Under Vijayanagara*, p. 100.
7. Viśvanātharāyani-Sthānādipati, 'Rāyavāchakam', *ASPII.*, III, p. 29.
8. *Ibid.*,
9. Girdharilāl Auqar, 'Tārikh-i-Zāfarah' (com. In 1771-72 A.D.), Ch. I, quoted from *Qutbshahi Dynasty*, pp. 654-57.
10. 'Rāya Vāchakam', *ASPP,* III, pp. 12-13.
11. *Studies in the Tird Dynasty*, pp. 110-11.
12. *SII.*, IV, no. 1352.
13. *Medieval Deccan* II, p. 407.
14. *Ibid.*, p. 514.
15. *Ibid.*, p. 514.
16. *Mac., Mss.*, 130, p. 8.
17. *SII.*, VI, no. 772.
18. *Ibid.*, V, no. 1194.
19. *Ibid.*, VI, no. 75.

20. *Ibid.*, no. 98
21. *Ibid.*, no. 246.
22. *Ibid.*, no. 287.
23. *Studies in the Third Dynasty*, pp. 344-35.
24. Quoted from *Fruther Sources*, I, p. 42.
25. EC., IV, ch. 99.
26. *Ibid.*
27. Quoted from *Further, Sources*, III, p. 154.
28. *SII.*, XVI, nos. 109, 174, 199 & 200, respectively.
29. See Chapter V. pp. 227-28.
30. *SII.*, VI, no. 751.
31. C. V. Ramachandra Rao, *Administration and Social Life in Medieval Andhra under Later Eastern Gangas and Survaynamsi Gajapati*, p. 348.
32. *SII.*, VI, nos. 759, 769, 751, 1036, 1047, 1000, 1179; *Ibid.*, V, nos. 1193, 1194 & 779.
33. *Ibid.*, XVI, no. 71.
34. *Ibid.*, no. 109.
35. The important officials in the Vijayanagara government like ministers, provincial governors, *Nāyakas* etc. appear to have engaged the services of secretaries known as *Kāryakartas* through whom they performed various functions (*Studies in the Third Dynasty*, p. 531).
36. *SII.*, no. 246.
37. *Cudd. Ins.*, p. 348.
38. 'Rāyavā chakm', *ASPP.*, III, p. 12.
39. *SII.*, XVI, no. 246.
40. *Cudd. Ins.*, p. 191.
41. *Studies in the Third Dynasty*, pp. 111 & 112.
42. *TTDE.*, V. pp. 407-06.

43. *SII.*, XVI, no. 55.
44. *Qutbshāhī Farmāns in Hazarat Bandā Nawāz Collection*, no. 15.
45. *Ibid.*, no. 18.
46. 'Rāyavāchakamu', *ASPP*, III, pp. 12-13.
47. *Mac. Mss.*, 133, pp. 42-49.
48. *SII.*, XVI, no. 38.
49. *TDER.*, p. 167.
50. *Cudd. Ins.*, p. 179.
51. *IAP, Cu.*, II, no. 220.
52. *SII.*, V, no. 100.
53. Bavappayya, an official under Krishnadeva Raya of Vijayanagara made a special provision for the wages of Temples watchmen in a grant made to the Temple of Chennakesava of Erragudi in the year 1523 A.D. (*Mac. Mss.*, 252, p. 13-14).
54. *LR.*, (Rōllamadugu), p. 148.
55. *LR.*, 18, (Gōtur), p. 513.
56. Quoted from *Aravīdu Dynasty*, p. 315.
57. *Mac. Mss.*, 108, pp. 57-60.
58. *SII.*, XVI, no. 296.
59. The Portuguese governor Mortin Alfonso thought of sending a fleet of 45 ships under 27 captains via east coast to plunder this Temple. But due to the precautionary measures taken by the Vijayanagara government, it was directed against some other Temple in Kerala country. (Quoted from *Aravīdu Dynasty*, pp. 60 & 61).
60. The recipients of this endowment were supposed to enjoy all their proprietory rights in perpetuity without the obligation to pay any taxes.
61. *SII.*, X, no. 492.

62. *Ins., Gloss.*
63. *SII.*, XVI, no. 586.
64. *Mac. Mss.*, 60, pp. 64-65.
65. H.H. Wilson, *A Glossary of Judicial and Revenue Terms and c. of British India.*
66. 'The Punjāi Inscription of Krishnadēva Rāya of 1517', *EI.*, XXV, p. 297.
67. *SII.*, XVI, no. 132.
68. *Studies in the Third Dynasty,* pp. 230-31.
69. *Ins. Gloss.*
70. *SII.*, X, no. 509.
71. *SII.*, IV, no. 709.
72. *AR.*, 1913, no. 170.
73. *NI.*, (Drasi), 73,
74. *SII.*, X, no. 509.
75. *AR.*, 1926, B. no. 388.
76. *Ibid.*, 1943, B. no. 131.
77. *TDER.*, p. 208.
78. *SII.*, XVI, no. 17.
79. Altekar, *State and Government in Ancient India,* p. 223.
80. (a) A record from Sattravada (Chittoor dist. of A.P.), *AR.*, 1912, p. 78.

(b) A record from Jambukēśvaram (Tiruchirapalli dist. of Tamilnadu), *SII.*, XVI, no. 201.

81. *SII.*, XVI., no. 212.
82. *Mac. Mss.*, 115, p. 47.
83. *Studies in the Third Dynasty,* p. 229.
84. *Mac. Mss.*, 140, p. 101.
85. *SII.*, XVI, no. 91.
86. *Ibid.*, no. 139.

87. *Studies in the Third Dynasty*, p. 215.
88. *SII.*, XVI, no. 108.
89. *Cudd. Ins.*, p. 373.
90. *AR.*, 1942, B. no. 139.
91. *SII.*, XVI, no. 139.
92. *NI.*, (Ongole), p. 132.
93. *Studies in the Third Dynasty*, pp. 253-55.
94. *SII.*, XVI, no. 149.
95. *Ibid.*, XVI, no. 201.
96. *Ibid.*
97. *NI.*, (Ongole), p. 31.
98. *ED.*, IV, p. 111.
99. *NI.*, III, p. 1121.
100. *SII.*, XVI, no. 52.
101. *AR.*, 1942, B. no. 34.
102. *Mac. Mss.*, 30, p. 53.
103. *SII.*, X, no. 496.
104. *MER.*, 1913, 179.
105. *Mac. Mss.*, 19, pp. 1-4.
106. *Studies in the Third Dynasty*, p. 242.
107. *LR.*, 40, pp. 209-10.
108. *SII.*, XVI, no. 160.
109. *Ibid.*, no. 91.
110. *Ibid.*, no. 201.

CHAPTER-6

1. *Cudd. Ins.*, p. 267.
2. *IAP.*, Cu. II, no. 30.
3. *Cudd. Ins.*, p. 443.

4. Quoted from N. R. Kulkarni, 'Advaita Philosophy of Karnataka' in *Karnātaka Darsana*, p. 276.
5. *TDER.*, f. n., p. 213.
6. *Ibid.*
7. *TTDE.*, nos. 157-159.
8. A *Ghatikāsthāna* is referred to in an inscription of the period of Vishnukundini Vikramendravarma II (*EI.*, IV, 24).
9. *SII.*, V, no. 10; Kandukuri Isvara Dutt in his '*Inscriptional Glossary of A.P.*' (p. 102) gives the meaning of the word '*Ghadiyaramu*' referred to in this particular epigraph, as a school or *Vidya-satram* and differentiates it with the same word (*Ghadiyāramu*) used in another inscription of 1505 A.D. to denote a clock (*Ibid.*). The word *Ghaḍiya Sāsi* used in an inscription of 1132 A.D. to denote a teacher employed in a *Ghaṭika*, also lends support to this hypothesis (*Ibid.*).
10. *SII.*, VI, no. 904.
11. *Ibid.*, no. 1096.
12. *Select Stone Inscriptions of A.P.*, (Arch. Series 9), no. 4.
13. *TDER.*, p. 305.
14. *Mac. Mss.*, 254, pp. 60-61.
15. *TDER.*, p. 134.
16. *Ibid.*, p. 258.
17. *SII.*, VI, no. 962.
18. *Ibid.*, no. 1022.
19. *SII.*, VI, no. 1040.
20. 'Malkāpuram Inscription', *JAHRS.*. IV, pp. 147 ff.
21. *TDER.*, p. 214.
22. *Sources*, p. 223.
23. Srikanta Sastri, 'Sanskrit Literature under Vijayanagara, *Vij., Sex. Comm. Vol.*, pp. 312-13.
24. *TDER.*, p. 207.

25. T. Ramalingesvara Rao, (trans.), *Brahma Vidhyā Simhāsanamu,* p. 49.
26. *Ibid.,* p. 39.
27. *EI.,* XII, p. 41.
28. Srinatha, *Śivāratrimahatmyam,* (Intro.), p. iii, iv.
29. *Sources,* pp. 146-49.
30. *Ibid.,* pp. 138-42.
31. *TDER.,* p. 211.
32. 'Malkāpuram Inscriptions', *JAHRS.,* IV, p. 147 ff.
33. *Ibid.,*
34. *Studies in the Third Dynasty,* p. 325.
35. *Ibid.,* p. 326.
36. *AR.,* 1927, p. 369; *AR.,* 1936-37, p. 284.
37. *AP., AR.,* 1937, B. p. 283.
38. Aubalayya, the donee of an *Agrahāra,* is referred to in an inscription of 1545 A.D. from the village Koruvanipalle (Cuddapah dt.) as *'Satkarma Niratudu (Yājana, Yajana, Adhyayana, Adhyapaka, Dāna* and *pratigraha).* (*Cudd.* Ins. 149).
39. *Studies in the Third Dynasty,* p. 407.
40. *Ibid.,*
41. *Ibid.,* p. 408.
42. M. Soma Sekhara Sarma, 'Mana Prācheena Vidyā Saṃsthalu' (Tel. article), *Bharati,* Vol. 16, 1926, Ugadi Issue, p. 242.
43. *AP., AR.,* 1939, A. no. 5.
44. *Ibid.*
45. *Studies in the Third Dynasty,* p. 409.
46. *JAHRS.,* III, p. 221-33.
47. Quoted from M.A. Muid Khan, *Arabian Poets of Gōlkonda,* p. 27.

48. Anononimous author, *Tuzuk-E-Qutb Shāhi,* p. 6.
49. Quoted from *Qutbshāhi Dynasty,* (f. n. no. iii), p. 368.
50. *Ibid.*, pp. 316-17.
51. M.S. Siddiqui, 'Syed Muhammad AL Hussāini Gēsu Darāz' in *IC.*, 1978, July, pp. 175-76.
52. K. A. Nizami, 'The Sūfi Movement in Decean' in *Medieval Deccan,* II, p. 175.
53. *Qutbshāhi Dynasty,* p. 605.
54. M. S. Siddiqui, 'Origin and Development of the Chisti order in Deccan (A.D. 1300-1531) in *IC.*, 1977, July, pp. 215-16.
55. *Ibid.*,
56. *ASPP.*, II, pp. 93-112.
57. *Ibid.*
58. *Bhārati,* Bhāva Samvatsara, Jēsthamāsa, pp. 1-14.
59. 'Puvvāda grant of Prōlaya Vēma Reddy of Kondavīdu' in *Copper plate Inscriptions of A.P. Government Museum,* Vol. I, p. 173.
60. *Mac.*, *Mss*., 103, p. 5.
61. See Chapter III, pp. 123-125.
62. Assumed by Govinda Bharati of Puspagiri, *Mac. Mss.*, 105, pp. 101-102.
63. Assumed by Vyasatirtha, *Mac.*, *Mss.*, 115, p. 29.
64. Assumed by Mukti Santa Bhiksavritti of Srisailam, *Reddi Kingdoms,* p. 320.
65. The Sringeri *Peetham,* because of its pre-eminent position among its branches, was known during this period as *Dharma-Simhāsanam* and *Vyakhyāna Simhāsanamu* (Foreward page, T. Ramalingesvara Rao, *Brahma Vidyā Simhāsanam* Trans.). Similarly, Mukti, Santa Bhikshavritti, the pontiff of Bhiksha Vritti, *Maṭha* (Saiva) of Srisailam is described in an inscription of 1449 A.D. from Srisailam (p. 32-33. *Mac. Mss.*, 137, *Kaifiyat* of Kandanavolu) as ruling over the kingdom of

penance. (*Tapōrājyamu*) and occupying the religious throne (*Samaya Simhāsanamu*) at Srisailam.

66. T. Ramalingesvara Rao, *op. cit.*, p. 45.
67. *Mac, Mss.*. 15, p. 19.
68. *Descriptive Catalogue of Telugu MSS* no. 1079, p. 1410.
69. *Sūryavamśi Gajapatis,* p. 45.
70. *Vv. Vm.*, p. 51.
71. Quoted from *Copper Plate Inscriptions of A.P. Government Museum,* Vol., I, p. 136.
72. *Ibid.*, no. 65.
73. *C.V. Ramachandra Rao, Administration and Society in Medieval Andhra under L.E. Gangas & S. Gajapatis,* pp. 88-90.
74. *EI.*, XXXVI, p. 79.
75. *Sources,* p. 158.
76. *Aravīdu Dynasty,* p. 15.
77. *Ibid.*
78. M.S. Siddiqui, 'Social Role of the Sūfis Saints in the Deccan during the Bahmani period', *Itihās* IV, I, 1976, p. 86.
79. *Ibid.*, p. 86.
80. *Malkāpūri,* pp. 272, 73.
81. *Qutbshāhī Dynasty,* p. 293.
82. *Ibid.*, pp. 601-602.
83. *Medieval Deccan.* II, pp. 183-84.
84. 'Malkāpuram Inscriptions of Rudramadēvi's period' *JAHRS.*, IV, p. 147. ff.
85. *Ibid.*
86. *Ibid.*
87. *SII.*, XVI, no. 175.
88. *Ibid.*, XVI, no. 38.

89. *Medieval Deccan,* I, p. 220.
90. M. S. Siddiqui, 'Origin & Development of the Chisti order in the Deccan (A.D. 1300-1538)', in *IC.,* 1977 July, p. 218.
91. M.S. Siddiqui, ' Social Role of the Sufi Saints in the Deccan during the Bahmani period', *Itihāhs* IV, 1976, p. 96.
92. *AR.,* 1911, pp. 87-90.
93. *Medieval Deccan,* II, p. 175.
94. *SII.,* VI, no. 243.
95. *Ibid.,* X, no. 728.
96. *Select Stone Inscription of A.P. (*Arch. Ser. No. 6*),* no. 4.
97. *TDER.,* p. 49.
98. These Ramanuja-kutams derived their name from Ramanuja the famous Srivaishnava *Acharya* of the 12th c. A.D.
99. 'Chadipirēla *Kaifiyat', Mac. Mss.,* 136, pp. 154-55.
100. *Manual of Nellore,* p. 429.
101. *AR.,* 1926, B. no. 414.
102. *TDER.,* p. 51.
103. *Relations,* p. 20.
104. *AR.,* 1944, B. no. 13.
105. *TTDE.,* V. no. 125.
106. T.K.T. Veeraragavacharya, *History of Tirupati, I,* (1977) p. 59.
107. *TDER.,* p. 46.
108. *Sastra-Mathapati,* that is the Superintendent of the choultry is mentioned in an inscription of 1291. A.D. from Simhachalam (*SII.,* VI, no. 904).
109. *TDER.,* p. 46.
110. *Ibid.,* p. 47.
111. *Ibid.,* p. 260.
112. *TTDE.,* V, no. 39.

113. 'Chadipirēla *Kaifiyat', Mac. Mss.*, 136, pp. 154-55.
114. *TDER.*, p. 94.
115. *SII.*, V. no. 128.
116. *Ibid.*, XVI, no. 288.
117. *Cudd. Ins.*, pp. 636-37.
118. Chpater II, pp. 42.
119. *Ins. Gloss.*, p. 102 (f.n.). The *Ghaṭika Yaṅtra* and *Ghaḍiyāra* referred to in this epigraph to denote the clock which was a cup measuring the hours by sinking in water.
120. 'Malkāpuram Inscription', *JAHRE.* IV, p. 147, ff.
121. *TDER.*, p. 46.
122. *SII.*, X, no. 388.
123. 'Malkāpuram Inscription', *JAHRS.*, IV, p. 147, ff.
124. Epigraph of 1496 A.D., *SII.*, IV, no. 271.
125. *Studies in the Third Dynasty,* p. 408.
126. *ASSP.*, III, pp. 12-13.
127. Quoted from, *Qutbshāhī Dynasty,* p. 316.
128. 'English Summaries of Farmāns & Sanads', in *Farmāns and Sanads of the Deccan Sultāns,* p. 13.
129. Bilgrami & Wilmott, *Historical and Descriptive Sketch of H.H., the Nizāms Dominions,* p. 542.
130. Anon., *Tuzuk-E-Qutbshāhī,* f. 6.
131. *Landmarks,* p. 41.
132. *EIM.*, 1935-36, p. 27.
133. *Landmakrs,* pp. 79-83.
134. *Qutbshāhī Dynasty,* p. 47.
135. Girdhāri Lāl, *Tārikh-E-Zāfrah,* p. 12.
136. *Landmarks,* p. 84.
137. *Mac. Mss.*, 104, pp. 70-711
138. *Malkāpūri,* I, pp. 274-75.

139. *Landmarks,* p. 40.
140. *IAP.,* Cu, II, no. 278.
141. *Ibid.,* no. 138.
142. *TTDE.,* III, no. 89.
143. Chapter V, pp. 264-269.
144. *NI.,* (Ongole), p. 31.
145. Quoted from *Medieval Deccan,* I. pp. 220-21.
146. *SII.,* XVI, no. 52.
147. *NI.,* III, p. 1121.
148. *Mac., Mss.,* 112, pp. 61-63.
149. *Kr. Rm.,* p. 40.
150. *Sources,* pp. 149-151.
151. *Vij. Sex. Comm. Vol.,* p. 75-85
152. *Qutbshāhī Dynasty,* p. 320.
153. *SII.,* V, no. 1052.
154. *Reddi Kingdoms,* p. 477.
155. *Kr. Rm.* Pp. 96, 97.
156. *Ibid.,* pp. 36-40 (My translation and parentheses).
157. *Ibid.,* pp. 45-48.
158. Pulkurki Somanatha, *Śrīpaṇditārādhya Charitra,* pp. 252-263.
159. *Relations,* pp. 20, 21.
160. *Kr. Rm.,* pp. 86-88.
161. *SII.,* X, no. 473.
162. 'Srisaila Vrittantam', *Mac. Mss.,* 127, pp. 174-75.

Bibliography

1. Original Sources

Inscriptional

Andhra Pradesh Annual Reports on Epigraphy, 1965, onwards.

Annual Reports of the Archaeological Department of H.E.H. the Nizam's Government. From 1914-15 to 1940-41.

Annual Reports of the Archaeological Department, Southern Circle, Madras.

Annual Reports of the Archaeological Survey of India.

Annual Reports on India Epigraphy.

Annual Reports on South Indian Epigraphy.

Copper Plate Inscriptions of Andhra Pradesh Government Museum, Volume I & II, ed. N. Ramesan, 1962, 1970.

Corups of Telingana Inscriptions, ed. Hyderabad, I, II and III by P. Srinivaschari, 1940, 1958 & IV by M. Somesekhara Sarma, 1973.

Cuddapah Inscriptions ed. N. Venkataramanayya, Madras, 1972.

Epigraphia Andhrica, Volume I to IV.

Epigraphia Carnatica.

Epigraphia Indica.

Epigraphia Indo-Moslemica.

Inscriptions of Andhra Pradesh, Hyderabad, Warangal District by N. V. Ramanayya, 1974, Karimnagar District by P.V.P. Sastry,

1974., Cuddapah District, Part I & II by P.V.P. Sastry, 1977, 1978., Nalgonda District.

Madras Epigraphical Reports.

Memoirs & Reports of the Archaeological Survey of India.

Mysore Archaeological Reports.

Nellore District Inscriptions, 3 Vols. By Messers. A. Butterworth & Venugopal Chetty, Madras, 1905.

South Indian Inscriptions, Vols. (Archaeological Survey of India, New Imperial Series).

Telingana Inscriptions, I & II, Hyderabad, 1960.

Tirumala Tirupati Devasthanam Epigraphical Series, Vols. Madras.

Topgraphical List of Inscriptions from the Madras Presidency, 3 Vols. Till 1915, by V. Rangacharya, Madras, 1919.

Literary

Anantāchārya, K. ed. *ŚrīSannidhi Guruparampara* (Tamil), Madras, 1914.

Dūrjati, *Śrīkālahasti Mahatmyamu,* ed. Bulusu Venkataramanayya, Madras, 1966.

Ēkāmranātha, *Pratāpa Charitra,* ed. K. Laxmiranjanam, Tanuku, A. P. 1969.

Errāpragada, *Nṛsimha Purānamu,* ed. Divakarla Venkatavadhani, Hyderabad, 1967.

——, *Harivamsamu,* ed. Puripandu Appalaswami, Hyderabad, 1969.

Laxmi Narasimha Charyulu, S. *Śrīmadādi Vān Sathakōpa Yatīndra Mahādēśika Vaibhavamu* (Telugu), tra. from Tamil by Manam Sesachalamnayudu, Pentapadu, A.P. 1928.

Pālkurki Sōmanātha, *Anubhava Sāramu,* ed. T. Kodandaramayya, Madras, 1955.

——, *Basava Purāna,* ed. G. V. Subrahmanyam, Hyderabad, 1969.

——, *Śrī Panditārādhya Charitra,* ed. Ch. Narayan Rao, Reprint Andhra Patrik, 1974, Madras.

Piduparti Sōmanātha Kavi, *Basava Purānam,* ed. Ganga Pattanapu Subrahmanya Kavi, Madras, 1925.

Prabhakara Sastri, V. *Chātupadyamanjari*, Madras, 1919.

Rājanātha, *Achyutarāyābhyudayam,* ed. R. V. Krishnamachar, Srirangam, 1907.

Śrīkrishnadēva Rāya, *Āmuktamālyada (*Vishnu Chittiyamu), ed. Vavillas, Madras, 1969.

Śrīnātha, *Śivarātri, Mahatmyamu,* ed. B. Ramaraju, Hyderabad, 1968.

——, *Hara Vilāsamu,* ed. Bulusu Venkataramanayya, Madras, 1973.

——, *Śrī Kāsi Khandamu,* Introd. N. Venkat Rao, Madras, 1958.

——, Palanāti Viracharitra, Vijayawada, 1961.

Tenāli Rāmakrishna Kavi, *Pānduranga Mahatmyamu,* ed. Rallapalli Anatakrishna Sarma, Hyderabad, 1967.

Vidhyānātha, *Pratāparudra yasōbhūshanamu,* trans., Ch. Rangacharya, Hyderabad, 1972.

Vinukoṇda Vallabharāya, *Krīdābhirāmamu,* ed. V. Prabhakara Sastri, Hyderabad, 1960.

Virūpāksha Paṇdita, *Chenna Basava Purāna,* Mangalore, 1851.

Viśvanathanayani Sthānādhipati, 'Rāya Vāchakamu', *Andhra Sāhitya Parishat Patrika,* III, pp. 11-40.

Maunscripts

Anonymous Author, *Tuzuk-E-Qutbshāhī* (Persian), NO. 412 in the Sālārjuna Museum Catalogue of Persian MSS I (written probably during the period of First Nizām of Hyderabad, Vol. I).

Anonymous Historian, *Tārīkh-i-Qutbshāhī* (Perisan), Copied at Hyderabad in 1161—A.H., A.P. Government State Archives Copy.

Brown, *Local Records,* Govt. Oriental Manuscript Library, Madras. *Mackenzie Manuscripts,* Copies of A.P. Sāhitya Academy & A.P. State Achieves.

Persian Chronicles & Other Works

Amīr Kushrau, 'Khazainul-Futūh', trans. *ED.,* III, pp. 67-93).

——, 'Nūshiphir', (trans. *ED.,* III, pp. 557-65).

Abdul Jabbār, Khān Malkāpūri, *Mahbūbu-i-dhil-manam Tadhkira Āuliya-I-Dakhan* (Urdu) 2 Vols. Hyderabad, 1331, A.H.

Briggs, J. *History of the Rise of the Mahomedan Power in India* (trans. From the Original Persian of Mahomed Kāsim Ferishta), Vols. I, II & III, Calcutta, 1908, 1909 & 1910.

Elliot, M. *The History of India* (as told by her own historians) The Mohammadan period (Tārīk-i-Ferōshāh by Ziāuddin Bārni).

Elliot & Dowson, *The History of India as told by its own Historians,* Vols. Allahabad, rpts. 1964-69.

Ferishta Mohammad Qasim bin-Hindushāh, *Tārikh-i-Ferishta* (Persian), 2 Vols. Bombay, 1832.

Girdhārilāl Ahqar, *Tārīkh-E-Zāfrah,* (Persian), Gorakpur, 1927.

Ghulām Hussāin Khān, *Gulzār-i-Āsafīya* (Persian), 1260 A.H.

Gulām Imām Khān, *Tārīkh-e-Rashīduddin Khān* (Urdu), Hyderabad, 1282 A.H.

Gulām Samdāni Gauhar, *Tuzuk-i-Mahboobiya* (Urdu), Hyderabad, 1319. A.H.

Isami, *Futūhus Salātin* (or Shāhnāmah-i-Hind) trans. & commentary ed., Agha Mahdi Hussain, Aligrah Muslim Univ. 1967. Muhammad Ali Khān, *Tazkara-E-Zakīrian* (Urdu), Hyderabad, 1361 A.H.

Nizāmuddin Ahmad Mirzāh, *Hadīqatus-Salātin* (Urdu), Hyderabad, 1961.

Shams-i-Shirāj Afīf, *Tārikh-i-Firūzshāhi, ED.,* III, pp. 269-74.

Syed Ali Tabātabā, *Burdān-i-Mā'asir* (Persian), Hyderabad, 1936.

Foreign Accounts

Foster, *Early Travels in India* (*1583-1619*), ed. W. Foster, London, 1927.

Ibn Battūta, *Travels in Asia & Africa 1325-54,* trans. & selected by H.A.R. Gibb., London, 1953.

Jean Baptiste Taverniers, *Travles in India-1640-67,* 2 Vols. Trans. V. Ball, London, 1189, New Delhi, 1977 Indian edn.

Jean De Thevenot, *The Indian Travels of the Venot and Careri,* ed. S. N. Sen, New Delhi, 1949.

Moreland, W.H. *Relations of Golkonda in the Early Seventeenth Century,* ed. 1608-22, London, 1931.

Nuniz Fernao, 'Chronicle of Fernao-Nuniz', trans. R. Sewell, *Forgotten Empire,* pp. 291-395.

Paes Domingo, 'Narrative of Domingo-Paes, trans. R. Sewell, *Forgotten Empire,* pp. 236-93.

Purchas, *His Pilgrims,* Glasgow, 1905-07.

FARMāNS AND SANADS

Farmāns of Bahmany and Qutbshāhī periods in the Bande Nawāz collection (Persian), copies preserved in A.P. Govt. State Archives.

Yūsuf Hussain Khān, ed. *Farmans & Sanads of the Deccan Sultaans,* pub. State Archives, A. P. Hyderabad, 1963.

II. SECONDARY SOURCES

Modern Works

Abdul Muid Khan, M.A. *Arabian Poets of Gōlkonda,* Bombay, 1963.

Ahmad Ali Syed Shah, *Hazrat Hussāin, Shāh-Wāli* (Urdu), Hyderabad, n.d.

Aiyangar, S. K. ed. *Sources of Vijayanagara History,* Madras, 1919.

——, 'A little known chapter of Vijayanagara history', Madras, 1916.

——, *South India and Her Muhammadan Invaders,* Madras, 1921.

——, *History of Tirupati,* Vol. I & II, Tirupati, 1940-41.

——. *Some Contributions of South India to Indian Culture,* Calcutta, 1923.

Anandamurti, Veturi, *Tallapāka Kavula Krutulu Vividha Sāhiti Prakriyalu,* I & II (Telugu), Hyderabad, 1974.

Ayangar & Seshagiri Rao, *Studies in South Indian Jainism,* I & II, Vijayanagaram, 1922.

Arudra, *Samgrāhandra Sāhityamu* (Tolirāyala Yugam and Malirāyala Yugam), (Telugu), Madras, 1965.

Banerji, R. D. *History of Orissa,* Calcutta, 1930.

Barth, A. *The Religions of India,* trans. Rev. J. Wood, London, 1921.

Bava V. K. ed. *Aspects of Deccan History,* Institute of Asian Studies, Hyderabad, 1975.

Bhandarkar, R. G. *Vaisanavism, Śaivism and Minor Religious Systems,* Poona, 1928.

Bhattacharya, H. ed. *The Cultural Heritage of India,* IV, (The Religions), Calcutta, 1969.

Bilgrami, A. A. *Māsir-E-Deccan,* (Urdu), Hyderabad.

—, *Landmarks of the Deccan,* Hyderabad, 1927.

Bilgrami & Willmott, *Historical & Descriptive Sketch of H.H. The Nizām's Dominions,* I, & II, Bombay, 1884.

Burton Stein, ed. *South Indian Temple,* New Delhi, 1978.

——, *All the Kings' Mana: Papers on Medieval South Indian History,* Madras, 1984.

Campbell, A.C. *Glimpses of the Nizām's Dominions,* Bombay, 1898.

Chattopadhyaya, S. *The Evolution of Theistic Sects in India,* Calcutta, 1962.

——, *Evolution of Hindu Sects* (upto the time of Sankaracharya), New Delhi. 1970.

Cousens, Henry, *Medieval Temples of Deccan,* Arch. Survey of India Imperial Series, Vol. 48 Calcutta, 1938.

——, *List of Antiquarian Remains in H.H. Nizam's Territories,* Calcutta, 1900.

Eliot, Charles, *Hindusim and Buddhism,* Vol. II (in three Vols). London, 1921.

Danielou, Alain, *Hindu Polytheism,* London, 1964.

Derret, J.D.M. *The Hōyāsalas,* Madras, 1957.

Desai, P. B., *Jainism in South India,* Sholapur, 1957.

——, *Basavesvara and his times,* Dharwar, 1968.

Feibleman, James, K. *The Institutions of Society,* London, 1956.

Ferguson, James, *History of Indian & Eastern Architecture,* Vol. I (rev. James Burgess), London, 1910.

Fyzee, A.A.A. *A Shī'ite Creed,* London, 1942.

Geroge Michell, *The Hindu Temple* (an introduction to the meaning and forms), Delhi, 1977.

Gopala Krishnamurty, S. *Jaina Vestiges in Andhra,* Hyderabad, 1963.

——, *The Art of Lepakshi,* Hyderabad, 1970.

——, *The Sculptures of Kakatiyas.* Hyderbad, 1970.

Gribble, J.D.B. *A History of the Deccan,* 2 Vols. London, 1895-1924.

Gururaja Bhatt, P. *Studies in Tuluva History & Culture,* Kalianpur, Karnataka, 1975.

Haig, W. *Historic Landamrks of the Deccan,* Allahabad, 1907.

Hanumantha Rao, B.S.L. *Religions in Andhra,* Guntur, 1973.

Haripada Chakraborti, *Asceticism in Ancient India,* Calcutta, 1973.

Heras, H. *The Aravīdu Dynasty of Vijayanagara,* Madras, 1927.

Hirananda Sastri, *Shitāb Khān of Warangal,* Calcutta, 1932.

Hussaini, S.A.Q., *Bahaman Shāh: The founder of the Bahmanī Kingodm,* Calcutta, 1960.

Iswara Dutt, K. *Inscriptional Glossary of Andhra Pradesh,* Hyderabad, 1967.

Iyer, C. V. Narayana, *The Origin and Early History of Śaivsim in India,* Madras, 1936.

Jagadesan, N. *History of Sri Vaishnavism in the Tamil Country,* Madurai, 1977.

Jaiswal, Suvira, *The Origin & Development of Vaiśnavism,* Delhi, 1967.

Kameswar Rao, V. *Select Vijyanagara Temples of Rāyalaseema,* Hyderabad, 1976.

Karmarkar, A. P. *The religions of India,* Vol. I (The Vratya or Dravidian Systems), Lonavla (India), 1950.

King, J. S. *The History of the Bahmanī Dynasty founded on the Burhān-i-Mā'asir,* London, 1900.

Krishna Sastri, H. *South Indian Images of Hindu Gods and Goddesses,* Madras, 1916.

Krishnaswami Ayyar, R., *Śrīsārada Pītham* (Telugu), trans. T. V. Ranagacharyulu & Tirumala Ramachandra, Madras, 1977.

Major, R. H. *India in the 15th Century,* London, 1858.

Mahadevan, T.M.P. *Outlines of Hindusim,* Bombay, 1960.

Mahalingam, T. V. *Economic Life in Vijayanagara,* Madras, 1951.

——, *Administration and Social Life Under Vijayanagara,* Madras, 2nd edn., 1969.

Majumdar, A. K. *Bhakti Renaissance,* Bombay, 1965.

Mallaiya, N. V. *Studies in Sanskrit Texts on Temple Architecture with special reference to Tantra Samuccaya,* Annamalai Univerasity, 1949.

Max Weber, *The Religion of India,* London, 1958.

Mazhar Hussain, *List of Uruses, Mēlas, Jātras, etc. in H.E.H. the Nizām's Dominions,* Hyderabad, 1940.

Mishra, K.C. *The Cult of Jagannātha,* Calcutta, 1971.

Mirza Abul Fazal, trans. *The Korān,* (a new trans. From the Original), Bombay, 1955.

Monier Williams, *Religious Thought and Life in India* (Vedism, Brahmanism & Hindusim), New Delhi, 1974.

——, *Sanskrit English Dictionary,* Oxford, 1951.

Mujeeb, M. *The Indian Muslims,* London, 1967.

Nadvi, S. S. *Indo-Arab Relations* (English trans. of his Urdu book 'Arab-Wo-Hind Ke Tāllūqat'.), Hyderabad, 1962.

Nandinath, S.C. *A Handbook of Viraśaivism,* Dharawar, 1942.

Nandi, R.N. *Religious Institutions and Cults in the Deccan,* Delhi, 1973.

Nrasimha Rao, R. *Corporate Life in Medieval Āndhra Dēśa,* Hyderabad, 1967.

Nicholson, R. A. *The Idea of Personality in Sūfism,* Cambridge, 1923.

Nizami, K.A. *Some Aspects of Religions and Politics in India during the Thirteenth Century,* Aligrah, 1961.

Pai, D. A. *A Monograph on the Religious sects in India among the Hindus,* Bombay, 1958.

Pathak, V. S. *Śaiva Cults in Northern India,* Varanasi, 1960.

Pratapa Reddi, S. *Āndhrula Sānghika Charitra,* (Telugu), Hyderabad, 1949.

Parabrahma Sastri, P. V. *Siddhōdvāha of Nṛsimha,* Hyderabad, 1965.

——, *The Kākatīyas of Warangal,* Hyderabad, 1978.

Rabindra Kumar Siddhanta Shastree, *Śaivism through the Ages,* New Delhi, 1975.

Radhakrishna, S. *Religion and Society,* London, 1966-67.

——, *Hindu View of Life,* Delhi, 1928.

——, *Heart of Hindusim,* Delhi, 1932.

——, *Indian Philosophy,* Vols. 2, London, 1948, 1960.

Radhakrishna Sarma, M. *Temples of Telengāna,* Hyderabad, 1972.

Ramachandra Rao, C.V. *Administration and Society in Medeival Āndhra (A.D. 1038-1538) Under the Later Eastern Gāngas and the Sūryavamśi Gajapatis,* Nellore, (A.P.), 1976.

Ramakrishna Aiyer, V. G. *The Economy of South Indian Temple,* Annamalainagar, 1956.

Ramakrsihna Sastri, S. *Virasaiva Literature in Telugu,* Tirupati, 1952.

Ramarao, M. *Select Kakatiya Temples,* Tirupati, 1966.

——, *The Temples of Śrīśailam,* Hyderabad, 1967.

——, *Buddhism in Āndhra-dēśa,* Hyderabad, 1956.

——, *Śaivite Deities of Āndhra-dēśa,* Tirupati, 1966.

——, *Kākatiyas of Warangal,* Hyderabad, 1952.

——, *Temples of Tirumala-Tirupati and Tiruchanūr,* Tirupati, 1963.

——, *The Temples of Kalinga,* Tirupati, 1965.

——, *Select Āndhra Temples,* Hyderabad, 1969.

Ramaswamy, N.S. *Temples at Tādpatri,* Hyderabad, 1976-77.

——, *Mukhalingam Temples,* Hyderabad, 1976-77.

Ramesan, N. *Śrī Śankarāchārya,* Ponnuru, (A.P.), 1959.

——, *Temples and Legends of Āndhra Pradesh,* Bombay, 1962.

——, *The Tirumala Temple,* Tirupati, 1981.

Rangachari, K. Diwanbahadur, *Sri Vaisnava Brahmans,* (Bulletin of the Madras Government Museum), Madras, 1931.

Saletore, B. A. *Medieval Jainsim,* Bombay, 1938.

——, *Social and Political Life in Vijayanagara Empire,* 2 Vols. Madras, 1934.

Sarvappa, Kase, *Siddhēśvara-Charitra,* ed. Prof. K. Laxmiranjanamu, Hyderabad, 1960.

Sastri, K.A.N. *A History of South India,* London, 1958.

——, *Development of Religion in South India,* Madras, 1962.

——, *Foreign Notices of South India,* Madras, 1939.

Sastri, K.A.N. & Venkataramanayya, N. *Further Sources of Vijayanagara History,* Vol. I to III, Madras, 1946.

Sewell, Robert, *The Historical Inscriptions of Southern India collected till 1923 and Outlines of Political History,* ed. by S. Krishnaswamy Aiyangar, Madras, 1932.

——, *List of Antiquarian Remains in the Presidency of Madras,* 2 Vols. Madras, 1982-84.

——, *Sketch of the Dynasties of Southern India,* Madras, 1884.

——, *A Forgotten Empire,* Madras, 1924.

Shah Rocco, *Gōlkonda and the Qutbshāhīs,* Lahore, 1920.

Sharma B.N.K. *A History of the Dvaita School of Vēdānta and its literature,* Vol. I, Bombay, 1960.

Sherwani H.K. *The Bahmanis of the Deccan,* Hyderabad, 1953.

——, *Muhammad Qulī Qutbshāh: founder of Hyderabād,* 1967.

——, *History of the Qutbshahi Dynasty,* New Delhi, 1974.

Sherwani & Joshi, P. ed. *History of Medieval Deccan* (1294-1724), 2 Vols. Hyderabad, 1974.

Siddiqui Abdul Majeed, *History of Gōlkonda,* Hyderabad, 1956.

Sircar, D.C. *Śākta Pīthās,* Banaras, 1948.

——, *Indian Epigraphical Glossary,* Delhi, 1966.

Sitapati, P. *Śrī Venkatēsvara: The Lord of the Seven Hills,* (Tirupati), Bombay, 1972.

Sivapada Sundaram, S. *The Śaiva School of Hindusim,* London, 1934.

Somasekhara Sarma, M. *History of the Reddi Kingdoms,* Waltair, 1945.

——, *Forgotten Chapter of Āndhra History,* Waltair, 1945.

Sree Rama Sarma, P. *Sāluva Dynasty of Vijayanagara,* Hydeabad, 1979.

Srinivasan, K.R. *Temples of South India,* New Delhi, 1972.

Srinivas Rao, U.N. *Tirupati-Śrīvenkatēsvara-Bālāji,* (Origin, significance and History of the Shrine), Madras, 1949.

Stella Kramrisch, *The Hindu Temple,* University of Calcutta, 1946.

Sundaram, K. *The Simhāchalam Temple,* Waltari, 1969.

——, *Studies in the Economic & Social Conditions of Medieval Āndhra,* 1968.

Tatacharya, M.K. *Life and Writings of Vedānta-Dēśika,* Madras, 1911.

Thurston, Edgar & Ranga Chari, K. *Castes and Tribes of Southern India,* Madras, 1909.

Venkataramanayya, N. *The Origin of South Indian Temple and Rudrasiva* (two monographs), pub. Madras Univ. 1930.

——, *Kampili and Vijayanagara,* Madras, 1942.

——, *Studies in the History of the Third Dynasty of Vijayangara,* Madras, 1935.

——, *Early Muslim Expansion in South India,* Madras, 1942.

——, ed. *Velugōtivāri Vamśāvali,* Univ. of Madras, 1939.

Venkataraman, K.R. *Brahma Vidya (Vyakhyana) Simhāsanamu,* trans. T. Ramalingēsvara Rao, Madras, 1977.

Viraraghacharya, T.KT. *History of Tirupati,* Vols. I & III, Tirupati, 1977.

Waston, A. *The War of the Glodsmiths' Daughter,* London, 1964.

Whitehead, Rev. Fr. *The Village Gods of South India,* Oxford, 1921.

Wilson, H.H. *Sketch of the Religious Sects of the Hindus,* Calcutta, 1846.

——, *A Glossary of Judicial and Revenue Terms and c. of British India,* London, 1875.

Wm Thedore de Bary, *Sources of Indian Traditions,* comp. Newyork, 1958.

Yazdani, G. *Bīdar, Its History and Monuments,* London, 1947.

——, ed. *The Early History of the Deccan,* 2 Vols. 1960.

Ziaud-din, Desai, *Mosques of India,* New Delhi, 1971.

Zor, Hayat-e-Mīr Mūmin (Urdu), Hyderabad, 1941.

——, *Sair-e-Golkonda* (Urdu), Hyderabad, 1949.

Articles

Baba Mala, S. 'The Sūfi Convent & its Social Significance in the Medieval period of Islām', *Islāmic Culture,* V, 51, 1977, Jan. pp. 31-52.

Chandrasekhar, S. 'Jainism and Penugonda Jain Temples', *Journal of Āndhra History and Culture,* XVII, p. 162.

Hanumantha Rao, S. 'The Influence of the Religious School of Sri Mādhwa on the History of Vijayanagara', *Quarterly Journal of the Mythic Society,* XX, pp. 284-87.

——, 'Śrī Mādhwachārya (A.D. 1238-1318)', *Journal of Indian History,* 1949.

——, 'History of Religious Movements in Medieval Āndhra', *Journal of Indian History,* 1936, p. 103.

Hiralal, Raibahadur, 'Gōlaki Matha', *Journal of Bihar Oriental Research Society,* XIII, 1927, p. 138.

Iswarachandra Bhatnagar, 'Mystic Monasticism during the Mughal Period', *Islāmic Culture,* Vol. XV, 1961, Jan. p. 79-90.

Aspect of the South Indian Temple', *Journal of Andhra History and Culture,* VIII, p. 21.

Krishnamacharyulu, C. R. 'The Religion of the Vijayanagara House', *Indian Antiquary,* XLIV, Oct. 1915, pp. 219-25.

Nizami, K. A. 'Sūfi Movement in the Deccan', *History of Medieval Deccan,* Vol. II, ed. Sherwani & Joshi, Hyderabad, 1974, pp. 173-99.

Rahat Azmi, 'Hyderabād-ke-Muqaddas-Tabarrukat', *Sada-i-Jāfarīya,* (Urdu), (Special Issue on Muharram), Oct. 1978, pp. 37-56.

Rangachari, V. 'The life and Times of Śrī Vēdānta Dēśika', *Journal of the Bombay Branch of the Royal Asiatic Society,* XXIV, pp. 277-312.

——, 'The Successors of Rāmānuja and the growth of sectarianism among the Śrīvaishnavas', *Ibid.,* XXIV, p. 102-26.

Saletore, B.A. 'Vaishnavism in Vijayangara' *Dr. R. Bhandarkar,* Volume p. 183.

Siddiqi, M.S., 'Origin and Development of the Chisti Order in the Deccan, A.D. 1300-1538', *Islāmic, Culture,* 1977, July p. 209-19.

——, 'Social Role of the Sūfi Saints in the Deccan during the Bahmany period,' *Itihas,* Vol. IV, I 1976, p. 83-107.

——, 'Syed Muhammad Al-Husāini Gēsudarāz (727-825/1321-1422)', *Islamic Culture,* July 1978, p. 173-84.

Somasekhara Sharma, M. 'Religious traditions', *Telugu-Cyclopaedia,* Vol. III.

Srinivas Chari, P. 'Taxation of Vijayanagara' *Indian Historical Quarterly,* XII-3, 1936, p. 443-35.

Srinivas Rao, B.V. 'The Religious Policy of Sangama Rulers', *Journal of Āndhra History and Culture,* XXIX, p. 37.

Sundaram, K. 'The Artisan Community of Medieval Āndhra', (A.D. 1000-1600), *Journal of Indian History,* 1965, p. 905.

Venkatasubbaiah, A. 'The Rājā-guru Kriyāśakti', *Quarterly Journal of the Mythic Society,* VII, pp. 118-36.

Journals

Āndhra Patrika, Annual (Telugu).

Āndhra Sahitya Parishat Patrika, (Telugu).

Annals of Bhandarkar Oriental Research Institute, Poona.

Bhārati (Telugu).

Indian Antiquary, Bombay.

Indian Culture, Calcutta.

Islamic Culture, Hyderabad.

Indian Historical Quarterly.

Itihās, (Journal of the A.P. Archives), Hyderabad.

Journal of Āndhra History and Culture, Guntur.

Journal of Āndhra Historical Research Society, Rajahmundry.

Journal of Asian Studies.

Journal of Bihar and Orissa Research Society.

Journal of Bombay Branch of Royal Asiatic Society, Bombay.

Journal of Indian History, Trivandrum.

Journal of Madras, University.

Journal of Oriental Research, Madras.

Journal of Śrī Venkatēsvara University, Tirupati.

Journal of the Hyderabad Archaeological Society.

Journal of the Royal Asiatic Society.

Proceedings of All India Oriental Conference.

Proceedings of Indian History Congress.

Quarterly Journal of Mythic Society, Bangalore.

Sabras, (Urdu) Monthly, Hyderabad, 1940, March.

Sadā-e-Jāffarīya, (Special Muharram Issue), (Urdu), Hyderabad, Oct., 1978.

Gazetteers and Manuals

Francis, W. *Madras District Gazetters-Anantapur,* Madras, 1905.

——, *Madras District Gazetteer-Bellary,* Vol. 2, Madras, 1904, 1916.

Fancis, G. *Vizagapatam-Gazetter,* Madras, 1907.

Breakenbury, C.F. *Madras District Gazetteers-Cuddapah,* Madras, 1915.

Gazetter of the Nellore District, (brought upto 1938), Madras, 1938-42.

Hemingway, F.R. *Madras District Gazetteer-Godavari,* Madras, 1907.

Imperial Gazetteer of Hyderabad State, Calcutta, 1909.

Imperial Gazetteer of India, Oxford, 1908.

Boswell, J.A.C. *Manual of the Nellore District in the Presidency of Madras,* Madras, 1875.

Carmichael, D.F. *Manual of the District of Vizagapatam,* Madras, 1869.

Chetti, N.G.K. *Manual of Kurnool District,* Madras, 1886.

Gribble, J.D.B. *A Manual of the District of Cuddapah,* Madras, 1875.

Kelsall John, *Manual of the Bellary District,* Madras, 1872.

Mackenzie, Gordon, *A Manual of the Krishna District in the Presidency of Madras,* Madras, 1883.

Malidy, T.J. *Manual of the Ganjam District,* Madras, 1882.

Morris, *Mannual of the Godavari District,* Madras, 1878.

Unpublished Theses

Asgar Ali Ansari, *The Relations between South Arābia and the Deccan,* (from the 17th till the 20th c. A.D.),. Department of Islamic Studies, Osmania University, Hyderabad, 1971.

Madhusudhan Reddy, K. *Theory and Practice of Government in Medieval Āndhra Dēśa,* (A.D. 1000-1400), Department of Political Science, Osmania University, Hyderabad, 1973.

Narasimha Rao, R. *Social and Economic Conditions in Medieval Āndhra Dēśa,* (A.D. 1000-1400), Department of History, O.U. Hyderabad, 1956.

Siddiqi Mohammad Suleman, *Sūfis of the Deccan* (A.D. 1347-1538), Department of Islamic Studies, Osmania University, Hyderabad, 1975.

Ziauddin Ahmad Shakeb, *Diplomatic and Political Relations of Iran and Golkonda,* Department of History, Poona University, 1977.

Souvenirs and Others

A Guide to Hyderabad, Institute of Asian Studies, Hyderabad, 1976.

Budha Jayanti Souvenir, 1956, ed. M Rama Rao & P. Srinivasachari.

History and Legend in Hyderabad, Department of Information & Public Relations, Hyderabad, 1933.

Kākatīya Sanchika, ed. M. Ramarao, Rajahmundry, 1936.

Reddi Sanchika, ed. Vaddadi Appa Rao, 1947.

Vijayanagara Sexcentenary Commemoration Volume, Dharwar, 1936.

Encyclopaedias

Encyclopaedia of Islām, ed. M.T.H. Houtsma, A.J. Wensink T. Warnold, W. Hefening & E. Levi-Provencal, London, 1908-38.

Encyclopaeida of Religion and Ethics.

Shorter Encyclopaeida of Islām, Gibb, H.A.R. & Kramers, J.A. ed. London, E.J. Brill, 1974.

Vijnana Sarvasvamu, Vol. 7. Telugu Bhasha Samithi, Hyderabad.

Index